CRICKET

By

HORACE G. HUTCHINSON

First published in 1903

This edition published by Read Books Ltd.
Copyright © 2019 Read Books Ltd.
This book is copyright and may not be
reproduced or copied in any way without
the express permission of the publisher in writing

British Library Cataloguing-in-Publication Data
A catalogue record for this book is available
from the British Library

CONTENTS

A SHORT HISTORY OF CRICKET 5

PREFACE 9

SOME POINTS IN CRICKET HISTORY
BY THE EDITOR 18

EARLY DEVELOPMENTS OF THE CRICKETING ART
BY THE EDITOR 42

BATTING
BY P. F. WARNER 60

BOWLING
BY D. L. A. JEPHSON 95

FIELDING
BY S. L. JESSOP 132

COUNTY CRICKET
BY W. J. FORD 148

AMATEURS AND PROFESSIONALS
BY THE HON. R. H. LYTTELTON 194

EARLIER AUSTRALIAN CRICKET
BY THE EARL OF DARNLEY 217

ENGLISH AND AUSTRALIAN CRICKET FROM 1894 TO 1902
BY A. C. MACLAREN 244

UNIVERSITY CRICKET
BY HOME GORDON AND H. D. G. LEVESON-GOWER 279

COUNTRY-HOUSE CRICKET
BY H. D. G. LEVESON-GOWER 316

VILLAGE CRICKET
BY C. F. WOOD 332

FOREIGN CRICKET
BY P. F. WARNER..350

CRICKET IN SOUTH AFRICA
BY P. F. WARNER..362

CRICKET IN NEW ZEALAND
BY P. F. WARNER..373

CRICKET GROUNDS
BY MESSRS. SUTTON AND SONS, THE KING'S
SEEDSMEN, READING...................................378

A Short History of Cricket

Cricket is a bat-and-ball game played between two teams of eleven players each, on a field at the centre of which is a rectangular twenty-two-yard long pitch. Each team takes its turn to bat, attempting to score runs, while the other team fields. Each turn is known as an innings. Whilst this may sound reasonably simple – the game of cricket has a very long and varied history; changing with time and geographical location.

Early cricket was at some time or other described as 'a club striking a ball (like) the ancient games of club-ball, stool-ball, trap-ball or stob-ball.' The sport can definitely be traced back to Tudor times in early sixteenth century England though. Further written evidence exists of a game known as 'creag' being played by Prince Edward, the son of Edward I, at Newenden, Kent, in 1301. There has been speculation, but no distinct evidence that this was a form of early English cricket.

The earliest definite reference to cricket being played in England (and hence anywhere) is given at a 1598 court case which mentions that 'creckett' was played on common land in Guildford, Surrey around 1550. Here, the court coroner gave witness that 'hee and diverse of his fellows did runne and play [on the common land] at creckett and other plaies.' It is believed that it was originally a children's game but references around 1610 indicate that adults had started playing it and the earliest reference to inter-parish or village cricket occurs soon afterwards. In 1624, a player called Jasper Vinall was killed when he was struck on the head during a match between two parish teams in Sussex.

During the seventeenth century, numerous references indicate the growth of cricket in the south-east of England. By the end of the century it had become an organised activity being played for high stakes, and it is believed that the first professionals appeared in the years following the Restoration in 1660. The game underwent major development in the eighteenth century and became the national sport of England. Betting played a major part in that development with rich patrons forming their own 'select XIs'. Bowling only really evolved in 1760 though, when bowlers began to pitch the ball instead of rolling or skimming it towards the batsman. This caused a revolution in bat design because to deal with the bouncing ball, it was necessary to introduce the modern straight bat in place of the old 'hockey stick' shape. The nineteenth century saw underarm bowling replaced by first roundarm and then overarm bowling. Both developments were controversial.

Meanwhile, the British Empire had been instrumental in spreading the game overseas, and by the middle of the nineteenth century it had become well established in India, North America, the Caribbean, South Africa, Australia and New Zealand. In 1844, the first international cricket match took place between the United States and Canada (although neither has ever been ranked as a Test-playing nation. In 1862, an English team made the first tour of Australia and in 1876–77, an England team took part in the first-ever Test match at the Melbourne Cricket Ground against Australia. The resultant rivalry gave birth to 'The Ashes' in 1882, and this has remained Test cricket's most famous contest ever since.

The last two decades before the First World War have been called the 'Golden Age of Cricket' – a form of nostalgia in the face of mounting modernisation and destruction. It was (and is) a unique game where in addition to the laws of play, the sportsmen must abide by the 'Spirit of the Game.' The standard of sportsmanship has historically been considered so high that the phrase 'it's just not cricket' was coined in the nineteenth century to describe unfair or underhanded behaviour in any walk of life. In the last few decades though, cricket has become increasingly fast-paced and competitive, increasing the use of appealing and sledging, although players are still expected to abide by the umpires' rulings without argument, and for the most part they do.

Cricket entered a new era in 1963 when English counties introduced the limited overs variant. As it was sure to produce a result, limited overs cricket was lucrative and the number of matches increased. In the twenty-first century, a new limited overs form, Twenty20, has made an immediate impact; though its longevity is yet to be established. As is evident from this brief history of Cricket, it is a sport with a long and fascinating history which has firmly retained its popularity into the present day. We hope the reader is encouraged to find out more and maybe have a game of their own.

"DESIPERE IN LOCO"

*From a Painting by
R. James.*

TOSSING FOR INNINGS.

PREFACE

Surely it is sheer neglect of opportunity offered by an official position if, being an editor, one has no prefatory word to say of the work that one is editing. It is said that that which is good requires no praise, but it is a saying that is contradicted at every turn—or else all that is advertised must be very bad. While it is our firm belief that the merits of the present book—*The Country Life Cricket Book*—are many and various (it would be an insult to the able heads of the different departments into which the great subject is herein divided to think otherwise), we believe also that the book has one very special and even unique merit. We believe, and are very sure, that there has never before been given to the public any such collection of interesting old prints illustrative of England's national game as appear in the present volume. It is due to the kind generosity of the Marylebone Cricket Club, as well as of divers private persons, that we are able to illustrate the book in this exceptional way; and we (that is to say, all who are concerned in the production) beg to take the opportunity of giving most cordial thanks to those who have given this invaluable help, and so greatly assisted in making the book not only attractive, but also original in its attraction. In the first place, the prints form in some measure a picture-history of the national game, from the early days when men played with the wide low wicket and the two stumps, down through all the years that the bat was developing out of a curved hockey-stick into its present shape, and that the use of the bat at the same time was altering from the manner of the man with the scythe, meeting the balls called "daisy-cutters," to the straightforward upright batting of the classical examples. The classical examples perhaps are exhibited most ably in the pictures of Mr. G. F. Watts, which show us that the human form divine can be studied in its athletic poses equally well (save for the disadvantage of the draping flannels) on the English field of cricket as in the Greek gymnasium. The prints, too, give us a picture-history of the costumes of the game. There are the "anointed clod-stumpers" of Broadhalfpenny going in to bat with the smock, most inconvenient, we may think, of dresses. There are the old-fashioned fellows who were so hardly parted from their top-hats. These heroes of a bygone age are also conspicuous in braces. We get a powerful hint, too, from the pictures, of the varying estimation in which the game has been held at different times. There is a suggestion of reverence in some of the illustrations—a sense that the artist knew himself to be handling a great theme. In others we see with pain that the treatment is almost comic, certainly frivolous. We hardly can suppose that the picture of the ladies' cricket match would encourage others of the sex to engage in the noble game, although "Miss Wicket" of the famous painting has a rather attractive although pensive air—she has all the aspect of having got out for a duck's egg

More decidedly to the same effect—of its differing hold on popular favour—do we get a hint from the spectators assembled (but assembled is too big a word for their little number) to view the game. "Lord's" on an Australian match day, or a Gents *v.* Players, or Oxford and Cambridge, hardly would be recognised by one of the old-time heroes, if we could call him up again across the Styx to take a second innings. He would wonder what all the people had come to look at. He hardly would believe that they were come to see the game he used to play to a very meagre gallery in his life. But he would be pleased to observe the progress of the world—how appreciative it grew of what was best in it as it grew older.

Another thing that the collection illustrates is the various changes of site of the headquarters of the game, if it had a headquarters before it settled down to its present place of honour in St. John's Wood. There is a picture (*vide* p. v) of "Thomas Lord's first Cricket Ground, Dorset Square, Marylebone. Match played June 20, 1793, between the Earls of Winchilsea and Darnley for 1000 guineas." With regard to this interesting picture, Sir Spencer Ponsonby-Fane, in his catalogue of the pictures, drawings, etc., in possession of the Marylebone Cricket Club, has a note as follows:—"This match was Kent (Lord Darnley's side) *v.* Marylebone, with Walker, Beldham, and Wills (Lord Winchilsea's side). M.C.C. won by ten wickets. It will be noticed that only two stumps are represented as being used, whereas, according to *Scores and Biographies*, it is known that as far back as 1775 a third stump had been introduced; many representations, however, of the game at a later date show only two stumps." No doubt at this early period there was no very fully acknowledged central authority, and such little details as these were much a matter of local option. The wicket shown in this picture does not seem to differ at all from the wicket in the picture of "Cricket" by F. Hayman, R.A., in the possession of the Marylebone Club, though the date of the latter is as early as 1743. Neither does the bat appear to have made much evolution in the interval. It is on the authority of Sir Spencer Ponsonby-Fane, in the catalogue above quoted, that we can give "about 1750" for the date of the picture named "A Match in Battersea Fields" , in which St. Paul's dome appears in the background. Here they seem to be playing with the three stumps, early as the date is. Again, in the fine picture, "painted for David Garrick" by Richard Wilson, of "Cricket at Hampton Wick" , three stumps are in use, and the bat has become much squared and straightened. Of course the pictures obviously fall into two chief classes—one in which "the play's the thing"; the cricket is the object of the artist's representation; the other in which the cricket is only used as an incidental feature in the foreground, to enliven a scene of which the serious interest is in the background or surroundings. But the pictures in which the cricket is the main, if not the only, interest are very much more numerous. A quaintly suggestive picture enough is that described in Sir S. Ponsonby-Fane's catalogue as, "Situation of H.M.'s Ships *Fury* and *Hecla* at Igloolie. Sailors playing Cricket on the Ice." In this, of course, there is no historical interest about the cricket . The one-legged and one-armed cricketers make a picture that is curious, though not very pleasant to contemplate; and the same is to be said of the rather vulgar representation of the ladies' cricket match noticed above. The "Ticket to see a Cricket Match" shows a bat of the most inordinate, and probably quite impossible, length; but we may easily suppose that the artist, consciously or unwittingly, has exaggerated the weapon of his day. Here too are two stumps only. We may notice the price of the ticket as somewhat remarkably high, 2s. 6d.; but it was in the days when matches were played for large sums of money, so perhaps all was in proportion (length of bat excepted, be it understood). There is a picture of the "celebrated Cricket Field near White Conduit House, 1787" , which is named a "Representation of the Noble Game of Cricket." It is a picture of some merit, and evidently careful execution, and here too the players are seen with bats of a prodigious length; so it may be that these huge weapons came into fashion for a while, only to be abandoned again when their uselessness was proved, or perhaps when the legislature began to make exact provision with regard to the implements used. In this same picture of the "Noble Game of Cricket" a man may be seen standing at deep square leg, who is apparently scoring the "notches," or "notching" the runs, on a piece of stick. This at least appears to be his occupation, and it is interesting to observe it at this comparatively late date, and at headquarters. In the match between the sides led by Lord Winchilsea and Lord Darnley respectively, it is seen that there are two tail-coated gentlemen sitting on a bench, and probably scoring on paper, for it is hardly likely that they can have been reporting for the press at that time. England did not then demand the news of the fall of each wicket, as it does now. Nevertheless, that there must have been a good deal of enthusiasm for the game, even at a pretty early date, is shown conclusively enough by the engraving of the "North-East View of the Cricket Grounds at Darnall, near Sheffield, Yorkshire." What the precise date of this picture may be I do not know, but it is evident that it must be old, from the costumes of the players, who are in knee-breeches and the hideous kind of caps that have been reintroduced with the coming of the motor-car. Also the umpires, with their top-hatted heads and tightly-breeched lower limbs, show that this picture is not modern. And yet the concourse of spectators is immense. Even allowing for some pardonable exaggeration on the part of the artist, it is certain that many people must have been in the habit of looking on at matches, otherwise this picture would be absurd; and this, be it observed, was not in the southern counties, which we have been led to look on as the nurseries of cricket, but away from all southern influence, far from headquarters, in Yorkshire, near Sheffield. To be sure, it may have been within the wide sphere of influence of the great Squire Osbaldeston, but even so the picture is suggestive. The scorers are here seated at a regular table. A very curious representation of the game is that given in the picture by James Pollard, named "A Match on the Heath" . It is a good picture. What is curious is that, though the period at which Pollard was producing his work was from 1821 to 1846, the bats used in the game are shown as slightly curved, and, more notably, the wicket is still of the two stumps only. There are only two alternative ways of accounting for this: either they still played in certain places with the two-stump wicket, or else, which is not likely, Pollard was very careless, and no cricketer, and took his cricket apparatus from some older picture. I observe, by the way, that I have, on the whole, done less than justice to the ladies, as they are portrayed playing the game, for though it is true that the one picture is, as noticed, vulgar enough, there is another, "An Eleven of Miss Wickets" , that is pretty and graceful. While some of the pictures in this collection are interesting mainly for their curiosity, or as being something like an illustrated history or diary of events and changes in the game, there are others that are real works of art and beauty, sometimes depending mainly on their expression of the game itself, and sometimes only using it as an adjunct to the scenery. Of the former kind, we must notice most especially the remarkable series of drawings by Mr. G. F. Watts, R.A., which show the batsman in the various positions of defence or attack. To very many it will be a revelation that the great artist could lend his pencil to a matter of such trivial importance (as some base souls may deem it) as the game of cricket; but without a doubt that great knowledge of anatomy, which has been one of the strong points in all his paintings, has been learned in some measure from these studies, which also give it a very high degree of expression. There is a force, a vigour, a meaning about these sketches which are interesting enough, if for no other reason than because they show so vividly the inadequacy of the mechanical efforts of photography, when brought into competition, as a means of expression, with the pencil of a really great artist. You feel almost as if you must jump aside out of the way of the fellow stepping forward to drive the leg volley, or of the fearful man drawn back to cut, so forcefully is the force expressed with which the batsman is inevitably going to hit the ball . One of the most charming pictures of those who have taken cricket for their theme is that which is lent by His Majesty the King to the M.C.C., and is styled "A Village Match." It is by Louis Belanger, of date 1768 . Charming, too, is the picture attributed to Gainsborough, "Portrait of a Youth with a Cricket-bat"; it is said to be a portrait of George IV. as a boy, but it seems doubtful. The bat here is curved, but hardly perceptibly; it shows the last stage in evolution before the straight bat was reached . Our frontispiece is a jolly scene—the ragged boys tossing the bat for innings—"Flat or Round?" and the fellow in the background heaping up the coats for a wicket. We all of us have played and loved that kind of cricket. A wonderfully good and detailed picture is that of "Kent *v.* Sussex" . It is a picture of a match in progress on the Brighton ground, and Brighton is seen in the background; in the foreground is a group of celebrated cricketers in the spectators' ring, yet posed, in a way that gives a look of artificiality to the whole scene, so as to show their faces to the artist. Even old Lillywhite, bowling, is turning his head quaintly, to show his features. One of the most conspicuous figures is the great Alfred Mynn, who was to a former generation what W. G. Grace has been to ours. All the figures are portraits, and every accessory to the scene is worked out most carefully. The drawing is by W. H. Mason. Sir Spencer Ponsonby-Fane has a note on this picture: "As a matter of fact, this match, as here represented, did not take place, the men shown in the engraving never having played together in such a match, but they all played for their respective counties about 1839-1841." Very delightful, too, is the picture that is the last in our book , "At the End of the Innings"— an old veteran with eye still keen, and firm mouth, telling of a determination to keep his wicket up and the ball down "as well as he knows how," and with an interest in the game of his youth unabated by years. A jolly painting is that of "Old Charlton Church and Manor House" , with the coach and four darting past, and the boys at cricket on the village green. And last, but to many of us greatest of all, there is the portrait of Dr. W. G. Grace, from Mr. A. Stuart Wortley's picture, which sums up a modern ideal of cricket that we have not yet found ourselves able to get past.

There are other pictures, not a few, that we might select for notice, but already this ramble goes beyond due prefatory limits. There are the sketches in which the cricket is made to point or illustrate political satires. To do full justice to these, one would need to be well versed in the history (other than the cricketing history) of the period. But enough has been said. One could not let such a gallery of old masters go without an attempt to do the showman for them in some feeble way. They need neither help nor apology. They are good enough to win off their own bat.

In our modern instances we have been no less lucky: with Mr. Warner to bat, Mr. Jephson to bowl, Mr. Jessop to field, and the rest of the good company, we do not know that any other choice could have made our eleven better than it is; but after all, that is for the public to say; it is from the pavilion, not the players, that the applause should come.

CRICKET

From a Painting by Francis Hayman, R.A.

CRICKET, AS PLAYED IN THE ARTILLERY GROUND, LONDON, IN 1743

CHAPTER I

SOME POINTS IN CRICKET HISTORY
BY THE EDITOR

Cricket began when first a man-monkey, instead of catching a cocoanut thrown him playfully by a fellow-anthropoid, hit it away from him with a stick which he chanced to be holding in his hand. But the date of this occurrence is not easy to ascertain, and therefore it is impossible to fix the date of the invention of cricket. For cricket has passed through so many stages of evolution before arriving at the phase in which we find it to-day that it is difficult to say when the name, as we understand its meaning, first became rightly applicable to it. The first use of the name "cricket" for any game is indeed a matter entirely of conjecture. It is not known precisely by Skeat, nor Strutt, nor Mr. Andrew Lang. But whether the name was applied by reason of the cricket or crooked stick, which was the early form of the bat, or whether from the cross stick used as a primitive bail, or from the cricket or stool, at which the bowler aimed the ball, really does not very much matter, for all these etymological vanities belong rather to the mythological age of cricket than the historical. Neither is it of great importance whether cricket was originally played under another name, such as club-ball, as Mr. Pycroft infers, on rather meagre authority, as it seems to me, from Nyren. Nyren did not hazard the inference. The fact is that the form in which we first find cricket played, and called cricket, is quite unlike our cricket of to-day, so that we do not need to go seeking anything by a different name. They played with two upright stumps, 1 foot high, 2 feet apart, with a cross stump over them and a hole dug beneath this cross stump. The cross stump is evidently the origin of our bails. Nyren does not believe in this kind of cricket, but he gives no reason for his disbelief, for the excellent reason that he can have had no reason for his scepticism; and the fact is proved by the evidence of old pictures. He was a simple, good man; he never saw anything like cricket played in that way, so he did not believe any one else ever had. He did not perhaps understand much about the law of evidence, but he wrote delightfully about cricket. The fourth edition of his guide, which a friend's kindness has privileged me to see, is dated 1847, some time after the author's death.

THE ROYAL ACADEMY CLUB IN MARYLEBONE FIELDS.

CRICKET

A MATCH IN BATTERSEA FIELDS.

Yes, in spite of Nyren, they bowled at this cross-stick and wicket which the ball could pass through again and again without removing the cross piece, and the recognised way of getting a man out was not so much to bowl him as to catch or run him out. You ran him out by getting the ball into the hole between the stumps before he got his bat there—making the game something like rounders. Fingers got such nasty knocks encountering the bat in a race for this hole that bails and a popping crease were substituted—at least the humane consideration is stated to have been a factor in the change.

It is not to be supposed that even we, for all our legislation, have witnessed the final evolution of cricket. Legislate we never so often, something will always remain to be bettered—the width of the wicket or the law of the follow on. About the earliest records that have come down to us there is a notable incompleteness that we must certainly regret. The bowler gets no credit for wickets caught or stumped off his bowling. What would become of the analysis of the underhand bowler of to-day if wickets caught and stumped were not credited to him? But at the date of these early records all the bowling was of necessity underhand. Judge then of the degree in which those poor bowlers have been defrauded of their just rights. Whether or no the name of our great national game was derived from the "cricket" in the sense of the crooked stick used for defence of the wicket, it is certain, from the evidence of old pictures, if from nothing else, that crooked sticks, like the modern hockey sticks, filled, as best they might, the function of the bat. They are figured as long and narrow, with a curving lower end. There was no question in those days of the bat passing the four-inch gauge. They must have been very inferior, as weapons of defence for the wicket, to our modern bats—broomsticks rather than bats—more than excusing, when taken in connection with the rough ground, the smallness of the scores, even though the bowling was all underhand and, practically, there was no defence. The solution of these problems, however, is, I fear, buried in the mists of antiquity, and one scarcely dares even to hope for a solution of them, or the fixing of the date of the changes. There are other problems that do not seem as if they ought to be so hopelessly beyond our ken. In Nyren's cricketer's guide, one of the laws of cricket, therein quoted, provides that the wickets shall be pitched by the umpires, yet in part of his time, if not all of it—and when the change was made I cannot find out—it must have been the custom for the bowler to choose the pitch, for he records special praise of the chief bowler of the old Hambledon Club, that on choosing a wicket he would be guided not only by the kind of ground that would help him individually best, but also would take pains to see that the bowler from the other end had a nice bumping knob to pitch the ball on—for by this time "length" bowling, as it was called, had come into general use. Nyren's words are that he "has with pleasure noticed the pains he—Harris—has taken in choosing the ground for his fellow-bowler as well as himself."

In 1774 there was a meeting, under the presidency of Sir William Draper, supported by the Duke of Dorset, the Earl of Tankerville, Sir Horace Mann, and other influential supporters of cricket, to draw up laws for the game, and therein it is stated that the "pitching of ye first wicket is to be determined by ye cast of a piece of money," but it does not then say by whom they are to be pitched, nor does this function come within the province of the umpires as therein defined. This, therefore, is the first problem which I would ask the help of all cricketing readers towards solving—the date at which the pitching of the stumps ceased to be the business or privilege of the bowler. It was the introduction of "length" bowling, no doubt—previously it was all along the ground—real bowling as in bowls—that forced them to straighten the bats. Mr. Ward, in some memoranda which he gave Nyren, and which the latter quoted at large, says of these bats, used in a match that arose from a challenge on behalf of Kent County, issued by Lord John Sackville, to play All England in 1847: "The batting could neither have been of a high character, nor indeed safe, as may be gathered from the figure of the bat at that time, which was similar to an old-fashioned dinner-knife curved at back and sweeping in the form of a volute at the front and end. With such a bat the system must have been all for hitting; it would be barely possible to block, and when the practice of bowling length balls was introduced, and which (*sic*) gave the bowler so great an advantage in the game, it became absolutely necessary to change the form of the bat in order that the striker might be able to keep pace with the improvement. It was therefore made straight in the pod, in consequence of which, a total revolution, it may be said a reformation too, ensued in the style of play."

Then follows a record of the score of the match, which need not be detailed. England made 40 and 70, and Kent 53 and 58 for nine wickets, a gallant win. "Some years after this," Mr. Ward continues—it is to be presumed Nyren quotes the *ipsissima verba*, for whenever he wants to put in anything off his own bat it appears above his initials in a note—"the fashion of the bat having been changed to a straight form, the system of blocking was adopted"—that is to say, some years after 1740.

The date is vague. Let us say early in the second half of the eighteenth century, and I think we may go so far as to say that cricket, as we understand it, began then too. It can hardly have been cricket—this entirely aggressive batting. The next date of importance as marking an epoch, if we may speak of the next when we have left the last so much to conjecture, is 1775. On 22nd of May of that year there was a great match "in the Artillery Ground between five of the Hambledon Club and five of All England, when Small went in, the last man, for fourteen runs and fetched them. Lumpy"—a very famous bowler baptized Edward, surnamed Stevens—"was bowler upon the occasion, and it having been remarked that his balls had three times passed between Small's stumps, it was considered to be a hard thing upon the bowler that his straightest ball should be so sacrificed; the number of the stumps was in consequence increased from two to three."

Engraved in 1743 by H. Roberts. After L. P. Boitard.
AN EXACT REPRESENTATION OF THE
GAME OF CRICKET.

That is plain enough, but what is not plain is the height of the stumps at that time.

Mr. Pycroft puts the height of the stumps at 1 foot, with a width of only 6 inches, up to 1780, and it is evident from what Nyren says—

(a) that he had never seen stumps of 1 foot high and 2 feet wide;

(b) that they were not of 22 inches high until 1775.

Therefore here is evidence in support of Mr. Pycroft's 1 foot high and 6 inch wide wicket, to say nothing of the unimpeachable value of his own statements. But he himself adduces nothing that I can find in its support, nor does he attempt to give us the date of the first narrowing of the stumps; and with regard to the alteration from two low stumps to three 22-inch stumps I am obliged to find him at variance with Nyren.

The point, therefore, that I want to light on is the date and circumstances of the change from wickets of two stumps 1 foot high and 2 feet apart, to wickets of two stumps 1 foot high, and only 6 inches apart. This very drastic change appears to have been accomplished without a word of historical comment upon it. There was a deal of discussion at the time of the introduction of the third stump about the probable effect on the game of this change, some arguing that it would shorten the game—that every one would get out quickly.

Mr. Ward took the opposite view, that it would lead to more careful and improved batting, and cites a remarkable match played in 1777 between the Hambledon Club and All England, in which, despite the third stump, England made 100 and 69; and Hambledon, in a single innings, made the wonderful score of 403. Aylward, who seems to have gone in eighth wicket down, scored 167, individually, notwithstanding that he had the mighty "Lumpy" against him.

Mr. Ward's memoranda therefore give us some interesting facts.

So far as we can see back, the distance between the wickets has always been 22 yards, but up to about some time in the first half of the eighteenth century the wicket consisted of two stumps 1 foot high, 2 feet apart, with a cross stump, and a hole between them.

Later, this was changed for two stumps, first of 1 foot and then of 22 inches high, 6 inches apart, with a bail and a popping crease.

About 1750 "length" bowling was introduced, superseding the all-along-the-ground business, and nearly concurrently the bats straightened instead of curved. And I think we can scarcely say "cricket" began before that, whatever "club-ball" or "stool-ball" may have done.

In 1775 a third stump was added.

This last date, I know, does not agree with Mr. Pycroft, but I cannot quite make out what his original sources are. He writes: "From an MS. my friend"—he has mentioned so many friends in the previous paragraph that it is impossible to identify the one he means—"received from the late Mr. William Ward, it appears that the wickets were placed 22 yards apart as long since as the year 1700. We are informed also that putting down the wickets, to make a man out in running, instead of the old custom of popping the ball into the hole, was adopted on account of severe injuries to the hands, and that the wicket was changed at the same time—1779-80—to the dimensions of 22 inches by 6, with a third stump added." So, on the authority of the "MS. received by his friend"—it may have been the very memoranda given to Nyren, for Mr. Pycroft has mentioned Nyren in the preceding paragraph—Pycroft cites Ward as lumping together the double change from the two low stumps to the three higher stumps in 1779-80, whereas, in his memoranda to Nyren, Mr. Ward distinctly names 1775 as the date at which the third stump was added.

Curiously enough, Pycroft must have known all about this, really, but it slipped his memory, for, a page or two further, we find him quoting almost Nyren's or Ward's words: "In a match of the Hambledon Club in 1775, it was observed, at a critical point in the game, that the ball passed three times between Mr.

Small's two stumps without knocking off the bail, and then, first a third stump was added, and seeing that the new style of balls which rise over the bat rose also over the wickets, *then but 1 foot high*, the wicket was altered to the dimensions of 22 inches by 8, and again, to its present dimensions of 27 inches by 8 in 1817." Though I find all up to that point in Nyren, I do not find the italicised words, but I have no doubt they present the fact quite accurately. They tell us nothing, however, as to the date at which the wicket was first narrowed.

Another curious piece of information Mr. Ward gives us, by the way. "Several years since—I do not recollect the precise date—a player named White, of Ryegate, brought a bat to a match which, being the width of the stumps, effectually defended his wicket from the bowler, and in consequence a law was passed limiting the future width of the bat to 4-1/4 inches. Another law also decreed that the ball should not weigh less than 5-1/2 oz. or more than 5-3/4 oz." Nyren appends a note to this: "I have a perfect recollection of this occurrence, also that subsequently an iron frame, of the statute width, was constructed for, and kept by, the Hambledon Club, through which any bat of suspected dimensions was passed, and allowed or rejected accordingly." "Several years since," says Mr. Ward, or Nyren, writing, as I presume, about the year 1833, so that perhaps we may put this invention of the gauge about 1830, or a little earlier. I wonder who has this iron gauge now. Has it been sold up for old iron?

That is a third very practical problem that one would like answered.

And is it not curious to see how the rules were made and modified to meet the occasions as they arose. The misfortune of that

> Honest Lumpy who did 'low,
> He ne'er could bowl but o'er a brow—

in bowling so many times between the stumps of the too

greatly blessed Small—whence the introduction of the third stump. And White with his barn-door bat, from "Ryegate," as it pleases them to spell it, compelling the use of the gauge.

We are too apt to think of the laws as "struck off at one time," like the American Constitution, instead of regarding them as something of slow growth in the past, that will have to grow, with our growth, in the future. We shall get into trouble if we regard them as something too sacred to touch and do not legislate as occasion arises.

We have altered them greatly since that meeting at the Star and Garter in Pall Mall in 1774, when they seem first to have been committed to writing, and by the end of the twentieth century it is likely that we shall have modified them considerably from this present form. We have a notion that our forefathers played the game in such a sportsmanlike manner, taking no possible advantage but such as was perfectly open and above-board, that they required scarcely any rules to guide them, but some sad things that the stern historian has to notice about the influence that betting had at one time on cricket—this, and also a sentence or two from these very memoranda of Mr. Ward, whom Nyren extols as the mirror of all cricketing chivalry—may show us, I think, that our cricketing forefathers had something human in them too. How is this for a piece of artful advice? "If you bring forward a fast bowler as a change, contrive, if fortune so favours you, that he shall bowl his first ball *when a cloud is passing over*, because, as this trifling circumstance frequently affects the sight of the striker, you may thereby stand a good chance of getting him out." And again, a little lower on the same page: "Endeavour, by every means in your power—such as, by changing the bowling, by little alterations in the field, or by any excuse you can invent—to delay the time, that the strikers may become cold or inactive."

A very cunning cricketer, this Mr. Ward.

Previously he had said: "If two players are well in, and warm with getting runs fast, and one should happen to be put out, supply his place immediately, lest the other become cold and stiff." Now just compare these two last suggestions with each other, you will say, I think, that the last is fair and just and proper counsel, instilling a precaution that you have every right to take, but the former, according to the modern sense of what is right and sportsmanlike, seems to me to be counselling something perilously near the verge of sharp practice. You send your man out quickly, that the other may not grow cold, and what happens? Your purpose is defeated by the bowler and field purposely dawdling in order that the man *may* grow cold. It does not strike one as quite, quite right, though no doubt it is not against the rules. But it is tricky, a little tricky. And so again we draw a date, without his suspecting it, of a new moral epoch, from our invaluable Mr. Ward. About 1833, or a little later, we grew a trifle more delicate and particular in some small points of cricketing behaviour and sportsmanlike dealing. The betting, and the like evil practices at one time connected with the game, were a grosser scandal which carried their own destruction with them.

If any man, therefore, can throw light on these three dark points, I shall be very grateful to him—the date at which the first high wicket was narrowed down to 6 inches, the date at which the bowler ceased to have the pitching of the wicket, and the present habitation of that famous piece of old iron, the gauge used on the barn-door bat of White of Ryegate. Nyren, the matchless historian of the game, reveals himself, in his little history, as a very estimable man, of some matchless qualities for his task—an unbounded love of his subject and a sweet nature perfectly free of the slightest taint of jealousy. He writes of no other cricketing societies, except incidentally, than of those men of Hambledon in Hampshire. *Quorum pars magna fui*, as he says, with a single explosion of very proper pride, and a note appended thereto explaining apologetically that he has some certain knowledge of Latin. But after this single expression, very fully justified, for he was the beloved father of the Hambledon Club for years, he speaks of himself again hardly at all, just as if he had no hand in its successes, preferring to find some generous word to say of all the rest—of Beldham, Harris, Aylward, Lumpy. Beldham was not nearly so handsome to him, speaking of him to Mr. Pycroft. "Old Nyren was not half a player as we reckon now," was Beldham's verdict. However, the old man was fifty then.

At least he was a very good type of an Englishman and cricketer, whatever his class as a player, or he could never have written that book. And how much Hambledon may have owed to Nyren we can never know. As it is, Hambledon has the credit that Nyren specially claims for it of being the *Attica*, the centre of early civilisation, of the cricketing world. But there may have been other Atticas—only, like the brave men before Agamemnon, unsung, for want of their Homeric Nyrens.

The fact of the matter is, we know little but gossip of how the cricket world went before the year 1786, when Bentley takes up the running and records the scores. A sad fire occurred in the M.C.C. Pavilion—at that time the Club played where the Regent's canal now runs, after being built out of Dorset Square—and burnt all the old score books—irreparable loss.

Mr. Pycroft made an excursion into the home of the Beldhams, and brought out much valuable gossip, along with the unhandsome criticism on Nyren. "In those days," says Beldham—1780, when Mr. Beldham was a boy—"the Hambledon Club could beat all England, but our three parishes around Farnham at last beat Hambledon."

"It is quite evident," adds Mr. Pycroft to this, "that Farnham was the cradle of cricket."

Something that Beldham and others may have said to Mr. Pycroft may have made this fact "quite evident" to him, but I cannot see that he has transmitted any such evidence to us. This much, however, I think we may say with confidence, that all that was best of cricketing tradition and practice *in the south of England*—that is to say, as far as was in touch at all with its influences—clustered in the little corner of Surrey in which the parish of Farnham is. But that is not to say that there were not other nuclei of cricket in the north and elsewhere, and I think there is evidence to lead us to think there were other centres, perhaps less energetic.

The "county" boundaries were not so rigid in those days. "You find us regularly," says Beldham to Mr. Pycroft—"us" being Farnham and thereabouts—"on the Hampshire side in Bentley's book," and it is quite true.

Then, from this little nucleus, cricket in the south extended. Beldham had a poor opinion of the cricket of Kent at first. Crawte, one of the best Kent men, was "stolen away from us," in Beldham's words. Aylward, the hero of the 167 runs, was taken, also to Kent, by Sir Horace Mann, as his bailiff, but "the best bat made but a poor bailiff, we heard." Sussex was a cricketing county from an early date, but Beldham had a poor opinion of its powers likewise.

The elements of the nucleus formed round Farnham were disseminated, as much as anything, by the support that certain rich and influential people gave the game. We have seen how Sir Horace Mann stole away Aylward. Other great supporters of the game were Earl Darnley, Earl Winchelsea, Mr. Paulet, and Mr. East—all before the centuries had turned into the eighteens.

"Kent and England," says Mr. Pycroft, "was as good an annual match in the last as in the present century." But in those days, as even his own later words show us, "Kent," so called, sometimes had three of the best All England men given in, even in a match against "England." They were not so particular then—what they wanted was a jolly good game, with a good stake on it.

"The White Conduit Fields and the Artillery Ground," Pycroft goes on, "supplied the place of Lord's, though in 1817 the name of Lord's is found in Bentley's matches, implying, of course, the old Marylebone Square, now Dorset Square, under Thomas Lord, and not the present, by St. John's Wood, more properly deserving the name of Dark's than Lord's. The Kentish battlefields were Sevenoaks—the land of Clout, one of the original makers of cricket balls—Coxheath, Dandelion Fields, in the Isle of Thanet, and Cobham Park, also Dartford Brent and Pennenden

Heath; there is also early mention of Gravesend, Rochester, and Woolwich. The Holt, near Farnham, and Moulsey Hurst, were the Surrey grounds.

THE GAME OF CRICKET.

From an Engraving. Published in 1787.
THE CRICKET FIELD NEAR WHITE CONDUIT HOUSE.

But there was cricket further afield. In 1790 the Brighton men were playing, and in the following year we find an eleven of old Etonians, with four players given, playing the M.C.C. team; also with four professionals, in Rutlandshire. This M.C.C. team went on to play eleven "yeomen and artisans of Leicester," defeating them sorely, and in the same year the Nottingham men met with a similar fate at the hands of the Club.

From these matches and their results we are now able, I think, to infer two things—first, that cricket had been played for some long while, not as an imported invention, but as an aboriginal growth, in these northern counties before these teams visited them from the south, and secondly, that the southern counties had brought it to a much higher pitch of perfection, for they could never have gone down so ninepinlike before any eleven of the Marylebone Club. Likely enough the inspired doctrine, of the straight bat and the left elbow up, of that gifted baker of gingerbread, Harry Hall of Farnham, had not travelled so far as the home of these northern folk, and in that case they would have been at a parlous disadvantage to those who had been brought up by its lights. They had not perhaps been so long in the habit of coping with "length" balls, which made the adoption of the left elbow up almost a necessity of defence. When the bowling came all along the ground it did not matter. Also there was in the south that prince of bowlers, Harris, whose magical deliveries shot up so straightly from the ground that it was almost essential for playing them to get out to the pitch of the ball. And if they had not this bowling, what was to educate them, unassisted, to a higher standard of batting? But they were not left unassisted, for the masterly elevens from the south began to come among them, and taught them many things, no doubt, both by example and by precept.

This was in 1791. 1793 brings a wider ray of light on the scene of cricket history. Essex and Herts come on the scene as cricketing counties—of second class, as we should call them now, to Kent and Surrey, but players and lovers of cricket all the same. They combined elevens apparently, and played twenty-two against an eleven of England, which beat them in a single innings. Mr. Pycroft has a specially interesting note in this connection. He was told by two old cricketers, one a Kent man and the other an Essex man, that when they were boys, cricket in both these counties was a game of the village, rather than of clubs. "There was a cricket bat behind the door, or else up in the bacon rack, in every cottage." Of course in London it was a game played in clubs, for they only could find the spaces where land was valuable. It was in the year of 1793 that "eleven yeomen at Oldfield Bray, in Berkshire, had learned enough to be able to defeat a good eleven of the Marylebone Club."

I am scandalised by the wholesale way I have to steal early history from Mr. Pycroft's book. The only excuse is that I do not know where to go to better it, though probably I may supplement it from chance sources.

In 1795 he tells us of matches in which the captains were respectively the Hon. Colonel Lennox—who fought a duel with the Duke of York—and the Earl of Winchelsea. A munificent supporter of the game was my Lord of Winchelsea, and used to rig out his merry men in suits of knee-breeches, shirts, hosen, and silver caps. It was a kind of feudal age of cricket, when the great captains prided themselves on the powers of their retainers, and staked largely on the result.

"In 1797," says Pycroft, "the Montpelier Club and ground attract our notice," and then goes on to speak of Swaffham in Norfolk, as a country of keen but not very successful cricketers. Lord Frederick Beauclerk took down an eleven that appears to have beaten three elevens combined of the Norfolk folk, and that in a single innings. This Lord Frederick Beauclerk, with the Hon. H. and Hon. J. Tufton, got up the first Gents *v.* Players match in 1798; but though the Gents, after the generous fashion of the day, were reinforced by the three chief flowers of the professional flock—namely, Tom Walker, Beldham, and Hammond—the Players beat them. In the same year Kent essayed to play England, only to be beaten into little pieces, and in 1800 they began the new century more modestly by playing with twenty-three men against twelve of England.

THE LAWS OF THE NOBLE GAME OF CRICKET.
As revised by the club at st. Mary-le-bone.
From the frontispiece to the laws.

For of course, after all has been said, the centre of the national game, as of everything national, was then, as now, smoky London. Lord's Pavilion was then, as it had been since 1787, on the site that Dorset Square occupies now. In London the men collected who loved cricket, and had the money to bet on the game and to engage the services of the players. There were keener cricketers, more general interest in cricket, then than a little later in the century. Three to four thousand spectators sometimes came to see a match at Lord's, and royalties sometimes took a hand in the game.

In the first years of the new century, Surrey was the great cricketing county. Only two of the All England eleven, Lord Frederick Beauclerk and Hammond, came from any other county. Hammond was wicket-keeper to the famous Homerton Club—"the best," says Mr. Ward, quoted by Pycroft, "we ever had. Hammond played till his sixtieth year, but Brown and Osbaldestone put all wicket-keeping to the rout"—by the pace of their bowling, of course.

About the first decade of the century the counties seem to have been divided off more strictly, for cricketing purposes, than before. Hampshire and Surrey, as we saw, ran in double harness, the men of Hants helping Surrey in a match, and the Surreyites mutually helping Hampshire. But now they no longer play together. Broadhalfpenny and even Windmill Down have gone to thistles, and the gallant Hambledon Club is no more. Godalming is mentioned as the strongest local centre of the game, and in 1808 Surrey had the glory of twice beating England in one season. But in 1821 the M.C.C. is again playing the "three parishes," Godalming, Farnham, and Hartley Row, and it is in the accounts of this very same year that we tumble on a dark and significant observation. "About this time," said Beldham to Mr. Pycroft, "we played the Coronation match, M.C.C. against the Players of England. We scored 278 and only six wickets down, when the game was given up. I was hurt, and could not run my notches; still James Bland and the other Legs begged of me to take pains, for it was no sporting match, 'any odds and no takers,' and they wanted to shame the gentlemen against wasting their—the Legs'—time in the same way another time."

"James Bland and the other Legs." At this distance of time we may perhaps repeat the epithet or nickname, and even class a named man under it, without the risk of an action for libel. Perhaps even the term "Legs" did not imply all the qualities which attach to it to-day, but in any case it is surely something of a shock to come on the presence of these questionable gentlemen just casually stated, not with any note of surprise, but merely as if they were a common and even essential accompaniment of a cricket match.

Of course we knew quite well that our forefathers betted large stakes between themselves, often on single-wicket matches. This was a favourite style of match with Mr. Osbaldestone—the Squire,—because his bowling was so fast that no one, practically, could hit it in front of the wicket, and hits did not count for runs, in single-wicket, behind the wicket. In double-wicket matches he often "beat his side," we are told—beat his own side—"by byes," no long-stop being able to stop his bowling effectively. The chief check to the Squire's career seems to have been the discovery of the famous Browne of Brighton, who bowled, some said, even faster. Beldham, however, made a lot of runs off the latter on one special occasion. This is a digression, into which the consideration of single-wicket matches for money—and is it a wonder we do not have more of them now?—beguiled me. But perhaps it is a good thing that we do not have them, for they may well have been the root and source of all the subsequent "leg-work." The Coronation match is the first occasion on which Mr. Pycroft notices the "Legs," in his order of writing, but lower down on the very same page he quotes some words of Mr. Budd, who shared, with Lord Frederick Beauclerk, the credit of being the best amateur cricketer of the day, relative to a match at Nottingham—M.C.C. *v.* Twenty-two of Notts—in which the same evil influence is apparent. "In that match," he says, "Clarke played"—the future captain of the All England travelling team. "In common with others, I lost my money, and was greatly disappointed at the termination. *One paid player was accused of selling,* and *never employed after.*"

Mr. Budd must have done his level best to avert defeat, too, for Bentley records that he caught out no less than nine of the Notts men; but *one paid player was accused of selling,* and Clarke was on the other side! However it happened, Notts won. Mr. Pycroft also says that in old Nyren's day the big matches were always made for £500 a side, apart, as we may presume, from outside betting.

Nowadays a sovereign or a fiver on the 'Varsity match is about the extent of the gambling that cricket invites. The James Bland referred to above had a brother, Joe—*Arcades ambo*, bookmakers both. These, with "Dick Whittom of Covent Garden—profession unnamed,—Simpson, a gaming-house keeper, and Toll of Esher, as regularly attended at a match as Crockford and Gully at Epsom and Ascot."

Mr. Pycroft scouts the idea that a simple-minded rustic of Surrey or Hampshire would long hold out against the inducements that these gentry would offer them, "at the Green Man and Still," to sell a match, and indeed some of the naïve revelations that were made to him by rustic senility when he went to gossip with it, over brandy and water, might confirm him in a poor opinion of the local virtue.

"I'll tell the truth," says one, whom he describes as a "fine old man," but leaves in kindly anonymity. "One match of the county I did sell, a match made by Mr. Osbaldeston at Nottingham. I had been sold out of a match just before, and lost £10, and happening to hear it, I joined two others of our eleven to sell, and get back my money. I won £10 exactly, and of this roguery no one ever suspected me; but many was the time I have been blamed for selling when as innocent as a babe." Then this old innocent, with his delightful notions of *cavalleria rusticana* and the wooing back of his £10, goes on to tell the means—hackneyed enough in themselves—by which the company of the Legs seduced the obstinacy of rustic virtue. "If I had fifty sons," he said, "I would never put one of them, for all the games in the world, in the way of the roguery that I have witnessed. The temptation was really very great—too great by far for any poor man to be exposed to."

There is a pathetic dignity about this simple moralising that contrasts well with the levity of his previous confession, but the state of things that it shows is really very disgusting. It is another tribute to the merit of this first of English games that it should have lived through and have lived down such a morbid condition.

"If gentlemen wanted to bet," said Beldham, "just under the

pavilion sat men ready, with money down, to give and take the current odds. These were by far the best men to bet with, because, if they lost, it was all in the way of business; they paid their money and did not grumble." The manners of some of the fraternity must have changed, not greatly for the better, since then. "Still," he continues, "they had all sorts of tricks to make their betting safe." And then he quotes, or Mr. Pycroft quotes—it is not very clear, and does not signify—Mr. Ward as saying, "One artifice was to keep a player out of the way by a false report that his wife was dead." It was as clever a piece of practical humour as it was honest. What a monstrous state of things it reveals!

And then Beldham, inspirited by Mr. Pycroft's geniality and brandy and water, goes on to assure him—as one who takes a view which the majority would condemn as childishly charitable—that he really does not believe, in spite of all that has been said, that any "gentleman," by which he means "amateur," has ever been known to sell a match, and he cites an instance in which for curiosity's sake he put the honesty of a certain noble lord to the test by covertly proposing selling a match to him. But though his lordship, who seems to have been betting against his own side, had actually £100 on the match, even this inducement was not enough to tempt the nobleman from the paths of virtue.

We will hope that no amateur did fall, and may join with Beldham in "believing it impossible," but the fiction that they did was used by the Legs to persuade any man of difficult honesty to go crooked. "Serve them as they serve you," was the argument, or one of the arguments, used. That "fine old man" whom Mr. Pycroft drew out so freely gives no edifying pictures of the players of the day: "Merry company of cricketers, all the men whose names I had ever heard as foremost in the game, met together, drinking, card-playing, betting, and singing, at the Green Man—that was the great cricketers' house—in Oxford Street—no man without his wine, I assure you, and such suppers as three guineas a game to lose and five to win—that was then the sum for players—could never pay for long."

That was their rate of payment, and that their mode of life—perhaps not the best fitted for the clear eye and the sound wind.

It appears that this degrading condition of cricket was brought to an end by its own excesses; it became a crying scandal. "Two very big rogues at Lord's fell a-quarrelling." They charged each other with all sorts of iniquities in the way of selling matches, all of which accusations, when compared with the records, squared so nicely with the truth that they carried conviction, and "opened the gentlemen's eyes too wide to close again to those practices."

Mr. Pycroft has a note on his own account about the match at Nottingham in which his informant confessed to him that he was paid to lose. There were men on the other side who were paid to lose too, but, perhaps because there were twenty-two of them, they could not do it, but won in their own despite.

It must have produced funny cricket, this selling of a match both ways, and Mr. Pycroft picked up a story of a single-wicket match in which both were playing to lose, where it was only by accident that a straight ball ever was bowled, but when it came it was always fatal. It reminds us of the much-discussed wides and no-balls bowled in the 'Varsity match to avert the follow-on: but, thank heaven, there is no suspicion of fraudulent financial motives in even the queerest of cricketing tactics to-day.

It is truly wonderful how all heavy betting has gone out. Partly, no doubt, this is because men play more in clubs. When individuals used to get up matches the players' expenses came very heavy; therefore they made the matches for a considerable stake to cover them, but the practice cannot have comforted the losers much. Nowadays the club pays players out of the subscribed funds.

Why the single-wicket game is all given up is hard to say, for it is an age of individual emulation, but we are content with the better part of the game of eleven aside. And when first was that number, which seems to have some constant attraction for the cricketer, introduced? We cannot tell. It seems usual from the dawn of history. Moreover, the length of the pitch was always, so far as the historic eye can pierce, twenty-two yards—twice eleven, and twice eleven inches was the height of the stumps when they were first raised from the foot-high wicket.

Mr. Budd told Mr. Pycroft of a curious single-wicket match in which he was something more than *magna*, even *maxima, pars.* It was against Mr. Braund, for fifty guineas. Mr. Braund was a tremendously fast bowler. "I went in first, and, scoring seventy runs, with some severe blows on the legs—nankin knees and silk stockings, and no pads in those days—I consulted my friend and knocked down my wicket, lest the match should last to the morrow, and I be unable to play"—on account of the injuries to his nankin knees, I suppose. "Mr. Braund was out without a run. I went in again, and making the seventy up to a hundred, I once more knocked down my own wicket, and once more my opponent failed to score."

Another interesting match that Mr. Pycroft records was Mr. Osbaldeston and William Lambert against Lord Frederick Beauclerk and Beldham. Mr. Osbaldeston, on the morning of the match, which was fixed under "play or pay" conditions, found himself too ill to play, so Lambert tackled the two of them, and actually beat them. I am sorry to say I find a record of a little temper shown—perhaps naturally enough—in this match, as on another occasion, when he was bowling to that barn-door bat of the Hambledon Club, Tom Walker, by Lord Frederick Beauclerk; but after all, what man is worth his salt without a temper? And no doubt both occasions were very trying.

The date of these single-wicket matches was about 1820, which brings matters up to about the time at which a stopper should be put on the mouth of this gossiping and cribbing Muse of History, for we are coming to the days as to which men still living are able to tell us the things that they have seen.

From a Painting by James Pollard.
A MATCH ON THE HEATH.

The laws of the noble game of cricket as revised by the Club at St. Mary-le-bone.

CHAPTER II

EARLY DEVELOPMENTS OF THE CRICKETING ART BY THE EDITOR

When I first formed the presumptuous design of editing this work, it was my original purpose to divide this chapter into two parts, whereof the one should treat of the development of batting and the other of the development of bowling. But I very soon found that such a division would never do, for it would be a dividing of two things that were in their nature indivisible, from the historian's point of view, the one being the correlative of the other, and the effects of the one upon the other being ever constant. Of course those effects have been mutual; the bowling has educated the batting, and in his turn, again, the batsman has been the instructor of the bowler. No sooner has the one changed his tactics at all than the other has changed front a little in order to meet this new attack. Naturally, perhaps, it seems that the bowler has the oftener taught the batsman, than *vice versa*; the aggressor, by a new form of attack, forcing on the defendant a new line of defence. I think it is the generally accepted view to-day that it is the bowling "that makes the batting," but on the other hand one is inclined to think that the excellence of the Australian bowling, and also of their wicket-keeping and general fielding, is very much the result of playing on such perfect wickets that the batsman practically would never get out unless fielding, wicket-keeping, and bowling were all of the highest quality. Therefore, in that special instance it may rather be said that the batting, under specially favourable conditions of climate and wickets, has "made the bowling." Of course the natural effect of playing on perfect wickets in matches that last as many days as you please has had its effect, and to us not altogether a pleasing effect, on the Australian batting, but this is scarcely the place to consider that feature of the case.

The first point of interest to notice is that Beldham is quite at one with us in attributing the advance in batting to the advance of bowling, notably to the wonderful bowling of Harris, which was of that portentous character to which the name of epoch-making is not misapplied, and Nyren is of the same opinion with Beldham, whom he considers to have been the first to play Harris's bowling with success by getting out to it at the pitch.

We have seen, in another part of the book, that, setting aside the stool-ball, and the other legendary sports of the ancients, which were "not cricket," the first game worthy of the name of cricket that appears in the dim twilight of history is the game they played at the beginning of the eighteenth century—say for simplicity's sake in 1700. In 1700 and for some time later the wicket that men bowled at was formed, as we have seen, of two stumps, each 1 foot high, 2 feet apart, and with a cross-stump by way of a bail laid from one to the other. Between the two stumps, and below the cross one, was a hole scraped in the ground—the primitive block-hole. There was no popping-crease: the batsman grounded his bat by thrusting the end of the bat into the block-hole. Then he was "in his ground." But if the wicket-keeper, or any fieldsman, could put the ball into the hole before the batsman had his bat grounded in it, the batsman was out. Observe, it was not a matter of knocking off the cross-stump with the ball, but of getting the ball into the hole before the batsman grounded his bat in it. It takes no very vivid imagination to picture the bruised and bloody fingers that must have resulted from the violent contact of the bat when there was a race for the block-hole between wicket-keeper and batsman.

And the bowling? The bowling of course was *bowling*, all along the ground, as in the famous old game of bowls. Very likely it was in some respects the best sort of bowling for the business.

With a wicket only a foot high, anything between the longest of long-hops or the yorkiest of yorkers would have jumped over it. They found out this disadvantage later, when they began to bowl "length" balls, which, after all is said, must have been far the more puzzling for the batsman. And besides the chance of going over the wicket, there was also the excellent opportunity of going through the wicket, between two stumps set as far apart as 2 feet. Probably this occurred so often that it did not seem particularly hard luck. The batsman, more probably, deemed himself very hardly used if he did not get two or three extra lives of this grace.

And after all, though no records that I can find have come down to us from those times, it is safe to infer that the batsmen did not make an overwhelming number of runs. Had it been so we should almost certainly have heard of it by oral tradition, and Aylward's great score of 167 at the end of the century would not have stood out as such a unique effort. Nor have we far to seek for the reason that the scores were not prodigious. Though the wicket was low, it was very broad, and a ball running over the surface of bumpy ground, as we may suppose those wickets to have been, would very often have taken off the cross-stump only a foot above the ground. Perhaps, even, at a foot high it was more assailable than at two feet by these methods of attack. Then too the weapons of defence—the bats, so to call them—are figured more like the hockey-sticks of to-day—"curved at the back, and sweeping in the form of a volute at the front and end," Mr. Ward's memoranda of Nyren say. Of course these were very inadequate weapons of defence, and in point of fact no defence seems ever to have been attempted. It was all hit. And for actual hitting of a ball always on the ground a bat of this shape may not have been so very ill adapted after all.

We do not know what the wiles of these old all-along-the-ground bowlers may have been. Probably they were fairly simple. Yet there is a significant word that crops up in the pages of Pycroft, that delightful writer, that almost inclines one to suspect these old-fashioned fellows of some guile. He constantly uses the expression "bias" bowling. He speaks of it, it is true, in connection with "length" balls, breaking from the pitch. But why should he have used the word "bias" unless it were in common parlance, and how should that singular word have come into common parlance unless from the analogy of the game of bowls, in which it is a cant term. In the game of bowls the bowls are sometimes weighted on one side, for convenience in making them roll round in a curve and so circumvent another bowl that may "stimy" them, to borrow a term from golf, from the jack; but sometimes—and this seems a more scientific form of the game—there is no bias in the bowl itself, but "side" can be communicated to it, by a finished player, with the same result as before. Now if it was the habit of these old-fashioned cricketers to bowl their "daisy-cutters" with bias on the ball, so that it would travel in a curve as it came along, the reason for the term as used by Pycroft is simple enough; but if this is not the explanation, the only alternative one is that the term first came into use—never having been mentioned in cricket before—for balls that broke from the pitch, wherein the analogy from bowls would be very far-fetched indeed, and the term altogether not one that would be likely to suggest itself. Therefore I think there is a likelihood—I claim no more for my inference—that these old cricketers bowled their underhand sneaks with spin on them, just as we often have seen them bowled—and a very good ball too on a rough wicket—in country cricket matches to-day.

Then we come to a change, and the date of that change appears to involve some of the highest authorities in a certain disagreement. But I am going to stick to Nyren, or rather to Mr. Ward's memoranda as edited by Nyren, rather than to Pycroft, both because the former wrote nearer to the date of the occurrences treated of, and also because the latter—though I love and revere his book—seems to me to have lumped dates together in a certain scornful, contemptuous haste, as if they were scarcely worth a good cricketer's attention. Nyren, or Mr. Ward for him, is more careful in his discrimination, according to my judgment as a grave historian.

According to Nyren, then, it was some time about or before 1746 that the stumps were both heightened and narrowed. From 1 foot they sprang up to 22 inches in height, and from 2 feet across they shrank to as little as 6 inches in width. A bail crossed their tops, and a popping-crease was drawn for the grounding of the bat, to the great saving, as we cannot doubt, of the wicket-keeper's fingers. Still, however, unless Nyren was mistaken, there were not as yet but two stumps—virtually it is certain he was mistaken in declining to believe that the game ever was played with a wicket of 2 feet width, but that does not prove him wrong in another matter in which all the probabilities are in his favour.

We are not given any very clear reason for this change in the height of wickets, but we very quickly see its effects. Hitherto bowling had been all along the ground, the wicket being so low that it was almost necessary to bowl in this now derided fashion if it was to be hit at all. But a wicket 10 inches higher might have its bail taken off by a higher-rising ball, the higher-rising ball was found to be a more difficult one for the batsman to hit, the higher-rising kind of ball was thereby proved the best for the bowler's purpose; in a word, "length" bowling, as they called it—the bowling of good length balls, as we should say—was introduced.

And now, all at once, the position of the unfortunate batsman was found to be a very parlous one indeed. For, remember, he had in his hand, to meet this bowling, a thing that had more resemblance to a hockey-stick than a cricket-bat. There is a certain "invisible length" which, as we all know, is extremely difficult to play with a modern square-faced bat and with all the science of modern theories of wielding it. How much more helpless then, as Euclid would put it, must the unfortunate man with the bandy-stick have felt when he saw coming towards him through the air a ball of that length which he knew would make it impossible when it reached him. Batsmen must have had a most miserable time of it for a year or two.

At length, out of their necessity was produced a new invention.

It was about the year 1750 that the "length" bowling came into fashion, and very soon afterwards the form of the cricket-bat was altered to that straight and square-faced aspect which gave it a chance of meeting the new bowling—which was assailing comparatively new wickets—on equal terms. Obviously there ought to be some kind of relation between the shape of the bat and the contour of the wicket that it is concerned to defend, and the contour of the upright 22-inch wicket demanded defence by a straight bat—that is to say, at first, merely a bat straight in itself. The gospel of the left elbow up and the meeting of the ball with bat at the perpendicular had not been preached thus early.

Engraved by Benoist After F. Hayman, R.A .
CRICKET, "AFTER THE PAINTING IN
VAUXHALL GARDEN."

And I take it that virtually cricket, worthy to be called by any such great name, did not really begin before this. This game of trundling along the ground at a two-foot wide wicket, and a man with a hockey-stick defending it, is really rather a travesty of the great and glorious game. The origin of cricket it was, no doubt, and as such is to be most piously revered, but actual cricket—hardly. Consider that old print of a game in progress on the Artillery Fields, where the players are equipped with the curved bats, wear knee-breeches, and the wicket is low and wide, with two stumps upright and one across. There is not a fieldsman on the off side of the wicket—a significant fact in itself; but further, and far more significant, a spectator is reclining on the ground, entirely at his ease, precisely in the position that point would occupy to-day. There can be but one meaning to this picture—that such a thing as off hitting was absolutely unknown. Possibly it was difficult enough to hit to the off, even with the best intentions, off these bats like bandy-sticks; it is at all events certain that it was a style of stroke not contemplated by the gentleman reclining on the ground.

I have spoken above of the bat as an instrument of defence. So to style it when writing of this era is to commit an anachronism. The earlier cricketers, even of the straight-bat epoch, were guiltless of the very notion of defence. They were all for aggression, trying to score off every ball. The reason of this was, no doubt, in the first place that the idea of merely stopping the ball had not occurred to them—partly because the object of the game is to score, and because the bandy-stick style of bat must have been singularly ill designed for defence; but also there is this further reason, that chance was much more on the batsman's side in the old days than it is now. Nowadays, if a ball is straight and the batsman misses it, it is a simple matter of cause and effect that the bails are sent flying and he is out. But with the wicket 2 feet wide, and no middle stump, this was by no means so inevitable. On the contrary, it must have been a very frequent occurrence for the ball to pass through the wicket without any disturbance of the timber. Even when the wicket was narrowed to 6 inches, there was still room for the ball to pass between the stumps, of which the fortune of the before-mentioned Small was a celebrated and flagrant instance. The old-time batsman was therefore not so essentially concerned with seeing that no straight ball got past his bat. He did not bother himself about defence. He gallantly tried to score off every ball that came to him.

Yet, for all that, his slogging was not like the slogging of to-day. He had no idea of jumping in and taking the ball at the half-volley. His notions went no further than staying in his ground and making the best he could of the ball in such fashion as it was pleased to come to him.

"These men"—the "old players," so called in 1780—says Mr. Pycroft, quoting the authority of Beldham, backed by that of Fennex, "played puddling about their crease, and had no freedom. I like to see a player upright and well forward, to face the ball like a man"—at this time of day, the wicket had lately been raised from 1 foot to 2 feet high, but had for some while been only 6 inches wide, a small mark for the bowler.

Mr. Pycroft goes on, quoting Beldham again: "There was some good hitting in those days"—towards the close of the eighteenth century is the date alluded to, as far as I can make out—"though too little defence. Tom Taylor would cut away in fine style, almost after the manner of Mr. Budd. Old Small was among the first members of the Hambledon Club. He began to play about 1750, and Lumpy Stevens at the same time. I can give you some notion, sir, of what cricket was in those days, for Lumpy, a very bad bat, as he was well aware, once said to me, 'Beldham, what do you think cricket must have been in those days when I was thought a good batsman?'"

This is instructive comment, as to the style of batting previous to 1780—that is the date that it appears we must fix for the change of style that brought batting in touch with modern theories. But by the way we ought to notice that Beldham spoke of the fielding as being very good, even in the oldest days of his recollection, and Mr. Pycroft is careful to add a note saying that this praise from Beldham was high praise indeed, and eminently to be trusted, as Beldham's own hands were also eminently to be trusted, whether for fielding the ball on the ground or for a catch.

But with the year 1780 we come to a new era in the art of batting, associated more particularly with the name and art of a famous bowler, David Harris, the association being again an illustration of the truth, which has several times already been in evidence, that it is the bowling that is the efficient cause in educating the batsman—that it is the bowling that "makes the batting."

"Nowadays," said Beldham to Mr. Pycroft, "all the world knows that"—namely, that the upright bat and the left elbow up and forward is the right principle of batting—"but when I began there was very little length bowling, little straight play, and very little defence either."

Beldham was a boy in 1780, and even before this, Harry Hall, the gingerbread-baker of Farnham, of immortal memory, was going about the country preaching the great truths about batting. May be he was but little listened to. At all events it is certain that until men had the straight bat to play with and the length bowling to contend with there can have been little opportunity or demand for straight batting.

"The first lobbing slow bowler I ever saw was Tom Walker," Beldham says. "When, in 1792, England played Kent, I did feel so ashamed of such baby bowling, but after all he did more than even David Harris himself. Two years after, in 1794, at Dartford Brent, Tom Walker, with his slow bowling, headed a side against David Harris, and beat him easily."

AN EARLY TICKET.

From a Drawing by Wm. Fecit.
WILLIAM AND THOMAS EARLE.

And this Walker, by the way, was a wonderful fellow in more departments of the game than one. A terrible stick, but very hard to get out—very slow between wickets, so that one of the old jokers said to him, "Surely you are well named Walker, for you are not much of a runner"—a moderate jest, but showing the sort of man he was. Then he was "bloodless," they said. However he was hit about the shins or fingers, he never showed a mark. Only David Harris, that terrible bowler, made the ball jump up and grind Tom Walker's fingers against the handle of the bat; but all Tom Walker did then was to rub his finger in the dust to stanch the reluctant flow of blood. It is all very grim and Homeric. David Harris, rather maliciously, said he liked to "rind Tom," as if he were a tree stem withered and gnarled. And it is a marvellous fact that a man of this character, whom you would call conservative to the core of his hard-grained timber, should actually have invented something new. But he did. He first tried the "throwing-bowling," the round-arm, which was credited to Willes—probably an independent invention, and so meriting equal honour—many years after. Well may Nyren speak of the Walkers, Tom and Harry, as those "anointed clod-stumpers." Harry was a hitter, his "half-hour was as good as Tom's afternoon."

And meanwhile what has become of David Harris? David Harris, it is said, once bowled him 170 balls for one run. And what manner of balls were these? Let us consider a moment a description of David Harris's bowling culled from Nyren. Parts of it lend themselves to the gaiety of nations, and the whole description, if not very lucid, is full of terror. "It would be difficult, perhaps impossible, to convey in writing an accurate idea of the grand effect of Harris's bowling"—the effect, as a matter of fact, is conveyed a deal more clearly than the way in which it was produced. "They only who have played against him can fully appreciate it. His attitude, when preparing for his run previously to delivering the ball, would have made a beautiful model for the sculptor. Phidias would certainly have taken him as a model. First of all, he stood erect as a soldier at drill; then, with a graceful curve of the arm, he raised the ball to his forehead"—singular and impressive ritual—"and drawing back his right foot, started off with his left. The calm look and general air of the man were uncommonly striking, and from this series of preparations he never deviated. His mode of delivering the ball was very singular. He would bring it from under the arm by a twist, and nearly as high as his arm-pit, and with this action *push* it, as it were, from him. How it was that the ball acquired the velocity it did by this mode of delivery, I never could comprehend."

Nor any one else either, for Harris was a very fast bowler. But I am inclined to think that there must have been some explanation to be discovered out of the fact that he was by profession—before cricket became his profession—a potter. With the strength of fingers that the potter acquires through working at his clay, he may have had the power of putting an amount of spin on the ball impossible for men whose digits had not gone through this course of training. In underhand bowling such as, after all is said, Harris's must have been, the spin is almost entirely the work of fingers. The turn of wrist had little share in it; for one thing, it was forbidden to deliver the ball with the knuckles uppermost.

And so it may well have been that, whatever the pace with which the ball was propelled, by these singular and statuesque means, through the air, it may have carried so much spin as to leap up twice as fast off the ground, as a billiard ball with much side on will seem to gain twice as much life after touching a cushion. And all that we read of Harris's bowling shows that the balls did come off the ground with tremendous speed.

"His balls," says Nyren, in another place, "were very little beholden to the ground when pitched; it was but a touch, and up again, and woe be to the man who did not get in to block them, for they had such a peculiar curl that they would grind his fingers against the bat. Many a time have I seen the blood drawn in this way from a batter who was not up to the trick. Old Tom Walker was the only exception. I have before classed him among the bloodless animals."

We have seen, however, that even from him Harris occasionally drew blood.

In Harris's day it was the custom for the bowler to choose the wicket, and it was always his preference to have a bump to pitch on, and so help this rising tendency of the ball off the pitch. Of course this would be the recognised aim of a bowler of to-day, but it was not so recognised then, and indeed Stevens, nicknamed "Lumpy," generally regarded as the second-best bowler to Harris of his day, always liked to bowl "o'er a brow" in order to make his balls shoot. The result was, as Nyren points out, that Lumpy—Lumpy of the honestly avowed preference for bowling "o'er a brow"—would hit the wicket oftener, but that more catches were given off Harris, though his balls often went over the wicket. But there was no manner of doubt as to which was the finer bowler. Harris was the man.

And now as to its effect on the batting. Notice these words of Beldham, for really they contain the kernel of the whole matter: "Woe be to the man who did not get in to block them, for they had such a peculiar curl that they would grind his fingers against the bat."

And again he says the same in more distinct words: "To Harris's fine bowling I attribute the great improvement that was made in hitting, and above all in stopping, for it was utterly impossible to remain at the crease, when the ball was tossed to a fine length; you were obliged to get in, or it would be about your hands, or the handle of your bat, and every player knows where its next place would be."

MR. JAMES HENRY DARK.
(The Proprietor of Lord's Cricket Ground, 1836-1864).

T. HUNT, OF DERBYSHIRE, d. 1858.

In this connection Mr. Pycroft writes as follows: "'Fennex,' said he"—"he" being Beldham again—"'Fennex was the first who played out at balls; before his day, batting was too much about the crease.' Beldham said that his own supposed tempting of Providence consisted in running in to hit. 'You do frighten me there jumping out of your ground,' said our Squire Paulet; and

Fennex used also to relate how, when he played forward to the pitch of the ball, his father 'had never seen the like in all his days,' the said days extending a long way back towards the beginning of the century. While speaking of going in to hit, Beldham said: 'My opinion has always been that too little is attempted in that direction. Judge your ball, and when the least overpitched, go in and hit her away.' In this opinion Mr. C. Taylor's practice would have borne Beldham out, and a fine dashing game this makes; only, it is a game for none but practised players. When you are perfect in playing in your ground, then, and then only, try how you can play out of it, as the best means to scatter the enemy and open the field."

So says Mr. Pycroft, a very high authority, and one whose instructions to the batsman are very sound and worthy of the very highest respect. No doubt he is right in his cautious counsel—human nature is prone to err on the side of rashness—but he does not notice the indisputable fact that it is easier to meet the ball at the pitch, if you can reach it, than later—always supposing it is not a rank long hop. He is rather inclined to treat this principle of getting out to the pitch as a counsel of perfection, and perhaps it is more easily put in practice now that wickets are more perfect than in his day, though if you really go out far enough—and unless you can get so far as to command the ball, however it break, it is surely better not to go out at all—the most troublesome ball has not time to develop much of its dangerous eccentricity before you have met it. Of course there is always the chance of missing it, and then there's the wicket-keeper's opportunity.

But, all details of prudence apart, there is no doubt that we have here a totally new departure in batting, devised, as is usual, to meet some new requirements on the part of the bowler. A very kindly, genial, remarkably honest man—a really loveable man—was this potter, David Harris, though he did say, in chaff, that he liked to "rind" Tom Walker, and certainly he was an epoch-making bowler, for he made the ball come off the ground with an underhand action in the very way that is the study of our overhanders. He was a good sportsman too, and when he had the pitching of the wicket, tried to give Lumpy, at the other end, a brow to bowl over, while he chose for himself a brow to pitch against. No one ever seems to have hinted that Harris's action was a jerk, though there were jerkers in the world in those days.

Beldham and Fennex, then, were the first to pick up the new style of going in to meet the pitch of the ball, and so prevent its jumping up "and grinding their fingers on the bat." Hitherto there had been good hitting, but all inside the crease, cutting and drawing to leg. Small had his bat straightened for the special purpose of making the draw stroke better. But hitherto there had been no idea of driving a shorter ball than a half-volley. Now first was developed the idea of going in to drive the ball and of forward defensive play; and therewith, as I conceive, the batsman's art became, in its principles, pretty much as Mr. Warner found it when his school coach began his education

CHAPTER III

BATTING BY P. F. WARNER

It has been said that good batsmen are born and not made, but my experience is rather to the contrary. There are certain gifts of eye and hand which all really good batsmen must possess, but I am strongly convinced that early practice and good coaching have a very great deal to do in the acquiring of all-round skill. A. E. Stoddart, whose retirement from first-class cricket has proved such a loss, not only to Middlesex, but to English cricket, is the only batsman who has attained to the first rank who did not start to play the game quite early in life, and he is the exception that proves the rule.

Any success I may have had as a batsman I attribute to my devotion to the game from my youngest days. Early rising in the West Indies is the custom, but so enthusiastic about cricket was I that I often got up at half-past five, so as to practise to the bowling of a black boy on a marble-paved gallery which provided the fastest and truest wicket I have ever played on. Even now I am ashamed to recall the number of broken window-panes I was responsible for, and many was the time that my black hero and I have taken to our heels, to be speedily followed by an irate nurse, who never failed to report the damage I had done to headquarters. But despite many a scolding, and prophecies that I should come to a bad end, I persevered in my wrong-doing, and to that perfect marble wicket and a good coach I owe the fact that I was seldom guilty of running away to square leg, a fault so common among boys. Therefore the first essential is a thoroughly good wicket to practise on, and a good wicket is not a difficult thing to obtain nowadays, what with the improved condition of grounds all over the country. And let me urge on every young cricketer the absolute necessity of practising in earnest from the very beginning. Endeavour to play at a net exactly as you would in a match, and if you are bowled out, try to feel almost as disappointed as if a similar fate had befallen you in a game. Pay attention to details, and if you make a bad stroke, notice where your mistake lay, remember it, and take the lesson to heart. But practise, practise, practise, and, if you are a keen cricketer, batting at the net may be made almost as enjoyable as batting in a match. Well, then, practise in earnest from the start of your career, and if possible get some keen and intelligent cricketer—not necessarily a great one—to coach you, but one with infinite patience and tact, who will occasionally give a word of encouragement, for an encouraging word and look do a greater amount of good than is generally imagined.

Having got a good wicket and a capable coach, see that a suitable bat is in your hand, and I strongly advise every boy to play with a bat suited to his strength and style; and here I may mention that it is a thousand times better to play with too light a bat than too heavy a one, for with too heavy a bat one cannot cut or time the ball correctly; besides, it is hardly possible to play straight with it, and a straight bat is the very essential of good sound batting. Giving the young cricketer a good driving and well-balanced bat, see that he puts on two pads, and at any rate one, if not two batting gloves. Thus equipped, he will be ready to take his place at the wicket, and the first thing our imaginary coach will have to teach him will be his POSITION AT THE WICKET. No fixed rules can be laid down as to the position a batsman should take up at the wicket, but undoubtedly the best advice that can be given is to take up the position most natural to him. The most popular way of standing is to place the right foot just inside the popping-crease, with the left just outside it, pointing towards the bowler or mid-off; but no two players stand exactly alike, and as I have said before, the most natural position is the best.

There used to be a difference of opinion as to whether a batsman should stand with his weight equally balanced on both legs, or on the right leg only, but nowadays the universally accepted theory is that the weight should be chiefly on the right leg. At any rate, W. G. Grace, K. S. Ranjitsinhji, C. B. Fry, and A. C. Maclaren are all of that opinion, and they certainly ought to know. L. C. H. Palairet's method of standing at the wicket is generally supposed to be the model attitude, and another cricketer whose position might well be studied is R. E. Foster, who, like Palairet, stands straight, but with a slight easing of the knees, which helps him to get a quick start at the ball. Both these cricketers stand as near as possible to their bats, without being leg before wicket, and I am a strong believer in this, for the reason that the nearer one is to the bat the more chance is there of playing absolutely straight and getting well over the ball. I am quite aware that there are one or two first-class batsmen who do not play with a straight bat, but they are men of wonderful eyesight, and their success has not altered my conviction that a boy should be taught to play with a straight bat.

As for taking guard, it does not matter whether you take middle, middle and leg, or leg stump. I have taken all three in a season. It is a mere question of inclination.

The bat should be held, I venture to think, in the manner most natural to the batsman, but the most common method is with the left hand nearly at the top of the handle, and the right hand somewhere about the middle; but there is no golden rule on the subject, and G. L. Jessop, for instance, holds the bat with his right hand at the very bottom of the handle. But Jessop is a genius, and his method should certainly not be copied by the young cricketer, unless the style of play Jessop adopts comes quite natural to him; then by all means he should be allowed to cultivate it. I rather believe myself in holding the bat as high up the handle with the right hand as possible—that is to say, about an inch or an inch and a half interval between the two hands.

This is the manner in which L. C. H. Palairet holds his bat, and I have always regarded and always shall regard him as the model for young cricketers to copy.

The first principle the coach has to instil into our young batsman is that he *must never move his right leg backwards* in the direction of short leg. He may move it to jump out to drive or to cut or to play back, but *never should he move it away from the wicket.*

This is the first point to be mastered by the beginner, for if the right leg is withdrawn away from the wicket, it is impossible to play with a straight bat, which, as I have said before, is the very essence of good batting. If a young batsman cannot refrain from running away, he should have his right leg pegged down.

CRICKET

From a Drawing by G. F. Watts, R.A.
BLOCK OR PLAY.

CRICKET

From a Drawing by G. F. Watts, R.A.
FORWARD PLAY.

The second principle to be inculcated is that *a straight bat is essential to success in batting*, though I do not mean to say that the bat should be held straight for every stroke, for the cut and the pull, for instance, are not made with a straight bat; but what I mean is that for defensive strokes, and in some scoring strokes, the bat must be held straight. A batsman who plays with an absolutely straight bat is nearly always a strong defensive player.

The third maxim is, *watch the ball*. Watch the bowler's arm as he runs up to bowl, and then the ball as it leaves his hand. Watch it closely right on to your bat, and do not start with a preconceived idea of where the ball is going to pitch, and do not make up your mind to make a certain stroke before the ball is actually delivered.

Playing the Ball

All strokes may be conveniently divided into two kinds, back and forward, and back play and forward play may be further divided into back and forward play for defensive purposes and back and forward play with the object of making runs. I will deal first with *Forward play*, and I will imagine that a good length ball has been delivered on a hard, true wicket. To play this ball correctly the batsman should get his left leg well out in the line of the ball, and then bring his bat as close as possible to his leg. This is the secret of all forward play, and the young cricketer cannot be too often urged to "get the left leg well out to the bat" when playing forward. Care should be taken not to overbalance oneself, but if body, wrist, and legs work correctly, the ball may be forced past the fielder, and it is really quite extraordinary the power that may be got into the stroke. The position of the hands changes during the forward stroke, the left wrist being on the side of the bat away from the wicket before the stroke is played, and on the opposite side at the expiration of the stroke. The ball must of course be kept down, and in order to do this the left shoulder must be kept well forward, pointing in the direction in which the stroke is made, and the bat must be at such an angle that the top of the handle is nearer to the bowler than the bottom of the blade. The whole weight of the body should be brought to bear on the stroke, and the batsman must make the most of his reach, and the whole thing should be one action and in one motion. Tom Emmett, the famous old Yorkshire cricketer, who was our coach at Rugby during the five years I was there, was never tired of teaching us this stroke. In playing forward the bat must be quite straight, and at the moment of actual contact with the ball the bat should be just behind the left leg. Now that the wickets are so good, forward play is a very effective weapon both of offence and defence to have in one's armoury, and it is therefore distinctly worth while for a batsman to acquire the highest efficiency in it.

The off drive may range anywhere from the left of the bowler to just in front of point, and the ball to be thus driven is one that is fairly well pitched up on the off side of the wicket, but not necessarily a half-volley. The great thing is to get well to the pitch of the ball, watch it, and not slash wildly at it. Care must be taken not to have a "go" at too wide a ball, for this is a favourite trick of slow bowlers, especially left-handers, and often results in an easy catch on the off side. There is one stroke, which is neither a genuine cut nor a genuine off drive, which may for convenience sake be dealt with here. The left leg is thrown out, as if the batsman were about to play a genuine off drive, but the ball is hit later than in the off drive, and with a horizontal rather than a perpendicular bat, the shoulders and forearm being brought into play rather more than the wrist. In some respects the stroke is very like the forward cut, of which I shall speak later, and many cricketers do not consider it an off drive, but rather in the nature of a cut. It is a useful stroke for a weak-wristed player. A good length ball on the off stump should be played in the direction of mid-off. A ball just wide of the off stump in the direction of extra cover, and a ball about a foot wide on the off side, should be played towards cover-point. The farther the ball is pitched outside the off stump, the farther ought the left leg to be thrown across the wicket, and the farther ought the left shoulder to be thrown forward. The wider the ball is, the more difficult it is to play, and a mistake common amongst beginners is that, without considering the direction of the ball, they advance the left leg straight down the wicket, just as if, in fact, the ball had pitched on the off stump, and not, for instance, a foot outside it. The left leg should be thrown *across the wicket almost in a line with the flight of the ball*. If the batsman plays forward at a ball a foot outside the off stump with his left leg straight down the wicket, he will find that the weight of his body will play no part in the stroke, and that should the ball break back he will be bowled out; therefore always remember to get the left leg well out to the bat, for apart from this being the golden rule for all forward play, there is an added advantage to be gained from the fact that, if the ball breaks enough to beat the bat, there will be little or no room for it to pass between the bat and the leg.

But in forward strokes, as in all other strokes, the great thing is to watch the ball carefully, for should you be playing forward with "your head in the air," that is to say, not looking at the ball, which at the last minute does something unexpected, either bumping or hanging on the pitch, you will for a certainty find yourself in trouble; and therefore, until you are thoroughly well set and have got the exact pace of the wicket, there should be a margin for emergencies, so that it should be possible to alter one's stroke at the last moment. The best way of playing a ball which one has gone forward to, and which one finds one cannot reach far enough to smother at the pitch, is to adopt the "half-cock" stroke. This stroke is made by holding the bat quite straight just over or slightly in front of the popping-crease and letting the ball hit it. It is a most excellent defensive stroke, and the proper way to play a ball whose length one has misjudged. W. G. Grace uses this stroke very frequently, as does F. S. Jackson. In making a forcing forward stroke the great thing is to swing the arms well and carry the stroke right through, which if well timed will send the ball very quickly to the boundary. Some batsmen play this forcing forward stroke so hard that it is difficult to distinguish it from a genuine hit, and I have a very vivid recollection of a grand innings of a hundred odd which A. E. Stoddart played at Lord's for Middlesex against Kent some five or six years ago. The wicket was hard and fast, and the power with which Mr. Stoddart forced good length balls from W. M. Bradley to the off boundary was astonishing. In offensive forward play great care should be taken not to bend the right knee, for with the bending of the right knee comes the sinking of the right shoulder, and if the shoulder sinks the batsman is very likely to get under the ball. When a batsman who is a strong forward player is thoroughly well set on a hard, true wicket, many of his runs will come from off drives, especially if the bowling be fast or medium paced, and the power one can get into an off drive, if body, wrist, and eye are working together, is almost as great as in the case of a genuine hit. It requires no great physique to be a powerful off driver, for a man of very slight build, if he is timing the ball well—and by timing the ball I mean the harmonious working of body, wrist, and eye—can make the ball travel to the boundary as fast as a strongly and powerfully built man. There are few better moments at cricket than when one has forced a good length ball through the fielders on the off side, standing well balanced where one is, and the ball making haste to the ring. There is a very conscious feeling that brain, eye, body, and hand have all acted in concert, and that a great deal has been accomplished with a minimum of exertion.

Back Play

As soon as a batsman has made up his mind to play a ball back, the weight of his body should be transferred to the left leg, and the right foot should be moved back towards the wicket and the left leg drawn up to it.

Many writers on cricket have laid it down as a rule that the right leg should never be moved in playing back, which may be all very well as an elementary principle for a boy who is just starting cricket, but which, I submit, with all respect, is altogether wrong if applied to one who has got over the initial difficulties of the game. For myself, were I coaching a boy, I should tell him to move the right leg in playing back, though of course I would never allow him to move it away from the wicket. With a moment's thought it will be seen that a batsman who moves his right leg towards the wicket must have a better chance of playing the ball correctly than one who stands with his right leg glued to the ground. In the first place, by moving back he makes the ball which he is shaping at shorter than it would have been if he had stood where he was by the distance that he stepped back. The ball is made shorter by two feet if the batsman moves two feet towards his wicket, instead of playing it where he originally stood, and the two feet more which in this case the ball has to travel gives the batsman so much the more time to judge and play it. Again, supposing a ball pitches on the off stump or just outside it, the batsman will assuredly play that particular ball more correctly if he moves his right leg across the wicket in a line with the off stump than if he keeps it firmly planted just off the leg stump. It stands to reason that if he moves his right leg across the wicket in a line with the ball, he will be nearer the direction the ball may take after pitching than if he adhered to his original position. Moreover, should the particular type of ball we are discussing break an inch or two from leg, the odds on his being caught at slip or the wicket are very great, should he not move his right leg across the wicket; whereas, should he bring his right leg across to the off stump and watch the ball closely after it has pitched, he will stand a far better chance of playing that ball in the middle of his bat than if he had remained with his right leg rooted to the earth. I well remember a very promising boy at Rugby, one who is now a county player, being nearly ruined by one of the cricketing masters insisting on his never moving his right leg, with the result that time after time was he caught at slip or the wicket, for the simple reason that he was too far off the ball when he played at it.

In playing forward, the golden rule is to get the left leg well forward to the direction the ball is taking, and the bat well up to the leg. The same rule applies in playing back. Get the right leg up to the line of the ball, and the bat as near as possible to the leg. The difficulty about moving back across the wicket is that the stroke requires considerable quickness of eye and foot, and quickness of foot is a point not half enough insisted on by the majority of coaches. All the best back players play back in this classical way—Victor Trumper, Ranjitsinhji, C. B. Fry, Tyldesley, A. C. Maclaren, and F. S. Jackson. If the ball in question breaks back into the batsman, he is equally well prepared for it, for he is well over the ball and better able to contend with the break, because more easily able to move his bat and get into position to play the stroke, than if he were standing firmly fixed on his right leg. Any one who thinks about the matter at all must see the advantage of playing in this way. It seems to me that in cricket the nearer the striker's body is to the ball, the more likely he is to make a correct stroke, for the reason that his eye is nearer to the object he is striking at. If then a batsman keeps his right foot firmly fixed just off the leg stump to a ball which pitches on the off stump or a couple of inches outside it, his eye is necessarily farther away from that ball than if he moved his right leg across the wicket in the direction the ball is taking. I do not think this point can be insisted on too strongly by coaches. Besides, let any cricketer compare the two methods of playing back, and he will, I am convinced, find the one I have urged the easiest and most natural.

I am a firm believer in this method of playing back, not only because all the famous players use it—and that in itself were sufficient—but because from one's own experience it has proved not only the easiest, but by far the most effective. By drawing back the right foot towards the wicket, not away from it, a batsman is often able to force the ball away between mid-on and the bowler, or between mid-off and the bowler, or between short leg and mid-on, the ball in the last instance being played away by a quick turn of the wrist at the last moment.

"It is a mistake to play back behind the legs, for it is impossible to put any power into a stroke when the bat is held nearer the wicket than the batsman himself is standing." These are the words of K. S. Ranjitsinhji in the *Jubilee Book of Cricket*, and as Ranjitsinhji is about the best back player in the world, he ought to know.

It is comparatively easy to play back as a defensive stroke, but any one who aspires to be a really good batsman must learn to make his back play a means of scoring runs. On a difficult wicket back play is everything; in fact, it may be safely said that a good rule to bear in mind on a sticky wicket is *to play back or hit*.

A batsman, unless he be an experienced one, ought not to try and hook short balls round to leg, especially if the bowling is fast, but a "rank long-hopper" may be hit to any point of the compass with a horizontal bat; though, however short and bad a ball, it should be carefully watched all the way, in case of an unexpected hang or rise. Short and straight balls, if they do not get up to any height, may be flicked round on the on side by a quick turn of the wrist.

In making the hook stroke the batsman should move back towards the wicket, turn almost square to the ball, and hit with a horizontal bat to the on side. The ball should be watched right on to the bat, so that, if it does anything unexpected, an ordinary back stroke may be substituted. Even a very short ball outside the off stump may be hooked round to leg, especially if there are seven fielders on the off side and only two or three on the on side. Shrewsbury, Tyldesley, A. C. Maclaren, C. B. Fry, K. S. Ranjitsinhji, and Victor Trumper are, or were, very good at this stroke, which may be made, by using the wrists, with an almost straight bat. Men who play the stroke with their arms, like A. C. Maclaren, hit across the ball. To hook a fast bowler is a proceeding fraught with no little danger, and ought only to be indulged in very occasionally, for it is a stroke that requires no little skill and nerve, for often the ball comes shoulder or head high to the batsman. A. E. Stoddart was particularly good at hitting this type of ball round to leg. Indeed, all round there have been few finer players to fast bowling than Stoddart. On slow wickets the hook stroke is simply invaluable, and short straight balls may be despatched to the boundary quite easily.

The Back Glance

A ball rather short of a good length pitching just outside the leg stump should be played away on the leg side with a backward movement. The right foot is put well back in a line with the leg stump, and the left foot drawn up beside it, but different cricketers play the stroke differently. Ranjitsinhji, for instance, moves his left leg across the wicket towards point, faces the ball, and plays it at the last instant by a quick turn of the wrist. Other batsmen turn almost right round, and others get right in front of the wicket. The ball must be watched right on to the bat, and the ball should glance away somewhere behind the umpire, or in the direction of long leg. It is a most useful and fascinating stroke, and can be employed to balls pitching on the middle and leg stumps, especially to a break-back bowler, though of course there is a danger here of being given l.b.w.

The Forward Glance

A good length or slightly overpitched ball just outside the leg stump should be played in the following manner: The left leg should be thrown down the wicket in a line with the ball, and the moment the ball touches the bat, the bat should be pushed forward by a quick turn of the wrist, the whole weight of the body being put into the stroke. The body is thrown well forward, with the result that the ball will go round to leg at a great pace.

I have found this a very useful stroke to bowlers like Mold, Richardson, and Lockwood, who break back into one, and, as in the case of the back glance, the stroke may be made to a ball pitching on the middle and leg stump to a break-back bowler. At Lord's it is a particularly effective stroke if one is batting at the end opposite the Pavilion, for the slope in the ground tends to accentuate the off break of any bowler who is on at the Pavilion end. Altogether it is a very productive stroke in first-class cricket. The back glance and the forward glance have practically taken the place of the leg hit, though, with the new-fashioned type of leg-break bowling as practised by Vine, Braund, Armstrong the Australian, and others, the genuine leg hit was more often seen last season than in some past years; but with six or seven men on the on side, it is extremely difficult to hit a leg ball without running the risk of being caught somewhere on the leg side, especially as the Braund type of bowler bowls a good length outside the batsman's legs.

The square leg hit is made by advancing the left leg down the wicket, and hitting the ball just as it passes the left leg. It is either just before the ball pitches or on the rise, according to the length of the ball. It is a very difficult matter to keep the ball down, the complete success of the stroke depending upon perfect accuracy of timing. This hit ought only to be attempted to a ball short of a half-volley. If the ball is a half-volley or well up, the correct stroke is in front of the wicket or square to leg with a vertical bat.

I am inclined to think that the glance stroke is preferable to the square leg or long leg hit, for it is quite as good for scoring purposes, and the ball can be watched right on to the bat, and placed and kept down with far greater certainty.

CRICKET

From a Drawing by G. F. Watts, R.A.
THE DRAW OR PULL.

The Pull

differs from the hook stroke in that it is more in the nature of a drive. The pull stroke is used to hit a ball pitched outside the off stump round to leg, and the stroke may be applied either to a half-volley or a good length ball outside the off stump.

W. W. Read used to be the great exponent of this stroke, and Ranjitsinhji also plays it with wonderful certainty. It is a dangerous stroke, for the ball which can thus be treated requires very careful choosing, and it is the difficulty of choosing the right ball which makes the stroke dangerous. The left foot should be thrown out to the pitch of the ball, and just as the ball rises from the ground it should be hit round on the on side with a horizontal bat. It is often a very useful stroke on a sticky wicket, to a bowler who is breaking back, though there is some risk of being caught at deep square leg, rather in front of the wicket, by the fielder who is almost invariably placed there when the wicket is helping the bowler.

A straight half-volley is a ball which every player ought to be able to drive, and it should always be hit in the most natural direction. It is a mistake to try and pull a straight half-volley. The chief point to remember in hitting a half-volley is to get as much swing as possible into the stroke. One or two batsmen swing the bat so far back that they occasionally hit themselves with the back of the bat on the head. The shoulders should come greatly into play in the drive, for they give added power to the swing of the arms, and throw the weight of the body with great force on to the left leg at the moment of hitting the ball.

In driving, the back of the left hand remains facing the bowler, instead of being on the opposite side of the handle, as in the case of forward play. The bat, as in forward play, must be kept as near as possible to the left leg. Batsmen who are quick on their feet often jump out to the pitch of a ball, and thereby make it a half-volley. Victor Trumper, the finest batsman Australia has ever produced, is the great exponent of this stroke, and the rapidity with which he gets to the ball is astonishing.

It is, if successfully played, a very useful stroke, for nothing is more apt to put a bowler off his length than by thus attacking him. It is of course a stroke more suitable for slow bowling than for fast.

From a Drawing by G. F. Watts, R.A.
THE LEG VOLLEY.

From a Drawing by G. F. Watts, R.A.
THE CUT.

The On Drive

Nearly every batsman prays for a half-volley on the leg stump, or one pitching within three or four inches of the leg stump, for, if properly timed, it is a stroke which sends a thrill of joy through the batsman. If the ball pitches on the wicket, the hit should be made between the bowler and mid-on, though with a break-back bowler the ball may often be forced wide of mid-on's right side. If the ball pitches outside the leg stump, it should be hit anywhere to the right of mid-on.

The whole body should work in agreement, the arms should swing freely, and the stroke should be well followed through. Nearly all the great batsmen play this stroke to perfection, but none better than F. S. Jackson.

The Cut

There are three classes of cuts: the forward cut, the square cut, and the late cut.

The forward cut is made at a shortish ball outside the off stump, the right foot being kept still, but the left foot brought across in the line of the ball. It is a stroke that requires very accurate timing, but when timed well, the ball often goes to the ring like a flash of lightning, somewhere between point and cover-point. W. L. Murdoch plays this stroke particularly well, as do A. O. Jones, H. K. Foster, and W. Gunn, while C. H. B. Marsham made the great majority of his fine 100 not out in the 'Varsity match of 1901 by its means. It is a somewhat dangerous stroke, for should the ball hang or bump unexpectedly, an uppish hit will in all probability follow.

The square cut sends the ball just behind point, and is made by moving the right foot across the wicket in a line with the off stump; and just as the ball is passing the batsman's body, the bat is brought down by a quick movement of the arms, while more power is added to the stroke by a sharp flick of the wrists. The bat should be slanting downwards towards the ground, in order to get well over the ball.

Tyldesley of Lancashire plays the same cut as well as any one else, though he often hits across the ball rather than over it, a fine stroke, harder than if he had got over the ball, being the result. His method is, however, a little dangerous, as there is a chance of the ball going up, though Tyldesley seems to have brought the stroke to perfection.

In the late cut the right foot is moved across to the same position as in the case of the square cut, but the ball is hit *after* it has passed the batsman's body. The most suitable ball for the late cut is one pitched wide of the off stump, not quite so short as the ball for the square cut, but still short of a good length. It is essentially a wrist stroke, and a man with a weak wrist will be wise not to attempt it. Late cutting requires a little manœuvring-ground, and care must be taken to avoid cutting at a ball too near the wicket.

There are few players who cut late really well, for the stroke requires the greatest nicety in timing and a strong, flexible pair of wrists. Ranjitsinhji makes this stroke with great certainty and brilliancy, but then he possesses an extraordinarily supple pair of wrists.

There is another kind of cut, called the "chop," which should be used to a short ball outside the off stump which keeps low after pitching. The bat should be brought down with great force horizontally, and if well timed the ball will go very hard. This is a favourite stroke of Sir T. C. O'Brien, K. G. Key, Victor Trumper, and R. E. Foster, who in the 'Varsity match of 1900 brought off this stroke on several occasions off E. M. Dowson's bowling. On a hard, true wicket, against fast or medium-paced bowling, forward play is the best; against slow bowling and lobs play back or hit is, generally speaking, the soundest advice that can be given a young cricketer, though on some wickets slow bowling may be played forward to, and even forced forward. But every really good slow bowler varies his pace. Five out of the six balls may be more or less of the same pace; but one ball out of the over is generally a fast one, or at any rate medium pace. Rhodes, the Yorkshire left-hander, bowls a very good fast ball, which comes across quickly with his arm, and the same may be said of Blythe of Kent and Cranfield of Somerset; while amongst slow right-handed bowlers C. M. Wells, for instance, is constantly varying the flight and pace of the ball. But in distinguishing the different styles of play which should be adopted in playing fast and slow bowling, it is well to remember that to fast bowling one plays forward to score runs, while to slow bowling you play forward to defend your wicket; though, as I have said before, a slow bowler may often be pushed forward between the fielders for one and two and sometimes four runs.

I do not think that batsmen jump out enough to slow bowling, for there is nothing so demoralising to a bowler as a batsman who comes out of his ground and hits when the ball is at all overpitched. Remember, if you do make up your mind to jump out and hit, to get right to the pitch of the ball; forget, too, for the moment, that there is such a person as the wicket-keeper.

When the bowling is fast enough to compel the wicket-keeper to stand back, I have found it a good plan to stand a foot or two outside the popping-crease. This tends to put the bowler off his length, for he finds his good length balls hit on the half-volley, and this, for the time at any rate, is apt to disconcert him.

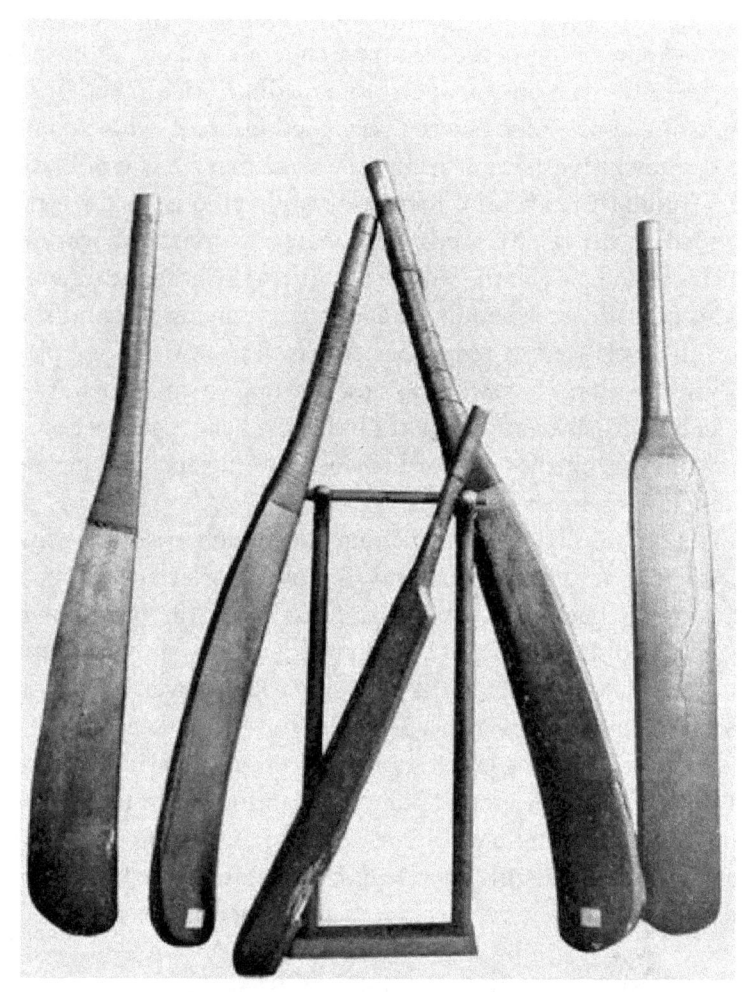

EIGHTEENTH CENTURY BATS, WHICH BELONGED TO THE FOURTH DUKE OF BUCCLEUCH.

CRICKET

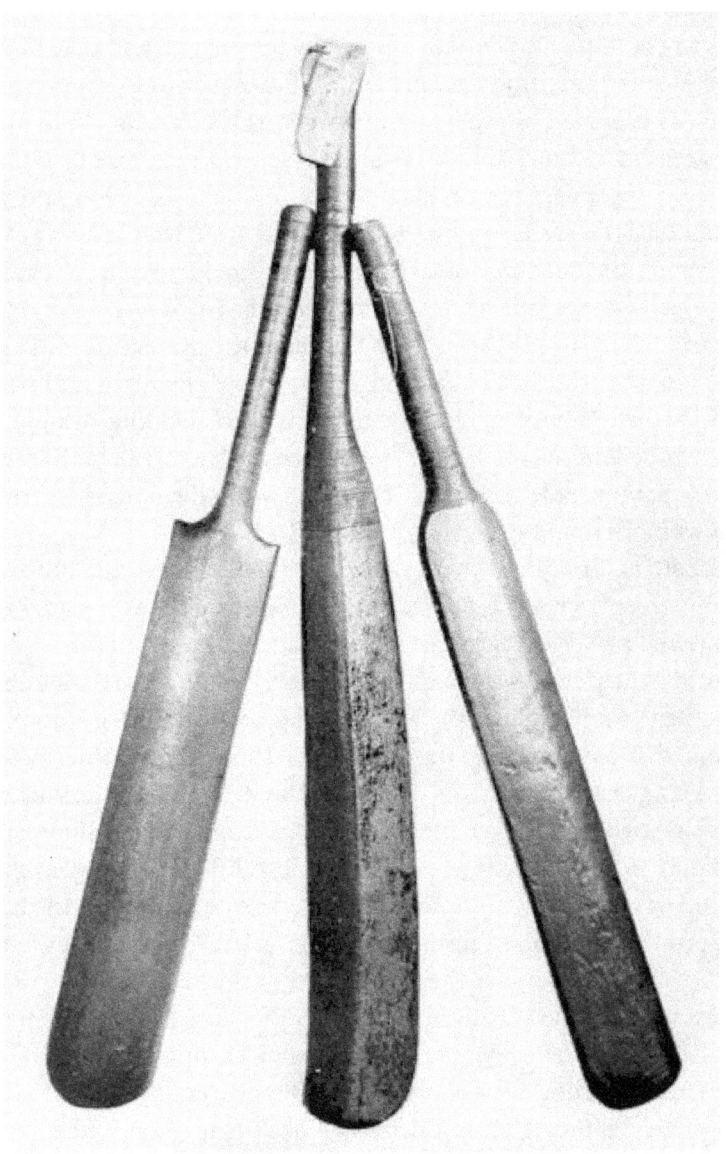

CELEBRATED BATS.
The one on the left belonged to Alfred Mynn, 1850; the centre one was originally used by Merser, of Kent (left-handed batsman); and the right-hand bat by E. Bagot, 1793.

In playing lobs you may stand in your ground and play back, occasionally scoring a single, but in dealing with lobs offensive tactics are the best, for, as a great general once said, "The best method of defence is to attack." Lobs should therefore be either hit on the full pitch or played back, and the batsman should stand a little easier on his right leg than if he were playing fast or medium bowling, so as to be ready to jump out and take the ball on the full pitch the moment he sees that it is slightly overpitched. By far the best lob bowler of the present day is D. L. A. Jephson, the Surrey captain, for he varies the flight and pace of the ball extremely cleverly, often, indeed, sending in quite a fast good length ball. He can, too, make the ball break both ways, and many people think that he might with advantage to Surrey bowl more than he does.

Batting on a hard, true wicket and on a sticky, difficult one are two entirely different things, and one often sees a man who is a fine player on a fast wicket absolutely at sea when rain has ruined the pitch. A left-handed bowler like Rhodes is then in his element, for he pitches the ball a good length on the leg stump; it comes across quickly to the off, and you stand a very good chance of being either bowled, or caught by David Hunter at the wicket, or snapped up by eager and lengthy John Tunnicliffe at short slip. Haigh, also of Yorkshire, is an extremely difficult bowler on this kind of wicket, for the amount of off break he can get on the ball is prodigious; while Trumble, the Australian, is probably as hard a bowler to play under these circumstances as ever lived.

As a rule the hitting or "long-handle game," as it has been called, pays best under these circumstances, but some men who are really strong in their back and on side play can play their ordinary game. A strong defensive back player can often get a good length ball which breaks back away on the on side for two or three runs, while a good puller has a great advantage on this kind of wicket. The man who does not watch the ball, and watch it well, will have little or no chance on a sticky wicket. At one time there were very few men who could play at all successfully on a really difficult wicket, but of late years, what with the general improvement in back play—due chiefly to Ranjitsinhji's influence on the game—the number, though far from being large, has increased. Victor Trumper, F. S. Jackson, Ranjitsinhji, C. B. Fry, A. C. Maclaren, T. L. Taylor, and Tyldesley are the best batsmen we have under conditions favourable to the bowler, and I shall never forget an extraordinary innings Ranjitsinhji played at Brighton in July 1900 for Middlesex *v.* Sussex. When stumps were drawn on the second evening of the match, Ranjitsinhji was not out 37, the game up to that time having been played on a perfect wicket. Rain, however, fell heavily in the night, and with the sun coming out next morning, the wicket was altogether in favour of the bowler. Vine made 17, but no one else on the side that day got more than 5, excepting Ranjitsinhji, who was last man out, l.b.w. to Trott, for 202! He gave one chance in the long field when he had made about 160 runs, but apart from this, his batting was absolutely without a flaw. Most of his runs came from hard drives, chiefly to the on, and strokes on the leg side. It was an astonishing innings, and its full significance was possibly not appreciated until Tate, on an exactly similar wicket, dismissed a powerful Middlesex eleven for just over 100 runs.

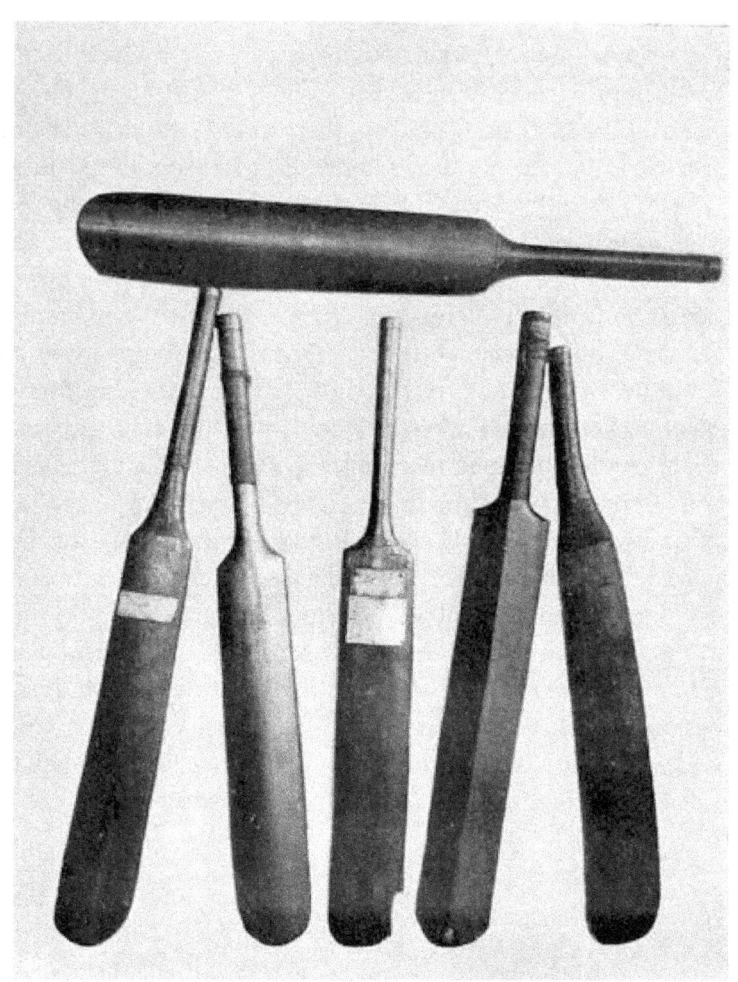

WAR-WORN WEAPONS.

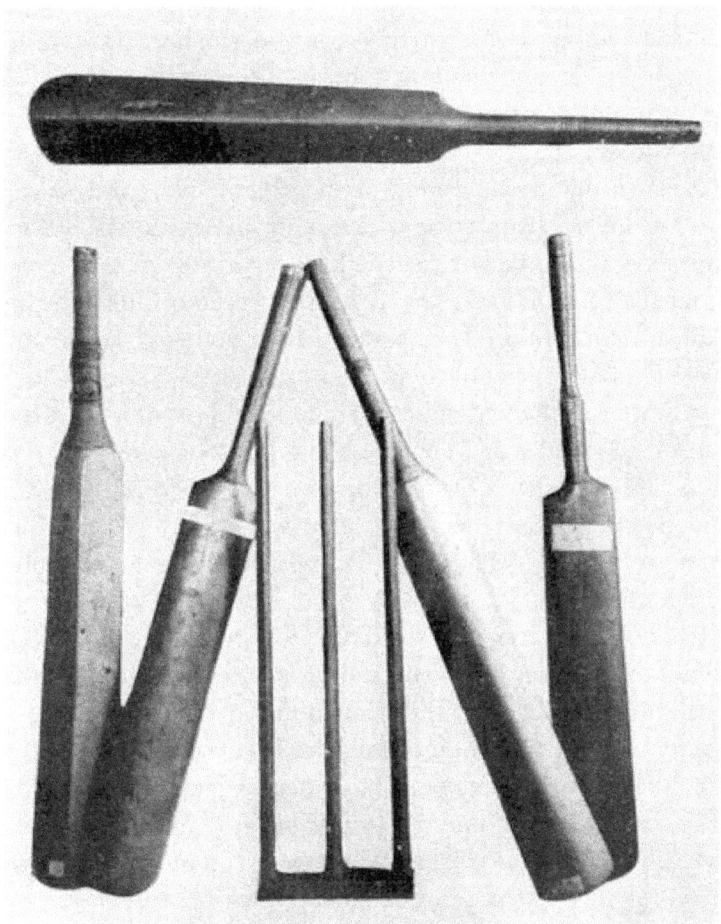

RELICS OF PAST ENGAGEMENTS.

A few words now on running. Never attempt a run if you feel any doubt as to its safety, for it is better to lose a possible single than to run out your partner. At the same time, I do not think that cricketers as a rule run as well as they ought to between the wickets. The Australians are an exception; they are extraordinarily quick.

Always back up two or three yards; when you call, call in a

decided manner. If your partner calls you, run hard if you intend to go; if you do not, stop him at once. The great thing is to make up your mind instantly.

If you are the striker, and you play the ball in front of the wicket, *always say* something—either "Yes," "No," or "Wait." If you hit the ball behind the wicket, your partner at the bowler's end should call, but as to whether the striker or non-striker should call the hit to third man many cricketers differ. The best plan, in my opinion, is to arrange with your partner. In that event a disaster is not likely to occur.

Always run the first run as hard as you can, and always look out for a second run when the ball is hit to the long field, for even to a Tyldesley, a Denton, or a Burnup, good runners, who understand one another, may often with safety get two for a drive to the long field when a slower runner would be content with a single.

There are, too, very few third men to whom one cannot run. I do not mean to say that a run should be attempted to third man when the ball goes hard and straight to him on the first bounce, but for a stroke a little to one side of him there is frequently a run. But the two batsmen must use their own discretion—and as has been said, *it is a thousand times better to lose a run than to risk running out your partner.* I was twice run out in the 'Varsity match of 1896—to a great extent my own fault in the second innings,—and since that game—memorable for the fact that Oxford, going in with 330 runs to win, hit off the number for the loss of four wickets, and for the no-ball incident which led eventually to an alteration in the follow-on rule—I have taken particular pains to improve my running between the wickets. I am not often run out now, and I hope I but seldom run my partner out—*Experientia docet sapientiam.*

Many batsmen, when nearing their 50 or 100, attempt the most absurd runs. This fault is more common amongst professional cricketers than amongst amateurs, for the reason that all the counties, with the one exception of Yorkshire, give their professionals a sovereign for every 50 runs they make. This so-called "talent-money" has been the cause of many a run-out. Yorkshire gives no "talent-money," but over and above the usual fee of £5 or £6 a match, each professional is "marked" according to his work in a particular game. For example, if a man made 25 runs on a bad wicket at a critical time, or even 10 not out in a one-wicket victory, he would be marked according to the merit of his performance in the eyes of his captain—in this case Lord Hawke. A fine bowling feat or a fine catch would be similarly rewarded. Each mark represents five shillings, and this system might with advantage be adopted by other counties.

GEORGE PARR, THE FAMOUS NOTTINGHAM BAT.

CRICKET

"N. FELIX" (N. Wanostrocht).

There is one thing that no coaching will teach a young cricketer, and that is confidence. Time alone can give him that, for confidence is a plant of slow growth. I do not believe the cricketer who says he has never been nervous—he is certainly not a first-class cricketer if he adheres to that statement; but nervousness will gradually disappear as a batsman gains confidence in himself. I have known men who when they first played county cricket were almost paralysed with nervousness, but who after two or three years' experience went out to bat with every confidence. Nervousness is undoubtedly a great handicap, and young players should try to overcome this weakness as soon as possible. Too much confidence is a mistake, for, to go back again to the Latin grammar, *nimia fiducia calamitati solet esse*. But too much confidence is better than no confidence—and by confidence I do not mean conceit, but a belief in one's own capabilities, founded on past deeds.

There are cricketers, too, who are so superstitious as to be almost a nuisance. There is the man who thinks he cannot make runs unless he goes in in a particular place. These men are somewhat annoying, but I think a captain should always try to humour them, if by so doing he is not upsetting the batting order of his side.

The typical instance of superstition affecting one's play at cricket seems to me to have been exemplified in the case of the Rugby boy who, alighting at the St. John's Wood Station on the Metropolitan Railway, for the Rugby and Marlborough match, saw the advertisement of Mr. John Hare's play, *A Pair of Spectacles*, staring him in the face. That boy had made heaps of runs during the summer at Rugby, but he came on to the ground fully convinced that he would make a pair of spectacles, and make them he did.

Again, G. O. Smith, to whose splendid batting Oxford were mainly indebted for their victory over Cambridge in 1896, had a firm conviction that he could only make runs in a certain pair of trousers; and G. J. Mordaunt, the Oxford captain of the previous year, took it as an evil omen, when, on awaking on the morning of the 'Varsity match, he saw from his bedroom window the flag with "Druce" in large letters on it flying from the Baker Street Bazaar. W. E. Druce was captain of the Light Blue eleven that year, and Mordaunt's feeling of coming disaster was, I regret to say, justified by the result of the match, for Cambridge beat us by 134 runs.

Coaches should be careful to avoid cramping the style of a young batsman, and of suppressing individuality and budding genius. Batsmen cannot be all of one type. Had G. L. Jessop been made to play according to the rules laid down, a great hitter would have been lost to the world, and England would never have won that last test-match at the Oval, for there would have been no Jessop on the side to accomplish what was, perhaps, the finest piece of hitting ever seen on a cricket-ground. It is useless trying to make a Barlow into a Lyons, or a Lyons into a Barlow.

Always endeavour to reach the ground in good time before a match begins, and to have five or ten minutes' practice; though there are some batsmen who do not believe in too much net practice. Every man must of course decide what suits himself best, but I cannot believe that a few minutes at a net can do anything but good, for one gains a sight of the ball, and gets the pace of the wicket.

If you are put in to bat anywhere but first, always remember that it is your duty not to take more than two minutes in getting to the wicket, for that is the limit allowed by law. This is most important, for you have no right to keep your partner waiting, and to waste time.

No one will ever become a great batsman without enthusiasm, and enthusiasm of the kind which will carry him through the inevitable disappointments and troubles of his early career. The path to success is not easy, and success comes only to the few. But the goal once reached, he must be a poor man indeed who does not feel a glow of pride on seeing the magic figures 100 going up on the big scoring-board at Lord's beneath his name; for believe me, the satisfaction is so great, and the applause such sweet music, that it is worth while taking the greatest pains to attain the proficiency necessary to the achievement of the feat. There is, too, a subtle charm and fascination about the game which creates among its devotees a bond of fellowship and *camaraderie* which nothing can alter.

From a Drawing by G. F. Watts, R.A .
THE BOWLER.
(Alfred Mynn).

CHAPTER IV

BOWLING BY D. L. A. JEPHSON

To those that have time hanging all too heavily on their hands, and in good truth know not what to do—to those perchance that may, through lack of occupation, be compelled amid adverse circumstances, finding that anything is occasionally better than nothing, to peruse these jagged, untrimmed sentences—I would say this: that for many days, with a deep determination of purpose, I have perused the writings of our great cricketers—I have read the golden words of Grace, of Steel, of Ranjitsinhji—and have arrived hot-haste, sick at heart, at the conclusion that I cannot retell what has so often been told by them, and told so clearly, so succinctly, with such prodigious insight into the profound ramifications of this art. And so, like some pale-faced curate sitting fear-bound beneath the terrifying presence of a ruddy bishop, I must perforce scratch with a rusty pen of the bowlers I have met. In the ten years of my cricket life I have met many.

Let us divide them into classes. We will take the old-time division; we will divide them into four—those that are of a slow pace, those that are of a medium pace, those that are fast, and those semi-moribund trundlers, the dealers in lobs.

Having myself started in my early days with the firm conviction that this old game of cricket was the best game for boys and men of moderate years that the ingenuity of generations had invented, I became also convinced that to be a great bowler was the highest pinnacle of fame, and at the same time of usefulness, that a cricketer could hope to rest on.

The work, without doubt, is hard, the labour of the day strenuous, but the pleasure of bowling a length with the wicket a bit in your favour, with a side that are trying to field, and not loafing as "little mounds of earth or waxen figures in a third-rate tailor's shop," is a goodly thing, a thing to dream of. And this craft of bowling is so sure, so certain. A great batsman may make a mistake, even on the Oval in the height of summer, even on the Oval in the height of perfection—and all those that have played there know the miraculous opportunities for run-getting this ground affords—he may make a mistake, let us say, bowled Richardson, 0! Well, for the day he is done—up to now of no use to his side, of no use to himself. Now, take the great bowler on a wicket of this excellence, or of any other. He can make a mistake, drop a slower one a bit too short, overpitch the well-intentioned yorker, falter in his stride and be placed to leg for four. What matter from a selfish point of view? His fun for the day has not departed. He bowls and bowls, and continues to bowl; and probably the blind goddess gives in the end the wherewithal to be cheerful. Therefore, on this miserable lowest ground of self-interest, be a bowler!

And then again, when he has done a noble thing—or perchance it is his birthday, and the elements give heeding to his call—there falls, let us say, a gentle rain in the early-bird hours, and a hot sun scorches from 10 to 12. He has got his money on a two to one chance (and nobody else in the race)—Peel, Rhodes, Haigh, Jack Hearne, the wonderful George Lohmann, and dozens more. What does the other side make? They are lucky to make 100—

lucky to make 70!

To be a bowler on a bit of bird-lime is the biggest certainty the cricket world has knowledge of. You may meet a Ranjitsinhji, a Bonner, a Jessop, or a Frank Crawford; but if you don't meet these, the odds on you are as the odds on an arc light to a farthing dip.

Again—for a moment to raise the platform on which we have been discussing so casually this selfish side of the bowler's existence—there can be little doubt that of the three branches of the game (batting, bowling, fielding), bowling is the pivot on which the other two turn. Who is the more use to his side—the great batsman or the great bowler? Nine out of ten intelligent beings answer unhesitatingly, the bowler; and rightly too, especially if he be of medium pace, or even slow medium, on a great variety of wickets, ranging from the fiery, cast-iron, stone-strewn rock of an Old Trafford wicket (I don't mean for a second that the Old Trafford ground is often in this state, but when it is, it is a little faster, a little more susceptible of bump, than anywhere else I know) down to Bristol or Southampton after a wet day, he is invariably of supreme assistance to his side. And what a number of graduated shades of differing wickets there are, from the sun-scorched cracking clay, where the fast bowler finds your fingers, or failing these your ribs, where your runs are made through the slips or first hop over their heads to the boundary, down through the varying degrees of good, natural, fast wickets to the Valhalla of batsmen, let us say Taunton, the Oval, or Bristol, where the ball rarely rises stump high, and where there is as much life in the wickets as there is in a barrel of oysters! On grounds like these the batsman assuredly cometh into his own, and metaphorically layeth the bowler by the heel, bruising him hip and thigh through the weary hours of an August day, till the welcome news of the last over revives the rag of a man that is left, and he slowly wends his way to the rabbit-hutch, in sore need of the well-earned bath and its ensuing rub down—in sore need of a ginger beer. Perhaps there are too many of these superexcellent wickets; perhaps, from certain batsmen's point of view, there are not. But the moment the rain appears, the bowler is another being; in the language of the cardroom, he wears a four-ace smile, and there is a corresponding depression in the countenance of the great batsman. All down the still more numerous phases of wet, sticky, and real bird-lime wickets (impossible for nine out of ten batsmen)—down through all these the four-ace smile remains, and it is only when we arrive at the thoroughly sodden ground, with a faint drizzle or slight showers at convenient intervals, when the ball is wet, the footholds greasy, and there are bucketfuls of sawdust besprinkled here, there, and everywhere, that the batsman again reverses the situation, and, like an overfed fox-terrier, has acquired another poor rat of a bowler.

I say overfed advisedly—not that he is replete with runs on too many occasions in an ordinary season, when a fair amount of rain falls, and the good and bad wickets are allotted us fairly evenly, and a decent percentage of catches are held (which is very seldom the case); but when he glues himself for a day or day and a half to some easy-paced billiard-table wicket, where a blind boy could stay with a toothpick, I say he is overfed—he gluts himself with runs; and though, as I have said before, he has, in my humble opinion, less chances of distinguishing himself than the medium-paced bowler, and is in consequence of less value to his side (which, after all, is the very essence of the game), yet when his opportunity arises he overeats himself to an astonishing degree, and often grouses to a similar extent as the rat of a bowler catches him by the tail with a duck and one on a wicket of sun-baked clay.

I have sorely digressed, but the trend of the digression was this, that if as a youth you wish to play cricket, devote all your time, all your energies, to bowling. A great bowler is born, not made; but though you may never soar to the heights of a Spofforth or a Lohmann, you can learn to bowl a good length, you can learn to bowl intelligently, and be a source of comfort to yourself, and, what is infinitely better, in all probability a source of comfort to your side.

We have divided the bowlers of to-day and yesterday into four: it were better to say three, leaving the few dealers in lobs to huddle themselves into a minute band that can nowadays follow many leagues behind the great cavalcade that comprises the real three divisions. Lobs are occasionally useful things to carry round with a side, but should in a healthy team be used medicinally.

They act as a stirring tonic to men in the field who have grown lazy and careless from lack of work, for with all the lobs I have ever seen there is always a blissful uncertainty as to where a good batsman will place the next one; and some players hit them so uncomfortably hard that it is best for the slackers to keep their weather eyes open, or they may experience a rude awakening. There is no more exhilarating spectacle on a cricket-field than to see a drowsy dreamer of a field receive the ball in a most unexpected place, on the wrist or the ankle, on the nose or somewhere where the injury is not likely to be serious.

Three years ago at the Oval, I remember, Sam Woods was watching a match, and a certain individual in an immaculate sweater, brilliantly decorated in front with letters a foot long, sauntered on to the field. It was evidently a part of the game with which he had no sympathy. Sam glared down on him, and in his terse phraseology commenced—

"Who's that feller?"

Some one mentioned a name. "I know," says Sam. "I know the silly bloomer.... He was fielding in the country—I was playing—up she went in the air—he was fast asleep—catch her, you fool!—and he caught her—*plumb on the nut.*"

WILLIAM LILLYWHITE.

From a Painting by W. Bromley.
JOHN WISDEN.

And this genial cricketer was pleased for the rest of the day at the mere recollection.

At last we have arrived, through devious paths, at our three great divisions. Many bowlers whom I class as slow may in reality consider themselves to be medium; many medium may prefer to be known as fast; and perhaps there may be a very few fast bowlers who prefer the description of medium—but I doubt it.

First and foremost we must place the Old Man, or Old 'Un, as we so endearingly like to speak of him. There can be but few people in this country who do not know this full-bearded, full-bodied figure of a man—the few short shuffling strides, the arm a little above the shoulder, the right hand a shade in front of him, the curious rotary action before delivery, *and the wonderful length.*

The hand is large and the ball well concealed, and as you face him, for he stands full fronted to you, it seems to leave by the back door, as it were, that is, over the knuckle of the little finger.

I have played with him many times, but he does not seem to me to do very much (of course I am speaking of a good wicket), but some come a little higher, others a little lower, some a little faster, some slower; on the middle leg is his favourite spot—two or three off the leg stick with a square deep who is not asleep, then a straighter one with a "bit of top on it"—the batsman tries to push to leg—there is a somewhat excited *'s that?* and the would-be run-getter is sauntering pavilionwards.

Certainly of all the slow bowlers I have met he is the most successful against *new faces*, whether they are young or old. He generally bowls them neck and crop, or else they are l.b.w., and it makes very little difference if the batsman is an Australian wonder, or a boy in a village school: they come in and they go out, and they can't understand it—it looks so extremely harmless. They forget the master-hand, with the master-mind to work it; they forget the wonderful perseverance! If you can't get them out over the wicket, try round; if you can't succeed this end, have a rest and try the other.

To-day he may bowl a trifle slower than he did twenty years ago. It seems to me, however, that he bowls with very much the same effect. He is a bowler that stands by himself. As long as I can remember, no one has ever compared "W. G." with any other bowler; he stands alone—it is a distinct form of attack. We hear of

Rhodes being contrasted with Peel, and Peel discussed in relation to Peate, and so on in thousands of instances, but the Old Man stands by himself, with a style, a method, a success of his own.

Of really good amateur slow bowlers, during the last twelve years, in which time I have been more or less nearly connected with first-class cricket, there has been a phenomenal dearth.

They can literally be counted on the fingers of a man's hand. As I write only two stand out—C. L. Townsend and C. M. Wells. Of course there have been others, and there are others, but unless I have missed my way through the long lists of bowlers through which I have passed, I have lighted on no names that, without some slight stretch of the imagination, one could place on anything like the same level with the two already mentioned. Should there be any, I sincerely apologise for their omission. A. G. Steel and E. A. Nepean never entered into my short first-class cricket experiences.

I have met them both, however, in club games, and even with the small amount of natural and acquired intelligence at my disposal, I could not fail to see how good they must have been at their best.

One feat of Nepean's I remember well. He was playing for the Gentlemen *v.* the Players at the Oval. Arthur Shrewsbury was batting, and Nepean was bowling, if my recollection fails me not, at the gas-works end, and, greatly to the astonishment of many of us present, *bowled him round his legs!*

Great as was the astonishment of the spectators, it paled before the wonder of the two in question, and the tale went round on the morrow that gentle sleep had failed to visit their respective couches on the evening of this memorable day. One was said to have lain awake all night marvelling *how on earth he had done it,* and the other *how on earth he had let it be done!*

Whether the tale be of truth or otherwise I know not, but it was a ball that probably Nepean will remember long after he has ceased playing even club cricket.

The one exception that proves the rule that great bowlers are born and not made is C. M. Wells. To the best of my belief, when he started his career at Dulwich as a bowler, he was of the shut-your-eyes, bang-'em-down, never-mind-where-but-plug-'em-down style. Only a slight success, I think, attended his efforts in this direction, and so, having seen some good slow bowler on the school ground, assiduously worked day after day at the nets, until up at Cambridge he proved himself to be on his day one of the finest slow bowlers we have seen. He possessed, and still possesses, a wonderful command of length, with plenty of spin from the off—a considerable variation of flight—a slower ball with several inches of break from leg, delivered, by the way, from almost the palm of the hand, and a ball that, as it comes sailing up the pitch towards you, has every appearance of being intended for a leg break, but which in reality is simply propelled with a large quantity of "top on. " It comes naturally quick off the ground, and it comes along straight as a die, and many a batsman has ceased from troubling, out l.b.w., through playing for a break that did not exist. I should perhaps not have said ceased from troubling, for it is a curious fact, and one for which there seems no adequate explanation, that though a batsman generally grumbles a little at being given out l.b.w. to a fast bowler, a *rara avis* is occasionally found agreeing with the decision; men as a rule grumble and trouble themselves vastly being dismissed in a similar manner to a slow ball, and a *rara avis* in this connection is almost as the dodo.

Of Wells' fast ball I am perhaps not so eulogistic, but no doubt he uses it as an astute hunter uses dead wood and briars to cover the many pitfalls into which his intended victims are to cast themselves. This end or that end, he never tires; if the laws of the game permitted it he would bowl both; and as regards fielding his own bowling, I think he is the best I have ever seen. I remember once at Cambridge in the Long Vac. playing with him—I think it was against the M.C.C. I know the side included Shacklock and Barnes. The latter was batting, and Wells let go a slow full pitch, and poor old Barnes dashed at it as a dog at a dinner. Wells, as he generally is, was well up the wicket, his legs well apart, looking for what he could find. Barnes found the full toss, and Wells the ball. As the veteran passed me at mid-off, his face was as the face of a man who stoops to pick up a sovereign and finds a brass button. It was the hardest catch, I should think, ever made at a range of 10 yards from the gun, and Barnes was no niggard with the wood!

Having played with and against Wells a great many times, I have had copious opportunities of watching him closely. He invariably starts with the ball in the left hand, and in the first stride or two throws it into his right. For the off break it falls into a cradle of fingers; the middle digits are spread open, while the first and fourth are bent double at the second joint. The ball rarely touches the thumb; the natural straightening of the first finger at the moment of delivery imparts the required break; but to bowl a length without the use of the thumb, and to train your fingers to fall at will into this cramped position, involves considerably more patience and practice than the average cricketer cares to give.

Here again I shall digress. In all the excellent works on cricket that at one time or another I have so diligently studied, I find most elaborate instructions on this same subject, the holding of the ball—"Always use your fingers," "Never use the palm of the hand," etc., etc.; but despite all this worthy advice, I have never yet seen two bowlers gather their fingers, or fingers and thumb, round the ball in such a manner that the hand of one could not for an instant be confused with the hand of the other. The length of their run may occasionally coincide, very occasionally their stride may be of the same compass, but these are the only two similar characteristics which any two bowlers may be said to possess. The action and method of handling the ball are as different in different bowlers as the features on the face of the one are unlike the features on the faces of the others. George Lohmann, one of the greatest bowlers that has ever lived, spread his long, sinuous fingers (in which I include the thumb) at almost equal distances round the whole circumference of the ball. Spofforth, on the other, held only half the ball, the little finger underneath, with the thumb on the top, both resting on the seam—believing, as at billiards, that a ball struck on one side will of necessity spin in its run or flight in the direction of the side to which the propelling force was given. Turner, on the other hand, covered the whole of the circumference, with the ball resting nearer the palm of the hand than is the case with the majority. Mead, again, being blessed with a long, strong forefinger, produces the same off break with this finger and the slight use of his thumb and second finger. Those who have played against Albert Trott know well the particular delivery when they see part of the ball projecting below his little finger, and the strong thumb standing straight up in the air; it is practically propelled by the second, third, and fourth fingers. I give these simply as a few instances. Every bowler, whether first class, second class, or "no class," has a peculiar method of his own, some idiosyncrasy, however slight, in his manner of gripping the ball, and this, too, *in addition* to the varying flexibility, the varying "flicks" or "whips" of the wrist, that each in his very own way employs.

Now for C. L. Townsend—by accident this is a suggestive phrase, and one that in his prime exactly describes the plan of action adopted by the incoming batsmen—"Now for Charles," "Go for him"—and they went; and a great number came back sorrowing—bowled round their legs with a two-foot break, stumped a couple of yards, caught at cover trying to drive, bowled with an off break or a fast one—out in every possible way. Bowling with a high, shambling action, he was very deceptive in the flight and very deceptive in the pace, the ball coming slow in air and fast off the pitch with as much finger leg break as he wanted.

On a sticky wicket, unlike the majority of slow leg break bowlers, he could, if he wished, leave it alone and rely almost entirely with very satisfactory results on the off break, bowled a bit faster. And, like Wells, he could bowl all day, and did until towards the end of his regular cricket career, when he forsook the stony path that a regular first-class bowler must tread for the scented groves where dwell our great batsmen, and, lapped in the luxury of 2000 runs per annum, forsook to a great extent his former mistress.

Among all the famous slow left-handers there is one that to me stands out more clearly than the rest, whether his striking personality—for who did not know that bouncing ball of a man?—whether his wonderful all-round skill, or his possession of that golden quality on a cricket field, the golden quality of *life*, stood uppermost in my mind, I cannot say, but to this day, as often as I think on the game, there always arises the short, thickset figure of poor Johnny Briggs.

Buffoon, perhaps, at times, but never with an obnoxious buffoonery. And what a bowler! The ball left his hand with a finger flick that you could hear in the pavilion, and here was every known variety of flight: three or four short, half walking, half running strides, and the ball was at you, spinning like a top; first a balloon of a ball that would drop much farther off than you thought, a lower one just on the same spot, both breaking away like smoke; then another, with nothing on, straight at the sticks; and then you saw the arm come round a shade faster, and, if you weren't on the watch, you found you had struck a snag in the form of a really fast yorker, bowled at a considerably greater pace than you have ever received one from either Peel or Rhodes. Poor Johnny! I have no space to dilate further on your wonderful gift of bowling with this indefinite "*you*." In conclusion, as this chapter seems rapidly to be casting itself into the mould of personal reminiscence, I will relate my last two meetings with you.

We were playing at Hastings in the Week. "W. G." was in command. It was my lucky day, having made 50 or so by blind slogging, and the liberal help of a sluggish field. The Doctor suggested you should try the Chapel end. I took 28 off the first three overs, six of them fours, mostly well off the off stump, bouncing up against the canvas at square leg. I remember the aggrieved look on your face as you remarked to the Old Man, "That's not much of a stroke, Doctor," and the Doctor answered, "It's all right if you can do it, Johnny"; and then, Johnny, you were taken off.

From a Painting by W. Bromley.
ALFRED MYNN.

JAS. COBBETT.

We were playing at Lord's, North *v.* South. It was a perfect wicket. I was in need of a few runs to end the season with. Poor Johnny was bowling, and bowling as well as ever, a bit faster on the fast wicket, and going considerably with his arm.

"W. G." had made as good a 130 as he ever made in his life. I went to the wicket, played two, and the leg stump leant wearily back with a ball that pitched on the middle and off—0!

The second innings, through the clemency of Ernest Smith, I avoided a pair. I got to the other end and faced Johnny: the same ball, the same languid attitude of the same stump, and the balance was mightily in your favour, Johnny, as it always was.

He was a great bowler on his day, a bowler that was never done with, and the void he has left on the cricket field will not be filled for many a day, if ever it be filled at all.

The mind of every cricketer naturally associates with the memory of Briggs the names of the other two great left-handers, Peel and Rhodes; and what a wonderfully successful trio they have been, and what an amount of amiable argument has been expended in the vain attempt to decide which is the greatest of the three! I prefer to bracket the three. And as no side is thoroughly equipped for attack without the inclusion of a bowler of this stamp, had the captain of a side the first call on the services of these two, he no doubt would include Peel on a fast wicket, and in the event of the rain falling, would give the preference to Rhodes. The smile on the face of either of them after a goodly shower, and an hour or two's stickying sun, has struck terror into the heart of many a creditable run-getter.

My first experience of Peel was at Cambridge. As usual, and rightly too, my place was number eleven on the list. There was six minutes to time, and the good MacGregor told me to buck up and go in. So into the dark I went, and, backed by the luck that sometimes falls to most undeserving persons, I stayed through an over and a half of Robert—not out 0 at night, and my last game for the 'Varsity! On the morrow, on not a very easy wicket, my marvellous luck remained with me, and stayed with me even until lunch! 41! It must have been a dreary show. I only instance this to once again emphasise the old old truism of what a game of chance this cricket is. Here was I playing in my last match, playing as a bowler, but, as the vulgar say, "couldn't bowl for toffee," or any other desirable sweetmeat. Here was I, number eleven, and by a kindly turn of fortune's wheel allowed to stop Bobby Peel for two hours and a half. Well, that six minutes in the dusk gave me ten years' cricket, so *I* have nothing to grumble at in the luck of the game!

As every one knows, Yorkshire owe much of their great success to the efforts of these two. Always to be relied upon—always ready to bowl either end for two or twenty overs at a stretch: bowlers that a captain can put on for an over, and knowing that neither of them will throw away a couple of fours trying to find their length. Should we compare the actions of the two, we must award the palm for style and easy rhythmic swing to Peel. To Rhodes we must allow the greater amount of spin.

Wilfred, as his intimates designate him, for some years had a bad time when he journeyed with his friends to the Oval, for he nearly always struck a fast wicket, and very few bowlers are affected to the same extent as he is by the varying conditions of the ground.

On the Oval we have generally managed to score against him, provided it is fine; but give him a little rain, and he gets his own and a bit more back. I remember, three years ago, at Kennington, Yorkshire and Surrey both made over 300. On the third day of the match there had been rain, and a blistering sun was doing its best to give the spectators their money's worth in the afternoon. In this it succeeded. Yorkshire held a lead of about 25. "Another drawn match, I suppose," was heard on every side; but the members and their friends don't quite realise the enormous difference of Rhodes, and of Rhodes and Haigh coupled, on a dry and on a sticky wicket.

Latterly, Surrey have been anything but a good side on a bad wicket, and those of us that knew this were by no means so happy in our minds, and our dismal forebodings came very nearly being realised. Haigh at the pavilion end and Rhodes at the gasometer did exactly as they liked. The former, with practically only three men on the off and innumerable short legs and silly mid-ons, bowled a perfect length off the off stump, coming back anything from three inches to a foot. Only once during the sorry rot that ensued did he get hit on the off. Rhodes, now a totally different bowler from the day before, plugged away on the off stump, and did exactly as he liked with the ball.

Four wickets for 8, and an hour and a bit to go! Poor old Surrey in the soup again! It certainly looked like it, for the mouldy eight runs on the tins were only hoisted there by a mighty effort and a considerable amount of luck. All out 15; and it would have been so had not Hayward stayed forty-five minutes, amassing another 8, and for Tom Richardson's pluckily slogged 17. The total, I think, reached by devious and rugged, very rugged paths, 51—and so Yorkshire were robbed of a well-earned victory. Rhodes had his own back, as he always does have it back when sun and rain put their heads together and strive strenuously for his welfare.

On another occasion that I recollect we made the handsome compilation of 37 against him and Wainwright at Bradford. The score-sheet was covered with "Stumped Hunter, b. Rhodes, 0." It was a most catching complaint, and five of us succumbed to it. It attacked us in two distinct varieties. We either played forward and slipped—"Stumped Hunter, b. Rhodes, 0," or we charged gaily up the pitch for home or glory. The result was precisely the same—"Stumped Hunter, b. Rhodes, 0."

But enough of Rhodes. Helped by his two good god-parents, sun and rain, the subject is a painful one to us of the south.

His co-helper in this match, Wainwright, is another bowler to whom the varying conditions of weather, and consequently of wickets, makes a phenomenal difference—perhaps more strikingly pronounced even than to Rhodes.

Harmless enough on a good wicket, on a bad one he could make the ball do what he liked. Many, of course, can do this; but they cannot make it turn with the astonishing rapidity from the pitch that Wainwright could. Slow in its flight, yet on touching the mud it would rush at you—I had almost said bite you—at any rate bowl you as you were playing back for the hang.

And now, my indulgent reader, we will make full sail

southwards, with the brave north wind full astern, to the headquarters of the cricketing world, the abode of the all-powerful M.C.C. Here we find a slow bowler; I call him slow, for though bowling every conceivable pace, I always maintain that he is at his best when four or five out of the six sent down are leisurely in their progress up the pitch, mixed up with one or two so exceedingly fast that "eye cannot follow them in their flight." I refer to Trott, or "Alberto," as he is generally called.

WILLIAM LILLYWHITE.

WILLIAM CLARKE,
Famous for Underhand Bowling.

A bowler of infinite resource—at times no doubt he gives many runs away through the persistence with which he tries new theories, new dodges, or a new action; but he is one of the few bowlers that the batsman is compelled to watch more closely than many another. Personally, I have retired from the conflict with Albert through every one of the exceedingly varied methods by which he has removed obstructing batsmen. As a rule he bowls with a decidedly low action, with any amount of off break on—with every degree of pace. Again the ball is held in the last three fingers, and a powerful upright thumb confronts the player opposed to him; this is generally a "pull-backed" one which hangs most uncomfortably in the air. The next comes as the lightning, and as likely as not catches you full pitch on the toe, or hits the bottom of the stumps as you are lifting the bat to play. At his best (for sometimes I have seen him bowl for hours without employing his fast one) it is as fast a ball as one wishes to meet, and its pace is made in the last of the few short steps Trott takes. Should he be unsuccessful, he will suddenly raise his arm and deliver one right over his head at a medium pace, which very often whips back sharply from the off, or, reverting to something like his original action, he will bowl an over or two of slow leg breaks, which, if their length is not all it should be, break about as much as Harry Trott was wont to break, and that is saying a good deal.

He is a bowler that I have never seen tired, and a wonderful gatherer of unconsidered trifles in the way of almost impossible "c. and b.'s." He stands in front of you like a brick wall, and you've got to hit it mighty hard for him to let it go by. Truly a great worker, this Anglo-Australian, as the papers so frequently call him.

At Taunton, a year or two ago, we invariably came across the slowest overhand bowler that has played in first-class cricket for ten years or so. Tyler was for a long time the stumbling-block in the way of many sides, more particularly of Surrey. Time after time he has bowled us out on all sorts of wickets—it was too slow, too high in the air, and consequently such a long time coming to you. Dozens of players I have seen bowled trying to sniggle one to leg, and if they were not bowled they were out l.b.w. Of course he has been "planted" again and again into the churchyard, but he knew what he was doing, and a ball a little higher or a little shorter found a resting-place in the safe hands of Palairet or Daniell on the pavilion rails. He has much to thank Sam Woods for. Wicket after wicket has he got at mid-off through Sam's fearless fielding, and run after run has he been saved. A great many cautious batsmen, too, have been irritated into hitting through the close proximity of Sam at silly point, and this silly point to a bowler of Tyler's pace is no sinecure, even with the most gentle of batsmen. I often wonder that this placing of a man right under the batsman's nose is not more often adopted, as the result seems always to justify it, for whether you get the man out or not, he is most decidedly put off his game. It is not, however, a place to go to sleep in, even with the mildest of performers. I was sorry that Tyler should have been no-balled at the close of his career, for the day on which he was penalised there seemed to be no difference whatever from the action he always had, and which was universally passed for years.

Of the leg-break bowlers there is Braund, one of the best all-round cricketers of the day. He is second only in the matter of pace to Vine, and he is easily first in the matter of length and direction—perhaps not so difficult as Vine is at his best, but he always bowls well, consistently well, on all sorts of wickets, and he is never punished to the extent the other bowlers of this class are when one is lucky enough to catch them on an off day.

There are many other slow bowlers of whom I should like to scribble, but time presses, and we must pass on to our second division, to the bowlers of the medium pace, whose numbers are as sands on the seashore.

There is very little doubt that the bowlers who comprise this our second division are in the majority of instances of more general value to their side than the faster bowlers, for the obvious reason that they can always obtain a foothold.

They can also bowl longer at a stretch, they can vary their pace, they can alter the whole principle of their attack to suit the varying stages of a wicket in a way that is given to very few of our really fast bowlers. There are, too, so many that one must include in this class, that it is a matter of considerable difficulty to make anything like an adequate selection. There are some, however, whose names will immediately occur to the minds of every average cricketer.

I asked W. G. Grace not long ago, "Who was the best medium-paced bowler you ever played against?" Almost without thought the answer came back, "George Lohmann"; and there is many another player who, asked the same question, would make answer in a similar strain.

We all knew that tall, fair-haired, broad, rather high-shouldered figure—a splendid worker in every section of the game. Great as the pleasure was in studiously watching the man bowl, or watching him bat, taking the extraordinary risks he did, to my mind an almost equally enjoyable thing was to watch him at extra slip. Before his time there were good slips, bad slips, fast-asleep slips, and since his time every variety of "slipper" has passed across the stage, but none ever had the same catlike activity, the same second-sight to practically foretell the flight, the pace of a ball, and the same safe pair of hands to hold it in.

But I am presumably writing on bowling and not fielding. The following description of George Lohmann by C. B. Fry is one of the very best things of the many that he has done:—

He made his own style of bowling, and a beautiful style it was—so beautiful that none but a decent cricketer could fully appreciate it. He had a high right-over action, which was naturally easy and free-swinging, but, in his seeking after variations of pace, he introduced into it just a suspicion—a mere suspicion—of laboriousness. Most people, I believe, considered his action to have been perfect. To the eye it was rhythmical and polished, but it cost him, probably, more effort than it appeared to do. His normal pace was medium; he took a run of moderate length, poised himself with a slight uplifting of his high square shoulders, and delivered the ball just before his hand reached the top of its circular swing, and, in the act of delivery, he seemed first to urge forward the upper part of his body in sympathy with his arm, and then allow it to follow through after the ball. Owing to his naturally high delivery, the ball described a pronounced curve, and dropped rather sooner than the batsman expected. This natural peculiarity he developed assiduously into a very deceptive ball which he appeared to bowl the same pace as the rest, but which he really, as it were, held back, causing the unwary and often the wary to play too soon. He was a perfect master of the whole art of varying his pace without betraying the variation to the batsman. He ran up and delivered the ball, to all appearances, exactly similarly each time; but one found now that the ball was hanging in the air, now that it was on to one surprisingly soon. He had complete control of his length, and very, very rarely—unless intentionally—dropped a ball too short or too far up. He had a curious power of making one feel a half-volley was on its way; but the end was usually a perfect length ball or a yorker. He had that subtle finger power which makes the ball spin, and consequently he could both make the ball break on a biting wicket and make it "nip along quick" on a true one. He made a practice of using both sides of the wicket on sticky pitches. If he found he was breaking too much, he would change from over to round the wicket, and on fast pitches he soon had a go round the wicket at a batsman who appeared comfortable at the other sort. But he was full of artifices and subtleties, and he kept on trying them all day, each as persistently as the others, one after another. With all his skill, he would never have achieved his great feats but for his insistence of purpose. He was what I call a very hostile bowler; he made one feel he was one's deadly enemy, and he used to put many batsmen off their strokes by his masterful and confident manner with the ball. He was by far the most difficult medium-pace bowler I ever played on a good wicket.

In the spring of a year eighteen summers ago three or four of us were playing cricket on the wilderness of Clapham Common. A young man watched the game for a little, and eventually took a hand. He bowled to us and he batted for us, and we learnt something. At the end of half an hour he left. We asked his name. "Lohmann," came the reply. We said, "Good-morning, and thank you." And to-day I think that there are dozens of committeemen all over the country, and especially in the county of Surrey, who would like to go out into the same or a similar wilderness and encounter another George Lohmann. They may go out hot haste to find one, but they will return empty-handed.

In reply to the same question that I asked W. G. Grace, Ranjitsinhji said, "Noble." Now of Noble I have not had sufficient experience to write, so I asked him again, and the next answer was, "Jack Hearne"; and for perfection of action, with its open-shouldered, almost three-quarter arm swing, I have never seen his equal. He has every variation of pace, and, on a wicket that suits him, as much off break as he wants; and he bowls, or did bowl at his best, a length that only a very few bowlers like Alfred Shaw ever excelled. It has been said that on a perfect wicket he plays a man in. Well, perhaps he does; but those of us who on a sticky wicket at Lord's—and at Lord's a sticky wicket spells perdition—have had the temerity to stand up against him, bowling as he nearly always is from the pavilion end, know with what difficulty he can be stopped, and with what superhuman effort scored off.

Two other great medium-paced bowlers appeal immediately to the player of cricket—Attewell and Mead—both of a wonderful length, and doing a bit either way, not in the same way as Jack Hearne, who is practically an off break bowler, with a fast ball going with his arm, but with distinctive finger or hand break going both ways.

Who does not remember Attewell's easy, full-faced run up to the wicket, the splendid control of length—a very machine, but a machine with an untiring human intelligence. Both these two are perfect gluttons for work—this end, the other end, both ends, all day and probably all night if the span of the hours for play were lengthened. Attewell I should have taken on a good wicket, and Mead on a bad.

The latter I remember years ago at Broxbourne, where he and I led the attack for the local club, and wonderfully successful he was; but in those days he bowled almost entirely leg breaks, and it was only, I believe, after journeying Leytonwards, that he developed the off theory, with an occasional straight one and with an occasional leg break, that ultimately gave him the position amongst great bowlers that he holds to-day.

Lancashire some seasons ago possessed a quartette that very few sides have been able to equal. I refer to Briggs, Hallam, Cuttell, and Mold. Each of the four obtained a hundred wickets. Lancashire were playing at the Oval; the wicket was on the slow side, not very difficult and not very easy; each of the four had a turn, and in this particular match Hallam bowled extremely well. In my own mind he was at his best one of the most difficult of medium-paced bowlers, for the flight was so deceptive. He has a good variation of pace, but the bad luck he has had in his health has clung to him in the matter of bowling—there seem to be more missed chances, more balls that beat the bat and evade the wicket, than fall to the lot of many another bowler in the same class.

LORDS GROUND EARLY IN THE NINETEENTH CENTURY.

From a Water-Colour by H. Alken.
ONE ARM AND ONE LEG MATCH.

In the matter of length, in the knowledge of the art of bowling, in his phenomenal success, there is one man in this our second division who occupies an almost unique position—Alfred Shaw. Every one knows the records that he holds, but there is one thing that at the time of its occurrence certainly was the subject of much gratifying comment, and this was Alfred Shaw's astonishing resurrection in first-class cricket, which hardly to-day receives the recognition that it merits. Sussex journeyed to the Oval. Shaw, who for a considerable time had given up first-class cricket, was included in the side, and those of us who were playing against him saw and realised one of the finest pieces of bowling ever given on a perfect Oval wicket. Surrey's score was well over 300. Shaw bowled one end and then the other till he had completed 50 overs. *During this time only 60 odd runs had been scored from him*, and there were seven Surrey victims labelled Shaw in the score-sheet. He bowled as only a marker could bowl, and every man that proceeded to the wicket either played a bit too soon or a bit too late at some period or other of his innings. It was a remarkable bowling performance, and remarkable evidence of stamina of a bowler not in the first flush of youth.

Another in this same class, and who at the start of his career was engaged on the staff at the Oval with his future club-mate Hulme, was George Davidson, a fast medium bowler with a longish run and an imperturbable length—full of life and vigour, and a man whose place in the side Derbyshire have not yet been enabled to fill.

Tate, like Rhodes, is again a cricketer to whom the state of a wicket makes a phenomenal difference, even more so than is usually the case. Given suitable conditions, there are few bowlers that can make the ball come up faster off the pitch than Tate. He bowls a really good length, and can apply the off break at will, and for years has stepped into the breach for Sussex and saved the rest of his side many many wearying hours of fielding. And now to make an end of our second division we will include F. S. Jackson and J. R. Mason. It is a very moot point whether they should be termed fast or medium—let us say they are fast-medium. It really does not matter much what we call them, for any one whose patience has held out thus far in this article has no doubt seen them both bowl again and again. F. S. Jackson is a confident bowler; he bowls with a confidence born of the past, and with an unlimited confidence in the future, and to this self-reliance I attribute a large proportion of his success. Bowling fast-medium, with an occasional off break and an occasional slow ball, he invariably manages to keep the runs down, and at the same time to take his quota of wickets; and a bowler that can go with Sam Woods through the whole of a Gentlemen *v.* Players match unchanged must be a really good bowler, even though as we watch him we cannot exactly determine how he succeeds as he undoubtedly does.

J. R. Mason is probably a bit faster than Jackson. He has a free upstanding delivery, an easy run up to the wicket, and a full-arm swing. He bowls a good length just off the off stump, and on his day and with a wicket in his favour can make the ball do a lot from the off. Sam Woods said that he had never in his life seen much better bowling than Mason's in the Somerset *v.* Kent match at Taunton in August 1901. The home side were dismissed for 74 and 78, Mason's share of the wickets being four for 26 and *eight for 29*, an excellent performance for any amateur on any wicket.

The last of our three divisions now claims our limited attention, and here it would be as well if I made yet another apology: the names of many of the great Australian bowlers have been omitted from these pages, from the fact that I have so seldom played against them. Of Giffen, Palmer, Turner, Ferris, Jones, and the "Demon Spofforth" I wish I could write, but what I could say of them would be as the sum of the runs I should in all probability have made against them. As I said before, to the cricketer who has got his heart and soul in the game, there is nothing much more exhilarating than the sleepy field being rudely awakened to a just sense of his duties. Speaking from a spectator's point of view, there is nothing more exciting than to watch the uprooting of the sticks, to note their gyration in the direction of the glorified long stop, and to follow the flight of a bail for fifty or sixty yards. To this end we must possess ourselves of a really fast bowler.

The best natural fast bowler, taken at the zenith of his fame, was Tom Richardson. Those of us that have watched him pounding away hour after hour and day after day at the Oval, have marvelled much at the wonderful natural spin, and have marvelled perhaps more at his inexhaustible energy and neverending fund of good-humour. He was never tired and never out of sorts, and when the wicket was badly broken I have known him time after time slacken his great pace for fear of injuring an opposing batsman. Always, and rightly too, one of the most popular players that ever stepped on to a cricket-field, still to-day, when perhaps his prime is past, there is no figure more welcome to the thousands that throng our grounds than the figure of "Long Tom," as the crowds delight to call him. It was indeed a gustable tit-bit to watch him in 1894 bowl Essex out at the Oval, taking the whole ten wickets himself.

A noteworthy fact in connection with Richardson, in the four years when he aggregated over 1000 wickets, was the great success he met with on all sorts and conditions of wickets. He could be quite as deadly in the slime or on a drying wicket as on the fieriest piece of asphalt. Now this ubiquitous wicket-taking is given to practically no fast bowler that I have ever seen, with the exception of Spofforth, and he did it not by bowling his usual great pace, as was the case with Richardson, but by slowing himself down to the speed of a Haigh or a Jack Hearne.

It is the general opinion of many of our greatest cricketers—W. G. Grace and Ranjitsinhji, for example—that on a fast good wicket, and when bowling at the top of his form, we have never known the equal of Lockwood. Bowling with a long bouncing run, he can make the ball flick higher and faster from the pitch than any other bowler in this our third class. There is at times the very devil in it, and when the ball is not rapping incontinently at your fingers, it is hitting the middle and leg from well outside the off stump. One of the finest balls bowled that failed to get a wicket was bowled by Lockwood to Ranjitsinhji at the Oval three or four seasons ago.

From an Engraving Published in 1784.
A MATCH AT THE GENTLEMAN'S CLUB, WHITE CON-
DUIT HOUSE, ISLINGTON.

I was standing at mid-off, and can see it to this day. Ranjitsinhji had just come in to bat, and was, I think, still on the mark. It was very fast; it pitched three to four inches off the off stump, and came back like lightning. I listened for the pleasing rattle of the sticks, but at the eleventh hour—no, I had better say the last hundredth part of a second—Ranjitsinhji's right leg was bent across, and he received it full on the thigh. There was no other player living who, having failed to stop it with his bat, could have got his leg there in time. He certainly acquired a bruise, but the pain of this surely and swiftly dwindled in an innings of over 190!

One of the finest victories Surrey ever won over Yorkshire was at the Oval. On a perfect wicket Surrey scored over 300 on the first day and a portion of the second. Richardson at the pavilion and Lockwood at the gasometer end started the attack, and on the same magnificent wicket *dismissed Yorkshire for 78!* Of these, Jack Brown made 48! Those of us who were playing, and those who were lucky enough to have visited the Oval that day, could never in their lives have seen finer fast bowling. Both bowled at a tremendous pace, both bowled at the top of their form; they seemed almost to be bowling man against man, to be vying for supremacy. It was a great day to catch the finest natural fast bowler in conjunction with the finest cultivated fast bowler making sad havoc of a very powerful side. It was in the second innings of Yorkshire that poor Frank Milligan made his last appearance at the Oval, and right well he played, making 64 out of a total of 170 odd. (I should have mentioned before that F. S. Jackson was unfortunately incapacitated from batting through an injured thumb. This of course greatly weakened the Yorkshire batting, but at the time Lord Hawke said he had rarely seen finer bowling.)

Of Arthur Mold this can be said with absolute certainty, that no bowler ever attained a similar pace with such a minimum of exertion—two or three long loose strides, two at a trot, and an arm swinging round like a flail, a good length, great pace, and on any wicket at times a considerable flick back from the off—a bowler that, like Richardson or Lockwood, might bowl a man at any period of his innings, however well set he might be. For as many of us know, there are certain bowlers, generally of the slow or medium class, that a respectable batsman, after an hour or so's stay at the wicket, can negotiate with safety, unless of course some violent risk be taken. With these three, and perhaps one or two more, it is quite possible to be bowled neck and heels when taking no risk whatever.

Of all the other fast bowlers I have met, the majority, and it is a large majority too, either go with the arm or go up the pitch straight as a die. Wass and Barnes are exceptions to this general rule, for under favourable conditions they bowl with a distinct leg break, and very difficult to play they are.

George Hirst, I think, stands in a section of fast bowlers entirely his own. It is a curious thing that we possess so few really fast left-handers. Hirst is equipped not only with great pace, but also with an extraordinary swerve, that is to say, he does not always have it under his immediate control, but when starting fresh and with a new ball, he swirls inwards in a stump-uprooting manner, and the swerve seems to take place in the last two or three yards of the ball's flight. I remember seeing Captain Bush confront him last year at Leeds for the first time. Hirst came up to the wicket with his swinging run, the ball left his hand; Bush's left leg shot out for his slashing stroke by cover, and it was only by astonishing luck that at the very last moment he stopped a yorker almost behind his right foot, and in stopping it overbalanced and lay prone—thus emphasising the luck he had experienced and the amount of the swerve. With a new ball it usually stays with him from twenty minutes to an hour, and it can occur again after a sufficient rest and the acquisition of another new ball. I think I am doing Rhodes no injustice when I say that for some time now Hirst has dismissed, largely through this swerve of his, more of the first five or six batsmen than have fallen to his, Wilfred's, lot.

Of all the really fast amateur bowlers none have given me so much pleasure to watch as Sam Woods. At Brighton College they tell me he was quite as fast as he ever was afterwards all through his first-class career as a bowler. Personally I experienced the same luck as many another would-be run-getter who met him for the first time, that is to say, I went in to bat and came out again without having heard the sound of the bat striking the ball, b. Woods 0! The pace was bewildering. At his best and in full health he was as fast as an ordinary player cares to encounter. Exceedingly even in temper for a fast bowler, there were only one or two little things that really worried him. One, however, was to see a man draw away as he came up to the crease with those short shuffling strides he always adopted. I shall never forget one day at Fenner's in some trial match a rather nervous performer against fast bowling wobbled to the wicket. Sam was bowling *over* the wicket, and the newcomer, who practically relied on a very late cut for scoring purposes, promptly planted him for two or three fours through the slips, having first withdrawn, at the approach of "the Terror," in the direction of the square leg umpire. The same sliding motion at right angles to the wicket, the same stroke, the same lucky four, and Sam goes round the wicket. If fast at first, he is faster now, and the nervous player is still more nervous. The ball comes down well clear of the leg stick, and is cut *behind the wicket and between the wicket and the stumper!*—a truly miraculous stroke, and one that I have never seen executed save on this solitary occasion. Four! but the next was straight, and it crept a bit, and the nervous batsman retired, having, however, before his departure credited himself with fifty or so on the sunburnt "tins."

Of W. M. Bradley, there is nothing to be said—a natural fast bowler with the mind of a man and the strength of a bull. I faced him two years ago at Canterbury. He was bowling against the pavilion and against the sun; the slope of the ground went with him, a new ball was in his hand, and it whizzed down the pitch as it left it. It was about the most uncomfortable ten minutes I ever spent. They came "down the vale" with a four-inch off break; they grazed one's ribs, one's chest, one's nose; and at last I was caught in the slips protecting my eye with my hand. It was on this occasion that I was truly convinced of what a grand player Tom Hayward is against really fast bowling. Though we were easily beaten, he made 97 not out! Good boy!

There are many more in this our third class that I should like to write about, but space and the clock forbid, and so perforce am I compelled to halt awhile and wait for the little cavalcade of "lobsters" that are so far behind, so very far behind, the pressing throng of modern bowlers.

CRICKET

To quote from *Wisden*:—

We, the solitary few who still strive to hold upright the tottering pillars in the ruined temple of lob bowling, unto whose shrine the bowlers of the olden time for ever flocked, to-day we are but of small account; there is scarcely a ground in England where derision is not our lot, or where laughter and jaunting jeers are not hurled broadcast at us. To-day perhaps to an all-powerful side we are of little use—to a side that is weak, to a side whose special weakness is its fielding, we are the strychnine of tonics. By himself stands Simpson-Hayward, for he "flicks" the ball as we have all seen many a wrathful billiard-player do when returning the white from a most unexpected pocket—it spins and spins and breaks sharply from the off, and it sometimes hits the wicket. There are two more, Wynyard and myself, and we both bowl in the old, old way, and we bowl with a persistence born of tentative success—occasionally we hook a fish, and great is our rejoicing. We are both fond of this bowling, I particularly so, and when on many a ground throughout the country there has arisen on every side the gentle sound of "Take him orf! Take him orf!" were it not that the side ever comes before oneself, I would bowl, and bowl, and bowl, until at eventide the cows come home.—

D. L. A. J., *Wisden*, 1902.

CRICKET

From a Painting by C. J. Basébe.
KENNINGTON OVAL IN 1849

CHAPTER V

FIELDING BY S. L. JESSOP

It has become almost an axiom of the game that more matches are lost by bad fielding than through any superexcellence of batting or bowling, and that this is really the case few will deny.

How many of those favoured mortals who participate in first-class cricket can call to mind instances of brilliant batting, followed up by capital bowling, all to be rendered null and void by the missing of a "sitter" by some lazy fieldsman whose thoughts were anywhere but on the game. Cricketers are but mortals, and catches will be missed as long as the game of cricket is played, but less mistakes would be made, especially in the slips, if fieldsmen would but pay the strictest attention to the game, and not allow their thoughts to wander. That chance that "Cain" gave to third slip, which might have turned defeat into victory, would in all probability have been accepted, had the culprit's thoughts not been too much engrossed in the choice of theatres that evening for his fiancée; and to such causes as these, if one could but read the thoughts of those at fault, many of the too frequent mistakes could be traced. Too much emphasis cannot be attached to this lack of attention, for one can but judge from one's own experience.

That fielding, the most important branch of the game, has deteriorated during even the past five or six years may be accepted as a true bill, and we can only look for improvement to those who have the rising generation under their charge. No one can expect to become a good fieldsman without assiduous and often irksome practice, and this, combined with the undue prominence bestowed on batting, may account somewhat for the deterioration. A batsman, by scoring 50 runs, feels that he may have had a material hand in the success of his side, and in the same way so does a bowler who takes five or six wickets, for they both have something tangible to show in the score-sheet. True, the fieldsman may have helped the bowler by a brilliant catch or two, but there is no record of the amount of runs he may have saved. Thus it is that a little selfishness may crop up, for whereas the fieldsman may feel that, like the spoke of a wheel, he is only part of a whole, the batsman or bowler feels that he is an individual. Be the reason what it may, there is no doubt that the practice of fielding is much neglected, and as there is not that monotony in it that so frequently crops up in batting achievements, it is difficult to understand the cause of that neglect. When one considers that the best batsman in the world is not absolutely certain of scoring a run, and that a good fieldsman nearly always saves 20 or 30, the importance of fielding can at once be appreciated.

From a spectacular point of view there is no more stirring sight than to see eleven players, each of whom is striving his utmost to outdo the other in his efforts to save runs, bringing off catches that an ordinary field would not even attempt, and saving runs in a manner which at times borders on the miraculous. It is such a sight as this that saves cricket from becoming too monotonous. As has been mentioned before, sufficient practice is not indulged in; players who take great pains to improve their batting look upon fielding in the light of a "something" that has to be put up with, and as such only to be tolerated. Let these same players take half an hour's practice every day for a month, and they will find an improvement in their fielding such as they would have hardly deemed possible. The only feasible way of obtaining practice is for some one to hit the ball to you from all sorts of distances, varying from 10 yards to 70, as this range will include different kinds of chances, from "slip" catches to catches in the long field. It is a good plan to use a light bat and hold it in the same manner that one would grasp a racquet, as by doing so one is able to impart a "cut" to the ball which closely resembles the spin that would result from a mis-hit to "cover" or a "snick" in the "slips." Excepting at school, throwing at the wicket is seldom practised, which is a great mistake, for many a run has been saved and many a wicket taken by the accuracy of a smart return.

In classifying fieldsmen, one can roughly do so by saying that there are two kinds, those that field near the wicket and those that field in the out-field, and these latter are in the minority. In the same manner, fielding may be dissolved into two parts, namely, ground fielding and catching. Ground fielding has been brought to a state of perfection for which the improvement in the modern cricket-grounds is in a large manner responsible. To become a good ground fieldsman one must be able to judge the pace of the ball to a nicety; otherwise, although one may succeed in stopping it, one will fail to gather the ball accurately, and consequently will not save the run. The fieldsman who excels is the one who, gathering the ball accurately, returns it to the keeper or bowler with one and the same action. The time saved by this almost simultaneous action of stopping and returning the ball is of immense value to fielders in the long field, not only in the saving of singles, but also in the running out of unwary batsmen. When a ball is travelling along the ground, the first duty of a fieldsman is if possible to get in front of it, drawing the legs close together, so that, should the ball through any irregularity in the turf bump over the outstretched hands, it will be impeded by the fieldsman's body. He must be equally certain with right or left hand in stopping those hits that he cannot get to with both hands, and there may be a time when it is absolutely necessary to use his foot in order to save runs. This method, useful and indispensable though it may be at times, is, one is sorry to say, becoming a little too general. Whenever possible the hand should always be used, and only as a desperate last chance should the foot be resorted to.

On the perfect grounds that now abound, in nine cases out of ten the chance of overtaking a ball that has been only moderately hit is very small, but it is worth while to pursue, even with the odds so great against one. And one should bear in mind that the quicker one starts in that pursuit, the more likely is that boundary to be saved, especially as to gauge the decrease in the pace of the ball is a most difficult matter. Grounds too must be taken into consideration, for it does not follow that a boundary which one might save at Birmingham would be saved at Brighton. When you are attempting to save a boundary by *pursuing* the ball, never try to seize the ball too soon, for you are only more likely to miss it altogether, and your chase to be rendered futile. Even should you succeed in grasping the ball, your effort of stooping down and diving forward so upsets your balance that to turn round and return the ball without unnecessary loss of time is extremely difficult. The method that should be adopted, and one that is more likely to meet with success, is for the fieldsman to overtake the ball, and when a little in front, or even level with it, to stretch the hand out and allow it to roll into the hand.

No matter how accurate one may be in returning a ball, accuracy is of little avail unless it be tempered with speed, for even though occasionally a man may be given out when the wicket has been hit and he has regained his ground, yet the fieldsman will find that it is the exception and not the rule. Without speed of return the fieldsman, be he ever so certain a catch or brilliant a ground field, will never reach a high point of excellence; he will be useful, but not great. Even this useful field is not so frequent as he should be.

Opportunities of running men out are often lost by the fieldsman becoming flurried, and returning the ball in a haphazard manner to whichever end he happens to be near. This is a most fatal mistake, and one that has been the cause of allowing many a batsman to proceed on his way safely when the reverse should have been the case. When an opportunity of running out a man does occur—and these, from the fieldsman's point of view, are too few and far between—the fieldsman should determine as to which end he is to return the ball before it reaches him. He will then have more time to make certain of the accuracy of his aim. Should he be fielding near the wicket, he should return to the wicket-keeper at the height of the latter's chest; if from the long field, on the first bounce, but always at the utmost speed. A time may come when it is imperative to aim at the stumps, for the time occupied in the keeper breaking the wickets may just suffice to give the batsman the benefit of the doubt in a close race; but as a general rule it is one's duty to rely on the keeper. The bowler at times has to fulfil the duties of a wicket-keeper in receiving the return balls, and as he does not possess the protection of gloves, one has to consider the question of damaging his fingers. With a bowler who is wont to flinch at a fast return, it is wiser in the end to leave the wicket entirely to the accuracy of the thrower and the nimbleness of the backer-up. Many "run outs" may accrue in this manner which might not have come to pass if too much reliance had been placed on the bowler. Preventing runs is made much easier by the faculty of being able to anticipate the direction of the batsman's stroke before he has actually played the ball, and this capacity is only acquired by most careful attention and experience. By being on one's toes, somewhat in the same manner as one would start for a race, it becomes much easier to cut off a ball than if one's foot is placed flat on the ground. The adoption of this attitude not only saves actual runs, but it has the further advantage of preventing batsmen from attempting those short runs which so often have the effect of demoralising a weak fielding side. Difficult as it is at times to judge to which end the ball will be returned, especially when a fieldsman feints to throw in at one end and then suddenly returns it to the other, some one should always be backing up both the wicket-keeper and bowler. Nothing is more annoying to the bowler than to see a sharp-run single converted into a two or even more by the lack of adequate backing-up. It is those who are fielding near the wicket who should be responsible for the prevention of overthrows, especially the man in that place to which it is usual to relegate a weak fieldsman, mid-on.

There is no hard-and-fast rule for the proper position to hold the hands when about to receive a catch. The hand should be so held as to form a cup, with the fingers extended, and the moment the ball is inside, the hand should be allowed to give, in order to minimise the impact. For catches in the long field one should thrust the hands up as high as one can, so that, if the ball should be fumbled, a chance may be left of securing it on a second attempt. One-handed catches must be made at times, even in the long field, but whenever possible two hands should be used. Confidence is a great factor of success at cricket, but even that quality may be overdone, especially in catching. To make a comparatively easy catch look difficult, in order to extort applause from the crowd, is a most unsportsmanlike act, jeopardising as it does the success of a side in order to gain a few moments of self-glorification. Fortunate is the side which does not possess one of these mountebanks. Catches should be looked upon as timely gifts of Providence, and as such not to be lightly treated, for in these days of concrete-like wickets chances occur all too infrequently.

In no branch of the game is the improvement so marked as it is in wicket-keeping, and for this improvement present-day cricketers have to thank that prince of wicket-keepers, the Australian, Blackham. Before he made his appearance in England, long-stops were looked upon as quite as indispensable to a side as the wicket-keeper himself, but on his arrival in 1878 the fallacy of that theory was quickly demonstrated. Wickets in those days were not quite the perfect wickets of to-day, and with Spofforth bowling his fastest and best, the manner in which Blackham stood close up to the wicket, and without the aid of a long-stop, was looked upon as something approaching the marvellous. Magnificent keepers as we have had, since he revolutionised the art of wicket-keeping, he is still without an equal.

No one, unless he possesses a natural aptitude for the position, is likely to achieve any considerable success, though it is a mistake to suppose that a wicket-keeper, like the poet, is born, not made.

Much can be done by practice, and by studying the methods of the many brilliant keepers that abound to-day. Excepting the captain of the side, no man is more open to criticism than the wicket-keeper, and in nine cases out of ten this criticism tends in the direction of abuse. By those who have been unfortunate enough to have been persuaded to don the gloves, the difficulties of the position are duly appreciated, but unless one has done so, one is hardly able to judge the great assistance that a good keeper can render a bowler. Besides his duties of stumping, running out, and catching, he is often able to inform the bowler as to the weak spots in a batsman's play, for from his very position he can more easily detect them. In the case of a good bowler and an equally competent stumper, it is a combination of two heads against one, the most valuable combination that a side can possess. The confidence that a good keeper inspires in a bowler is only equalled by the confidence that one would naturally possess in using one's own billiard-cue. An incompetent wicket-keeper will make a good bowler powerless, whilst a good keeper considerably strengthens a weak bowling side. A wicket-keeper without a good nerve may be likened to a ship without a rudder, for each is practically helpless. The slightest sign of flinching would result in an appalling amount of byes and missed opportunities. Very rarely indeed is a match concluded without the wicket-keeper having played an important part in either the winning or the losing of it. He should never lose sight of the ball from the moment it is out of the bowler's hand to the moment it reaches him, and above all, he should never snap at the ball.

CRICKET

THE CRICKET FIELD AT RUGBY.

From a Painting by W. J. Bowden.
A MATCH IN THE EIGHTIES.

He stands up in a stooping posture, with his hands close enough to the bails to allow him to remove them in almost the same action as receiving the ball. Until the ball has been struck or has passed the bat, he should remain stationary, for it is much easier to accurately judge the ball thus than when on the move.

Necessity compels him at times to jump to this or that side, but this should be done before the ball reaches him, in order to allow the body to be again stationary when his hands receive the ball. In order to run the least chance of injury to the hands, especially to the top joints of the fingers, the hands should be held at a downward angle, and allowed to "give" with the impact of the ball. This "give" should be very slight to slow or medium bowling, as the drawing back of the hands after taking a ball, even though occupying the slightest fraction of a second, often results in a missed opportunity of stumping. Wicket-keepers who are in the habit of allowing their hands to "give" considerably are, on account of their hands being farther back, invariably better catchers than stumpers. This is especially applicable to Board, the Gloucestershire keeper. He brings off some most wonderful catches, but from this very habit of drawing the hands back too far, he is often unable to outpace the batsman when a question of stumping arises. Considering how completely a batsman, especially a left-hander, often obscures the sight of the ball from the keeper's view, it is a distinct credit to his skill that he is able to perform his duties so ably. How many times has the explanation of a dropped catch by cover or mid-off been put down to want of a proper sight of the ball; but one rarely hears that excuse from the stumper, and yet he, above any of the other fields, has a right to use it. To a very fast bowler even the most proficient of wicket-keepers should stand back, for he is more likely to make catches there than if he stood up. Stumping off fast bowling is of rare occurrence, not on account of the pace of the bowling, but because in playing it a batsman rarely leaves his crease, and consequently the keeper gets few opportunities. The latter's most difficult duty is the taking of balls on the leg side. He rarely gets a clear sight of these, and consequently has to rely more or less on guess-work, especially to bowling above medium pace. The South African, Halliwell, was quite as much at home in keeping on the leg side as he was on the off, and frequently used to stump batsmen whilst attempting to glance fast bowling to leg. Thankless as the post of wicket-keeping is at times, yet from the frequency of his opportunities the wicket-keeper must often gain some solace.

Because a fieldsman is a good out-field, it does not follow that he will be equally successful in any position nearer the wicket, so that, though it may be an excellent plan for a fieldsman to become acquainted with other positions in the field, yet, as "use is second habit," it may be wiser for him to make a specialty of that position in which he has become accustomed to field. On account of the comparatively little movement that it requires, "point" is a much sought after position by those players who, either from stress of age or laziness, do not wish to indulge in much running or throwing. Such is really not the use for which this position was intended, for, from the very fact of its being so adjacent to the wicket, it requires extreme attention and activity. "Point" should never be farther away from the wicket than 12 yards, either to slow bowling or fast, and he should always be ready to take the place of the stumper whenever the latter, either because of the bad return or on account of his zeal in running after a "snick," leaves his post. Many "points" stand too far out, so much so that they encroach on the duties of "cover." If a "point" stands some 16 or 17 yards away from the wicket, the "cover" must of necessity stand much deeper, and by doing so he can rarely stop two determined batsmen from stealing many short runs during the course of a long partnership. No finer "points" than Noble, and Wright of Derbyshire, who stand rarely more than 10 yards from the bat, could be found, and the number of catches that they have brought off because of their propinquity to the wicket more than counterbalances the number of runs that they might have saved by standing back.

There is no position in the field that gives so many opportunities for a fine field to shine as does that of "cover-point." It is a most trying position for any one who may not be in the best of condition, as he has to be continually on the move, for he it is that is held responsible for the prevention of short runs, quite the most arduous part of his many duties. As he has a large area of ground to look after, he must be very exact in keeping in his right place, as even a yard may mean all the difference between taking or missing a chance, especially as the ball sometimes travels at great speed in his direction. The difficulty of the position lies in the amount of "spin" that is often imparted to the ball, not only when on the ground, but also when in the air. Catches which often appear to be going to one's right hand have suddenly to be attempted with the left, on account of the curve, and this curve being of a very sudden nature, these catches are extremely hard to judge. This curve is most pronounced when a slow left-hand or a leg-break bowler is bowling. One often sees apparently easy catches from mis-hits dropped at "cover" in a most unaccountable fashion, but in reality these simple "dolly" catches are much more difficult to hold than those from hard drives. An incredible amount of "spin" is put on a mis-hit ball, so that, unless the catch is received well into the middle of the hand, the spinning ball will act in much the same fashion as does a billiard-ball when "check side" is imparted to it. When assisted by an extra mid-off, "cover" should place himself much squarer with the wickets, as he will have a much less area of ground to guard, and he must be just deep enough to be able to save singles. He should be able to return the ball from below the shoulder with a fast wristy action, full pitch to the wickets. The introduction of extra mid-off has somewhat lessened "cover's" duties, so much so that often a brilliant field has very little to do in that position, this being especially the case with slow bowling. Naturally, strokes off slow bowling are made more in front than behind or square, so that to this class of bowling the extra mid-off is indispensable. To see Gregory fielding at "cover" is an object-lesson to those fielders who may have fallen into the disastrous habit of allowing the ball to come to them, instead of dashing in to meet it. There are many admirable cover-points, but for many years the Australian has been quite in a class by himself in that position. The duties of "third man" are of the same description as those of "cover," for the position calls for equal activity and dash. Short runs are invariably attempted if the "third man" is at all likely to be flurried, so that the fieldsman selected for the position must essentially be cool and collected. The pace of the wicket and the bowling should determine the exact position in which he should stand, and he should cultivate a stooping attitude, as the balls come to him as a rule very low. He will not get many catches, but when he does, it is extremely likely that they will be very difficult, on account of the "cut" that the ball will possess from being hit in that direction. When a short run is attempted, it is better to return the ball to the bowler, as the batsman who is backing up has less ground to cover than the striker. Any ball that goes to the left hand of "point" he has to attend to, and he must also back up the wicket-keeper when the ball is returned from the on side. One of the long fields is generally deputed to fill the position, often solely in order to save him from having to walk too far in order to fill some other position. Naturally it is a wise precaution to avoid tiring your fieldsmen, but unless the long field shows a marked aptitude for the position, he should not be placed there. Third men that one cannot occasionally steal runs from are very rare, but he would be a daring runner who would attempt to do so when such brilliant men as Trumper, Sewell, or Burnup are fielding in that position.

If one could trace the position of the field in which most catches are missed, "the slips," it would be safe to say, would pan out as the chief offenders. Excepting the wicket-keeper's, theirs are the most important places, and require quick-sighted fieldsmen who are certain catches. Attention is the most important quality, combined with the faculty of being able to judge the flight of the ball from the bat. One must adopt a stooping attitude, in order to reach low catches, and also because it enables one to spring in any direction with more ease than if one stands upright. Though two hands, as in other positions in the field, should be used whenever possible, yet one must be certain with either hand, as the majority of catches are brought off with one hand.

Two common faults are pretty general, namely, snapping at the ball instead of letting it come into the hand, and standing in the wrong place. The distance at which the slips should stand varies very much in accordance with the state of the pitch and the nature of the bowling. They would naturally be farther back to fast bowling than to slow. It is a moot point as to whether a slip should be stationary or occasionally on the move, in order to anticipate a stroke. An experienced slip has his own method, and he is wise to stick to it if he finds it meets with success, even though it be a method not altogether orthodox. Of present-day slips individually, R. E. Foster, A. O. Jones, Tunnicliffe, J. R. Mason, and Braund stand out very prominently, but collectively the combination of Braund, Maclaren, and Jones is all that one could desire.

An easy position, but one that requires considerable nerve and activity, is "mid-off." As a rule the ball comes straight to the fielder and at great pace, but usually with very little twist on, though occasionally, when a left-hander is bowling, the ball swerves a good deal. The most difficult catches that he has to deal with are those that rise from the very moment that the ball touches the bat, and unless he judges the ball very accurately, he will find that the tips of his fingers will suffer very considerably, and that success will not attend his efforts. "Mid-off" should be in such a position as to be able to back up the bowler when the batsman returns the ball hard, and also to save short runs. Like "cover" and "third man," he should be always ready to start, as he often gets chances of a run-out. The amount of runs that the Australian Jones and Hirst save in that position, and the catches that they bring off, are phenomenal.

In all the course of my experience I have never yet seen a really first-class "mid-on." It may be that I have been peculiarly unfortunate in that respect. It is an easy position to field in, because the ball is not often hit in that direction, and when it is, there is no twist, although there may be a good deal of pace on it. On account of the easiness of the position, the weak fieldsmen are deposited there. When a "short leg" is utilised, "mid-on's" duties are a perfect sinecure, but on fast wickets, when the short leg's services are dispensed with, he has a considerable amount of work to get through. He is often the only man fielding on the on side of the wicket, and accordingly he has to run for any ball that may be played on that side. He must be ready to back up both the wicket-keeper and the bowler, so that a great many runs can be saved by a smart field in this position.

On a bad wicket and with an off-break bowler the position of short leg is indispensable, as under these conditions many balls, though intended to be played straight, hit the edge of the bat and, on account of the break, proceed in his direction. Though weak fielders are also relegated to this position, it is a difficult post to fill adequately, as the ball comes often very quick and low, with a good deal of spin on. His position varies a good deal according to the style of the batsman, but he should not be too deep. As a general rule, he should be about 10 or 11 yards from the batsman. As so much leg-break bowling is now in vogue, he often gets bombarded in a dangerous manner. When a bowler of this kind is performing, it is just as well to place one of the best fieldsmen in that position.

Fielding in the "long field" requires more nerve and judgment than does fielding near the wicket. The ball is much longer in the air and on the ground, and it is on account of this fact that nerve plays such an important part. The ball is so long in coming to the fieldsman that he has time to conceive all manner of things that may happen, and it is for this reason that the knowledge of the temperaments of those playing under him is so useful to the captain. A fieldsman who is nervous in the long field need not necessarily be classed as a bad field, for cases have come under my own observation of the wonderful change that has been wrought in a "nervy" field when fielding close to the wickets. Generally speaking, there are two positions in the long field, "long on" and "long off," but now that the fashionable method of bowling wide of the leg stump has somewhat superseded the "off theory," the old position of "long leg" has lately been made more use of. In all three positions the duties are similar, and they require a safe pair of hands, speed in running, and great accuracy in returning the ball. Everything in the nature of a chance must be attempted, even at the risk of not saving a boundary, for often catches are made that at times look impossible. "Long field" must return the ball the moment that it is in his hands, and should never wait for the ball to come to him, but should dash in the moment it is struck. Few "out-fields" can throw a distance of 70 or 80 yards without going through some such preliminary as moving the arms round and round in order to gain sufficient momentum to aid them in propelling the ball, and even running 2 or 3 yards before returning it. This waste of time is simply a sign of lack of practice, and can easily be remedied by sufficient attention paid to it.

The importance of good fielding cannot be too greatly emphasised, for without it a good bowling side is rendered ineffectual and powerless to win matches, excepting on bad wickets. Unless a batsman or a bowler should possess great proficiency, he should not be included in a first-class match if he cannot attain to an average standard of fielding; *i.e.* he should be able to throw, not jerk, and catch reasonable catches. The time comes when a fieldsman, through advancing years, may not be so speedy in the field as he was wont to be in his younger days, though his powers as a batsman may be scarcely diminished. Provided he is still able to hold catches, in positions that require little or no running about, he may still be a powerful factor of success to his side. But for young fieldsmen who either from sheer laziness or inability cannot either hold catches or save runs, one cannot but have a feeling of disgust, and it is such players as these that are out of place in first-class cricket.

KENT v. SUSSEX, AT BRIGHTON.

A supposed Match played between 1839-41

CHAPTER VI

COUNTY CRICKET BY W. J. FORD

It has been always cast in the teeth of us Englishmen by our Continental critics that we take our amusements seriously—that our idea of recreation is to go forth and kill something, and that anything of the nature of excitement is unknown to us; even our wars seem to them to be conducted by us in a cold-blooded, business-like, almost saturnine fashion, such as the foreigner cannot understand. Our almost fanatical excitement over the relief of Mafeking and of Ladysmith might have served to disenlighten our neighbours to a certain degree, but they probably regarded those wild bursts of enthusiasm as a mere phase of a fever, as one of the periodic alternations of heat and cold that are characteristic of a severe attack of ague. It is for the historian and the student of human nature to decide whether our nature is phlegmatic or merely proud, and whether these rare outbursts are not in reality a genuine eruption of violent volcanic feelings which have long smouldered beneath the crust of our real nature. The true account seems to be that in matters of a public and, still more, of an international character, insular pride does not allow us to reveal the fact that the Englishman possesses a certain amount of that excitability which we choose to attribute to the southern and the Latin races: it is only a special stress that reveals this side of our nature. When, however, the Englishman's foot is on English soil, and when his only critics are of the same blood as himself, then and only then does he allow the true keenness of his disposition to run riot. The Englishman, in short, only casts aside his phlegm, his reserve, and his pride when he is in congenial society, and the presence of the necessary society is in no place more apparent than on the scenes of those sports that afford him the amusement and, in some cases, the means of life. Those scenes may be narrowed down to the football field, the race-course, and the cricket ground. It is with the last of these that our business at present lies.

It would be impossible to lay down any cast-iron reason for the fact that general interest in cricket has increased by leaps and bounds in the last twenty years. The fact is incontrovertible, whatever the cause may be, but to most of those who have watched the course of cricket events, the progress of county cricket will present itself as the primary cause of the progress of the game as a whole. At the same time, there is a fair field left for those who choose to maintain that the impetus given to county cricket is really due to the rapid spread of the game itself and the attendant enthusiasm of its admirers; while there is, as usual, a third course left to us, which is to maintain that the two things, general cricket and county cricket, have advanced *pari passu*, each owing much to the other. And at this point we may abandon the question as one that will produce abundant controversy and no conviction, especially as all the theorists can meet and agree as to the one common effect, differ as they may as to the cause, namely, that both players of the game and lovers of the game have increased by innumerable multiples during the last fifteen or twenty years. There are those who think it good to decry this desperate enthusiasm for a pastime—who declare that it is a symptom of national decadence, and declare that a mere game is an irrational thing, inasmuch as a rational treatment of it at once destroys its existence as a game in the true sense of the word. We are hardly prepared, however, to have our pastimes handled in this Socratic manner. A game is a game, and if it is a good game, we who love it consider that it deserves something more than casual and ephemeral treatment; hence we throw ourselves into it heart and soul, and those who like to see heart-and-soul work have only to go to the nearest county ground on a match day to see how energy and rivalry can, on the principle enunciated above, turn a game into a no-game.

Nor is it illogical at this point to assume that county cricket is to us the highest popular embodiment of our pastime; it is true that a certain and a limited number of special matches attract more attention, for sentimental reasons, than do mere county matches, but it is on the latter class of games that genuine and general interest is mainly expended, earning for those who exhibit it a certain amount of contempt from those who hold that to lavish interest on a game is to squander a valuable asset. Political economy and its votaries would doubtless tell us—indeed, they do tell us—that such labour as is expended on hitting, or on bowling, or on stopping, or on catching a mere ball, is unproductive labour, and consequently labour lost, while they show no limit to their contempt for those who, not being actual players themselves, squander—so they call it—valuable time in watching other people waste time that is equally valuable. However, the cynic and his butt, like the poor, are always with us; all that we can desire and all that we can hope for is that he will confine himself to his dwelling, and leave us to enjoy ourselves in peace, while we may fairly ask him to reflect in the recesses of his barrel as to what the watchers of cricket would do with themselves if there were no cricket to watch. That they would be better employed is possible; that they would be worse employed is probable; and he would be a poor philosopher indeed who would find fault with the open-air stage of Lord's or the Oval, and would yet allow the music-hall and the theatre to stifle their nightly victims. The strictest of Puritans could hardly find fault with bat and ball as being the inculcators of evil principles; rather, like the study of the ingenuous arts, do they "soften our characters and forbid them to be savage." The cynic and the rhymer have had their say, but cricket is still with us, and seems likely to stay, howl as they will.

In connection with the game's advance, it would be unjust not to acknowledge the fillip that has been given to it by the periodical visits of Australian elevens, the first of which occurred as far back as 1878, combined with the return of their calls by our men. It was a new truth to us that there was growing up in Greater Britain a race of men who, taught by ourselves, profiting by our lessons, and in the process of time perhaps improving on our methods, were able to withstand us to our face, the pupil often proving the superior of the master; and it may be that to this fact, and the perhaps unconscious conviction that "the old man" must not be "beaten by the boy" at cricket as at chess, is due the uprise of county cricket as the readiest means of ascertaining our strength and organising our resources, though it was not till several years after the first visit of Australians that any real attempt to organise county cricket into a formal competition succeeded. Such an attempt had been made in 1872 by the Marylebone Cricket Club, which offered a cup in that year for competition among the counties, but the offer was coldly received, the counties that entered were so few that such words as "competition" and "championship" became misnomers, and the offer was withdrawn. Not that the word "champion" had not been and still was applied to some county or another as soon as the last ball of the season had been bowled, but the expression was visionary; it was merely the outcome of the views of the press or of individuals, and it naturally happened that when these views conflicted there were "two Richmonds in the field," both styled champion by their respective supporters. It was not till the representatives of counties met in peaceful conclave, coded laws and bye-laws, with the request that the M.C.C. would exercise a fatherly and presidential rule over county cricket, that the latter became historical fact.

It seems to me that the growth and systematization of general cricket are due to the growth and systematization of county cricket, and the emulation which accompanied its increase. The counties, having set their hands to the plough, were in no mood to look back; those which, as exceptionally strong, were rated first-rate, set themselves to see that no weakness on their part should cause them to be degraded to the ranks; while the rank and file, on the other hand, spared no effort to secure their own promotion. And at this point it is well to remind those who profess to see a mere desire of money-making underlying the expansion of county cricket, that the then junior counties, many of which are now seniors, owed their existence and its prolongation not to gate-money or speculating syndicates, as is the case with many football clubs, but to the generous assistance of enthusiastic patrons, whose only motive for liberality was their own love of the game, as a game, and their desire to see it not merely extended, but perfected. At the present day there are county clubs which rely mainly for their existence on the voluntary subscriptions and donations of their supporters, men whose only reward is the opportunity of seeing good cricket brought home to their own doors, and the promotion, expansion, and improvement of the game. Gate-money is of course an important factor in a club's receipts, but it is sheer nonsense, it is almost mendacity, to declare that the county cricket of to-day is played for gate-money and for nothing else. Yet such assertions have been made, and are still made, by men who do not reflect that the patrons who subscribe to a club do not do so with the idea of providing the public with a gratis entertainment, though—I am thinking of one patron in particular—such an act would not be without precedent: their idea is, as stated before, to provide amusement for themselves, encourage the game, and help those who help themselves. The last people to grumble at the payment of gate-money are the payers themselves, who are not slow to recognise that sixpence is not a large sum to expend for a day in the open air, with a display of skill and activity thrown in, for which the spectator pays at the rate of about one penny per hour! Lastly, and briefly—for there is no satisfaction gained by dealing with misstatements—when accounts are balanced, the surplus that remains, if any, does not go to swell the speculator's income, but is devoted to the improvement of accommodation, the advancement of the game, or that prudent economy that provides against the cricketer's bugbear, in every sense of the word—a rainy day.

I have suggested that we owe the increase of cricket to the growth of county cricket, and the reasons are not far to seek. When once a county is included in the first class, or aspires to it, its first effort is to enlist all its available talent, and as the reward of the great cricketer is no mean one, whether that reward come in the shape of reputation and amusement to the amateur, or of good red gold to the professional, the aim and ambition of every promising player and of the club to which he belongs is to get at least a fair trial in the higher spheres of the game. Further than that, the executive does not merely wait to receive the applications of the ambitious, but, like Porsena of Clusium, it "bids its messengers ride forth, east and west and south and north," not exactly "to summon its array," but to ascertain what fighting blood there is in the county ready for immediate action, and what recruits there are whose early promise may be developed into disciplined effectiveness. In other words, the cricketing pulse of the county at once begins to throb, and the executive, like a wise physician, keeps its finger on that organ, to ascertain the condition of the patient. But it is not merely by inquisition into the talent that is available that the ranks of a county eleven are filled up: the promising players are invited to attend at the county ground for inspection, practice, and tuition, being drafted into the company of the "ground" bowlers, and given opportunities in minor matches of exhibiting their natural and their trained powers, a further impulse being given to cricket by the distribution of the big matches among different centres, where such distribution is possible, and by the mission of so-called second elevens to the most distant bounds, to play matches and to discover talent. These trips may well be compared to the marches of different regiments through those districts from which, under the territorial system, they hope to draw their recruits. When to these different forms of encouragement we add the sums spent in occasional subsidies, to say nothing of the salaries of players and officials, and of the expenses entailed by the upkeep of the club's ground and property, it will be seen that, though the sour may sneer, it would be and is impossible for a crack county to maintain its position unless its assured income from subscriptions were augmented by the humble sixpence of gate-money. It is not, of course, every county that can manage its cricket *en prince* in the way indicated: that implies a heavy rent-roll, a handsome and dependable income, and perhaps a snug little sum in the 2-3/4 per cents; only rich counties can do things with a lavish hand, and find themselves able to spare a lucrative match that will produce a bouncing benefit for some deserving professional. Others have to look rather wistfully at the small roll of cloth from which their coat has to be cut, and have to curtail expenses accordingly; but the county cricket club, even if run upon humble lines, recollects that Rome was not completed within the twenty-four hours, and that as nothing succeeds like success, its first and primary duty is to be successful, if possible; that it is only by pains and patience that the best men are to be discovered and utilised, and that its turn can only be served by inoculating as many people and clubs as possible with the most virulent type of cricket fever.

I am disposed to think that that county is likely to prosper which can find two or three grounds within its borders which are suitable for county cricket, and are in the centre of fairly populous districts; to which fact I attribute, in no small degree, the success of the Yorkshire County C.C. as an institution, and of its eleven as a fighting body. Not that the side has always had the pleasant experiences of 1900, 1901, and 1902, when in a series of eighty-three matches only two resulted in failure, for as recently as 1889 the big county and Sussex met at the fag-end of the season in an encounter which was to decide whether the northern or the southern county was to find its name at the bottom of the roll; but the county of so many acres has not only a large field of selection, but has also, in Sheffield, Leeds, Huddersfield, Bradford, Scarborough, York, Hull, and Dewsbury, so many centres of action that she can display her powers to tens of thousands, where other counties can only muster thousands, and can thus command a very large and consistent income. But in strict and strong relief stands out the figure of Nottingham, a county that, to the best of my knowledge, has never played a "home" match away from the Trent Bridge ground, and has never been blest with a superabundance of this world's goods, yet has for many years not only possessed a formidable eleven of its own, but has also been able to send out a full and steady stream of professional players of all classes, some of whom, though not exactly thankless children, have proved a veritable set of serpent's teeth when arrayed against the mother county. Nottinghamshire is a standing exception to the rule that great elevens are the outcome of great incomes.

There is no doubt that the true nucleus of a county eleven lies in the body of professional players that the executive has at its disposal. As men who are in receipt of a definite wage for their services, and as men who, by reason of their skill, obedience, and civility, have something like a right to expect a benefit match after some ten or twelve years of service, they find it a duty as well as a pleasure to keep themselves in good condition as well as in good practice, and, their services being always available, they are in the long run of more general use than the amateurs, many of whom, having other avocations, are unable to play regularly. Not that any eleven is complete without its amateurs. Among professionals a certain amount of professional jealousy is sure to arise, which sometimes grows into something stronger; while it has been proved by actual experience that in an eleven entirely composed of paid players, and of course captained by a professional, difficulties of discipline will occur, the management of the eleven being acridly criticised by those who think that in some form or other their abilities have not been duly recognised, which lack of recognition is attributable to the worst and meanest of motives. There is no such thing, fortunately, as a cricket trade-union, nor is there any place for it, but as a matter of history it is right to record that various secessions, almost amounting to mutinies, have occurred in the professional ranks at different times, which have sometimes taken the form of a strike, based either on a claim for higher pay, or on a demand that certain players who are regarded as obnoxious—almost as blacklegs— by their comrades should not take part in a given match, under no less a penalty than the refusal of the protestants to appear themselves. All these things have occurred, but just as the intestine disputes of bees may, according to Virgil, be allayed by the flinging down of a handful of dust, so a little diplomatic negotiation has settled the dispute. But nothing tends so much to bind a team together in the bonds of amity as well as of discipline as the presence of capable amateurs—men of tact and education as well as efficient cricketers, one of whom, acting as captain and supreme controller, can readily check the earlier symptoms of discontent, or, better still, by his wise administration of his office prevent the incubation of a disease so disastrous as indiscipline. The moral effect of the presence of amateurs is no whit less than their value as players, preventing as it does the somewhat sordid troubles that are apt to arise among those to whom cricket is a livelihood, and not merely a pastime. Further, a great deal has been said and written—mainly by those who know nothing of the subject—as to the exact relations existing between the amateur and the professional. Only ignorance permits a man to apply such a word as "snobbish" to the custom of providing separate accommodation for the two classes of players; worse is it when such a one hints at such a thing as stand-offishness on the part of the amateurs. There are certain differences in the education and the social position of the two classes that makes the closer intimacy of the pavilion undesirable, and undesired also by both parties. At any rate, cricketers are perfectly capable of making all such arrangements for themselves, without the intrusion and interference of others. They have their own code and their own method, nor does there exist any analogy between the regulations, especially as to the amateur *status*, of cricket and of other games. Cricket stands on its own pedestal, and it is good that it should.

A CRICKET MATCH (about 1750).

One of the troublous parts of cricket legislation has been the question of the residential qualification of cricketers for their counties, and the manner of defining what *bona fide* residence is. It has been always recognised, I believe, that a man may play for the county in which he was born, or for the county in which he resides, though for "or" might have been written "and" as recently as 1873. Up to that date a man might, and many men did, play for two counties in one and the same season, under the two qualifications, while it was an understood thing that when those two counties met he represented the county of his birth. There were, however, obvious objections to this dual license, though they only first took shape in the form of proposed regulation in 1868. Five years later it was made law that a man who was doubly qualified must elect at the beginning of each season to play for one of these counties, and for no other. It was undoubtedly an abuse that such a state of things should exist, but it must have been a convenient source of revenue to a few professionals in the days when fees were low and matches few. But the accurate definition of *bona fide* residence is still a difficulty: in some cases a man has taken a room, or a room has been taken for him, in the county for which he is desired to qualify, and he has, as occasion suited, occupied it for a night or two, while similar evasions or elastic interpretations of the law have existed; but the present solution of the question is probably the best one, *i.e.* to fall back on the patient and ever-willing committee of the M.C.C., which consents to adjudicate on all such questions as they arise. It should be added that proposals have been made several times, notably by Lord Harris in 1880, that the residential period should be reduced to one year; but though this reduction would have acted well in certain cases, especially in those of Colonial and army players who took up their residence in England, it has been held that objections outweigh the advantages, and the tale of years has not been reduced.

Some men consider that only the qualification of birth should be considered, so that only natives of a county should represent it; but, after all, this qualification is a mere accident as far as the individual himself is concerned; it would act hardly on a man born in a poor county—poor, that is, as a cricket-playing county; it would condemn many a first-class player to take little or no part in first-class cricket, which is the same thing as county cricket, and we might even have the anomaly of a county desiring, owing to its plethora of great players, to put two teams into the competition. As long as one county does not attempt to lure away men from its neighbours, as long as every club keeps its eyes wide open in its quest for its own young blood, and as long as every man feels that it is a primary duty to keep his allegiance to his native county, so long will the present rule be thoroughly satisfactory, and the "sporting spirit" must be trusted to see that the unwritten laws are not transgressed. At the same time, a hard case may readily be stated, the case of the man of true and tried merit, who has only the prospect of a small income and a small benefit as the reward his birth-county can give him, while by naturalising himself with its neighbour he may look for a large pecuniary reward. As a general rule, however, the present system works well: useful men are sometimes overlooked, and allowed, so to speak, to take foreign service as soldiers of fortune, but as the process is largely reciprocal, it reacts, to some extent, on all counties alike. To Yorkshire, and I believe to Yorkshire alone, belongs the credit of having been represented for many years by Yorkshiremen alone; but then Yorkshire is a very big land.

As soon as cricket became a part and parcel of English sporting life, the contesting sides naturally ranged themselves, in some cases at least, under the political subdivisions of England, viz. the counties, and consequently we find county cricket existing in a form as far back as 1730, when "a great match was played on Richmond Green, between Surrey and Middlesex, which was won by the former" (I quote from T. Waghorn's *Cricket Scores*). It is interesting, by the way, to note that two of the keenest rivals of to-day met in friendly combat some 130 years before Middlesex could boast of a county club, while the Surrey Club did not really come into existence till 1845. It may be added that Middlesex had its revenge three years later, *i.e.* in 1733, and that the then Prince of Wales, a great patron of cricket, was so pleased with the skill and zeal of the players, that he presented them with a guinea apiece.

Organisation, classification, championships, and all the paraphernalia of modern county cricket did not exist, of course, in the times when locomotion was difficult and matches consequently few, except among near neighbours; but it may not, on the whole, have been bad for cricket that at the outset many matches were made for money, and that all contests of importance were vehicles for universal and heavy betting.

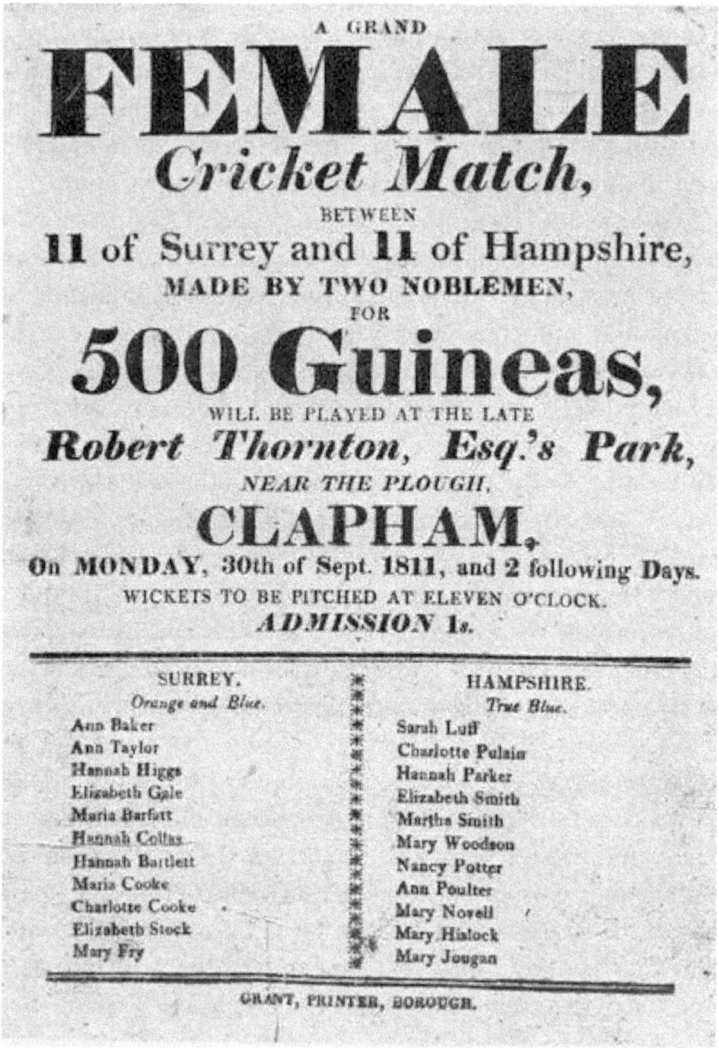

CRICKET

A GRAND FEMALE Cricket Match,

BETWEEN

11 of Surrey and 11 of Hampshire,

MADE BY TWO NOBLEMEN,

FOR

500 Guineas,

WILL BE PLAYED AT THE LATE

Robert Thornton, Esq.'s Park,

NEAR THE PLOUGH,

CLAPHAM,

On MONDAY, 30th of Sept. 1811, and 2 following Days.

WICKETS TO BE PITCHED AT ELEVEN O'CLOCK.

ADMISSION 1s.

SURREY.	HAMPSHIRE.
Orange and Blue.	*True Blue.*
Ann Baker	Sarah Luff
Ann Taylor	Charlotte Pulain
Hannah Higgs	Hannah Parker
Elizabeth Gale	Elizabeth Smith
Maria Barfutt	Martha Smith
Hannah Collus	Mary Woodson
Hannah Bartlett	Nancy Potter
Maria Cooke	Ann Poulter
Charlotte Cooke	Mary Novell
Elizabeth Stock	Mary Hislock
Mary Fry	Mary Jougan

GRANT, PRINTER, BOROUGH.

A CURIOUS COUNTY CLUB ADVERTISEMENT.

It may seem heterodox to approve of wagers and stakes, when nowadays it is the pride of those interested in cricket that it rises above such things, but it must not be forgotten that customs change with the times; that betting was universal in the eighteenth century and the early part of the nineteenth among all men who wished to be considered "smart"; and also that, but for the support and encouragement given to the game by "sportsmen" and "Corinthians," it would never have flourished in the fashion in which it flourishes to-day: indeed, there was nothing more absurd in Kent playing Hampshire for 500 guineas, than that the representatives of the two counties should fight a main of cocks for the same sum. We naturally find certain abuses which are due to the betting system, but on the whole, it kept the game alive, and soon quickened it into a more vigorous existence. Money had to be found somehow; gate-money was out of the question in the days when most matches, even the very greatest, were played on village greens or open commons; hence the natural sequence that in the men who found the stakes and laid the wagers cricket found its best and keenest patrons. To the love of betting we may probably attribute the formation of various matches in which curious combinations of numbers were made, or when certain men were played as "given" men, so that the strength of the contending parties might be equalised. Who, however, would care to go nowadays to see twenty-two of Surrey play twenty-two of Middlesex, a game that took place in 1802, and again in 1803? In 1797 we find that England played against *thirty-three* of Norfolk, and won in a single innings by 14 runs. Again, in 1800, twelve of England play nineteen of Kent, and we find about this period such matches as "Middlesex, with two of Berkshire and one of Kent *v.* Essex, with two 'given' men"; but a special interest attaches to this match, as being the first ever played on Lord's ground, the old "Lord's" of Dorset Square, in 1787. Perhaps it is not unfair to conjecture that the original match was to be between the two counties, but that the sides had to be patched up owing to defections. It seems hardly probable that monetary or other reasons would prompt such curious combinations of men and counties. Proper qualification can hardly have been insisted upon; indeed, we find that the famous Hambledon Club, practically Hampshire county, was largely composed of Surrey men who received enthusiastic invitations to visit the famous Broad Halfpenny Down. Harking back to some stray scraps of historical interest, we read that in 1739 Kent, "the unconquerable county," played England in the presence of 1000 spectators, but the match ended in a fiasco, owing to disputes; indeed, such terminations were not very uncommon when party feeling ran high and betting was rampant. In 1746 Kent again plays England, and wins by a short neck, *i.e.* by one wicket, while Sussex and Surrey seem great rivals; Surrey, indeed, beats England three years later, and in 1750 loses to Kent by 3 runs, but wins the return by nine wickets. From the names quoted, it is evident that cricket flourished in the south rather than in the north; but cricket was not unknown in the big manufacturing shires, for we find that Manchester and Liverpool were then, as now, desperate rivals, as were Sheffield and Nottingham.

Sheffield, indeed, was so strong that it could play, and used to play, the rest of Yorkshire single-handed. In a note to a match played between Hants and England in 1772, we find that "Lumpy," for England, bowled out Small, "which thing had not happened for some years"! Perhaps "Lumpy" had secured one of those wickets on which he could bowl—

For honest Lumpy did allow
He ne'er could bowl but o'er a brow.

Hence if the wicket had a "brow," and Lumpy pitched one of his "shooters" on it, Small's downfall is not remarkable. However, though Hambledon was the best club and Hants the best county, England was too strong to be tackled single-handed. Surrey first met Kent in 1772, and beat the county of cherries and hops, having previously done the same for Hants, though in the latter case the nuisance of "given men" crops up on both sides; yet such games were clearly popular, strength being thereby equalised, for we find numerous matches between Hambledon and England in which the former club was supported by the presence of outsiders. However, the Hambledon Club, "the cradle of cricket," with its "ale that would flare like turpentine"—what a use to put good "October" to!—"a viand (for it was more than liquor)" that was "vended at 2d. per pint," collapsed towards the end of the century, and it was many a long year before Hants became great again. Alas, too, for Hambledon cricketers! They were not content to play cricket for love or for glory, but for stakes, the stakes being pints, doubtless of the famous "viand"!

A few stray notes on the early half of the century may be not inappropriate, and most interesting seem to be the trio of matches played between England and Sussex in 1826. No such contest had ever taken place before, and the series was really arranged to test the relative merits of underhand bowling and the then new-fangled roundhand. The results may be regarded as conclusive. Not only did Sussex win the first match by seven wickets and the second by three wickets, but the third match was lost by the county by as few as 24 runs. More conclusive was the action of nine of the professionals, who refused, after the second match was over, to play in the third game, "unless the Sussex bowlers bowl fair—that is, abstain from throwing." The triumph of the new style was complete, though five of the recalcitrants played in the third match after all. It was in the Kent-Sussex match of this year, Kent having some given men, that wides were first counted, though they did not appear as a separate item. Three years later no-balls received a similar distinction, the match being, nominally, between Middlesex and the M.C.C.; but the county had no regular organisation till five-and-thirty years later. Indeed, it is illustrative of the then condition of some so-called "county elevens," that "Yorkshire" plays the Sheffield Wednesday C.C. and is beaten in 1830, while in 1832 Sheffield plays twenty-two of Yorkshire! However, in 1834 an eleven, called Yorkshire, consisting mainly of Sheffielders, lost to Norfolk by no less than 272 runs, Fuller Pilch contributing 87 not out and 73; yet Pilch was a Suffolk man, who was eventually induced to settle in Kent, though in this year he played for England and against Kent, which at this time was easily the strongest county. Next year Yorkshire had its revenge on Norfolk, as, though Pilch made 153 not out in the second innings, the Norfolk men surrendered, the game being hopeless, probably to avoid the necessity of coming up on the third day.

From a Drawing by G. F. Watts, R.A.
THE BATSMAN.
(Fuller Pilch).

It is unnecessary to dive more deeply into dates, figures, and facts, beyond the important fact that early in the last century there were many counties that played cricket between themselves, and in certain cases could challenge the rest of England, though they did not exist as regularly organised societies. The matches were arranged by the patrons of cricket, as an exciting form of contest in which money was to be won or lost by betting, and with a view to the increase of the excitement, men were given to one side or barred from another, or else extra numbers were allowed as a counterpoise to extra skill, till in due course counties began to exist as organisations of themselves, with a view to county cricket pure and simple. Their establishment, however, was a matter of time. Sussex led the way in 1839; Kent seems to have followed the lead in 1842, the year when the first Canterbury "Week" was held, under similar conditions to those that now exist; while the year 1845 saw the birth of the Surrey Club, with the Oval as its cradle. Then came a gap, but in the 'sixties county clubs sprang rapidly into existence—Notts in 1859 or 1860, Yorkshire in 1862, Hants in 1863 (though the club collapsed early, and was resuscitated in 1874). Middlesex saw the light in 1864, and so did Lancashire. Leicestershire dates back to 1878, Derbyshire to 1870, while Gloucestershire is only a year younger, being followed by Somerset in 1875, by Essex in 1876, and by Warwickshire in 1882. With the appearance of Worcestershire on the scene in 1899, at least as a first-class county, we have reached the last-joined of the present big cricketing counties; but it should be clearly understood that the dates given are as a rule only those of the years in which the clubs were originally formed. Their pretensions to be included in the privileged list of those who are entitled, as being "first-class," to take part in the championship competition were only gratified when they had by active service and doughty deeds established a claim to promotion.

The formation of county clubs, especially in the middle of last century, may fairly be traced directly to the success, in finance as well as in cricket, of those famous organisations, the All England and the United All England elevens. Originally founded as purely financial speculations, for the promotion and success of which the best cricketing talent of the country was enlisted, they made annual progresses through England, meeting the picked local talent of all cricketing centres, generally reinforced by imported men, and meeting each other at Lord's on Whit-Monday, this last match being regarded as at least the equal of the Gentlemen and Players fixture as a display of scientific cricket. The periodical visits of these skilled *troupes* not only excited the interest and improved the cricket of the local centres—Dr. Grace himself bears ample testimony to the keenness caused by their presence—but they also opened the eyes of cricket-lovers to the fact that good cricket could be made self-supporting. Further, they saw the immense progress that the game would make, and the enormous facilities that would be offered to that progress, in every county which had a club and a centre of its own. It may be said, indeed, that the success of these peripatetic teams, while it conduced to their own collapse, suggested and promoted the foundation of county cricket as it is played nowadays. The two great elevens did their work well and thoroughly, both for themselves and for the game, and when they dispersed, and their constituent members were drafted into the county elevens, they could at least claim that they had popularised the game, had improved the methods in which it was played, and had left behind them a valuable legacy to all those who either played or admired cricket. Think of this, all of you who are apt to remember only the pettinesses and schisms of those two great elevens! There were pettinesses, and there were schisms, but these must be forgotten in the recollection that the men who erred were likewise the men who put our first-class cricket on its present basis, who made the existence of county cricket feasible, possible, and profitable.

It should here be noted that though only fifteen counties have been enumerated, the cricket-playing counties are by no means restricted to that number. Norfolk and Suffolk have for many years been cricketing counties. Cambridgeshire was at one time, thanks to Hayward, Carpenter, and Tarrant, one of the strongest of counties. Northamptonshire, Durham, Northumberland, Lincolnshire, and many others, *quos nunc perscribere longum est*, have all fostered cricket and cricketers, and if they have not come into the forefront of the battle yet, there is no reason why they should not yet figure as champions, considering the vigour and keenness with which the game is played and watched. In fact, the question of classification is an extremely hard one, the uncertainty of cricket and the part that luck plays adding most materially to the difficulties. By the present system the general results pan out pretty well, and harmonise, as a rule, with public opinion, but accurate organisation and registration, with due regard to merit, is impossible in a game at which such curious results are possible as were seen in the Yorkshire-Somerset match of 1901. Yorkshire, undefeated, was at the head of the list then, as at the end of the year. Somerset, at the time the match was played, had won but one match out of eight; further, the game in question was played on Yorkshire territory, and Somerset, dismissed for 97, was headed on the first innings by 238 runs. In the end, Somerset won by 279! Who can classify, who promote, who degrade, when such extraordinary fluctuations are possible? It is clearly no solution of the promotion question to suggest that the lowest of the first-class counties should play the highest of the minor counties, the first-class certificate being the stake. Nor are matters facilitated when we remember that, for financial and other reasons, the minor counties contend in a competition in which only two days are allotted to a match instead of three. Doubtless public opinion, *i.e.* the opinion of the players who are before the public, offered the best solution of the difficulty of promotion by co-opting Worcestershire into their ranks, the formality being of the simplest nature; for Worcestershire, the fresh claimant for the highest honours, simply announced at the Counties' meeting that they had arranged to play the minimum number of matches that qualify for the first class with the requisite number of counties. The first-class counties co-opted Worcestershire; arbitration and adjudication were unnecessary.

In the infancy of county cricket the meetings of the different clubs were arranged by a sort of process which we may appropriately describe as natural selection. What could be more natural than the rivalry between the great professional sides—I am writing of the 'seventies—of Yorkshire and Nottingham, and of both with Lancashire, and of the amateur elevens of Middlesex and Gloucestershire? Geographical convenience brought certain counties into close contact, and pre-eminent strength tempted others to ignore all difficulties, geographical and sentimental, and to fight the good fight to the bitter end. All things, indeed, seemed to be working up for some form of county competition, when the M.C.C., in 1872, offered a challenge cup to be held by the leading county of the year. The conditions, put in an abbreviated form, were that a certain number of counties, not exceeding six, were to be selected by the M.C.C. as the competitors; that the matches were to be played at Lord's, and apparently on the "knock-out" principle; in the event of a draw, the match was to be replayed; the cup to be retained by any county that could win it three years in succession. The competition, however, fell through, several of the counties withdrawing their entries, and the Marylebone Club consequently withdrawing its offer. Kent, however, played Sussex at Lord's for perhaps the only time, and on "dangerously rough wickets," Kent winning by 52 runs.

It is not possible to give a list of champion counties that is absolutely accurate, as, until the competition was regulated by proper laws, and a recognised system of scoring points existed, the champions were selected partly by popular opinion, partly by the written opinions of the press, the two often differing, especially when party feeling ran high. In the following list, however, the opinion expressed by Dr. W. G. Grace in his *Cricket* has generally been regarded as paramount, and few will venture to dispute his authority.

Champion Counties, 1864-1901

Year	County		Year	County	
1864.	Surrey.		1883.	Yorkshire.	
1865.	Notts.		1884.	Notts.	
1866.	Middlesex.		1885.	Notts.	
1867.	Yorkshire.		1886.	Notts.	
1868.	Yorkshire.		1887.	Surrey.	
1869.	Notts.		1888.	Surrey.	
1870.	Yorkshire.		1889.	{ Surrey / Lancashire }	equal.
1871.	Notts.				
1872.	Surrey.			Surrey	
1873.	{ Gloucestershire / Notts }	equal.	1890.	Surrey.	
			1891.	Surrey.	
1874.	Gloucestershire.		1892.	Surrey.	
1875.	Notts.		1893.	Yorkshire.	
1876.	Gloucestershire.		1894.	Surrey.	
1877.	Gloucestershire.		1895.	Surrey.	
1878.	Notts.		1896.	Yorkshire.	
1879.	{ Lancashire / Notts }	equal.	1897.	Lancashire.	
			1897.	Yorkshire.	
1880.	Notts.		1899.	Surrey.	
1881.	Lancashire.		1900.	Yorkshire.	
1881.	{ Lancashire / Notts }	equal.	1901.	Yorkshire.	
			1902.	Yorkshire.	

Thus in the last thirty-eight years, if we reckon in the occasions when two or more counties have tied for the first place, we find that the championship has been held by Nottinghamshire thirteen times, by Surrey eleven times, by Yorkshire ten times, by Lancashire five times, by Gloucestershire four times, and by Middlesex once. Sussex did not lose a match in 1871, but only played its neighbours of Kent and Surrey, in a year when the three northern counties were particularly strong. The above list is of course given for what it is worth, but may be regarded as fairly accurate, though the conditions and the methods of calculation have differed so widely at various periods. Up to 1888, no special system for reckoning the "order" seems to have obtained, the results being practically arrived at "by inspection"; in that year and in 1889 the proportion of wins to the matches played was the accepted process, losses being ignored, and drawn games counting half a point, so that Notts, with nine wins and three draws in fourteen games, tied with Surrey and Lancashire, both of which had ten wins and one draw, ten points and a half, in the same number of matches. Next year, and till 1895, defeats were deducted from victories, and the points thus obtained decided the award, but in the latter year the present system was adopted: a win counts a point for, and a defeat counts a point against; losses are deducted from wins, and a ratio is calculated between the figure thus obtained and the number of finished matches, draws being ignored. Thus, if a county plays 20 matches, wins 11, loses 4, and draws 5, the figure is 11-4, *i.e.* 7; the proportional fraction is 7/15 (15 being the number of completed matches), and the figure of merit 46.66, the original vulgar fraction being, for the sake of convenience, multiplied by 100 and reduced to a decimal.

Referring back to the list once more, we note that Gloucestershire was not beaten in 1876 or 1877. Lancashire lost no match in 1881, and won six games with an innings to spare. Lancashire and Notts had identical figures in 1882; but critics were inclined to favour the superiority of Lancashire, as having beaten Notts on one of the occasions when the two counties met, while the other match was drawn. Notts in 1884 won nine games out of ten, and drew the tenth—a great record, eclipsed by Yorkshire, who lost no match in 1900, and only one in both 1901 and 1902. Yorkshire's career since 1889 has been curious: in that year she played Sussex at the very end of the season, the "wooden spoon" depending on the result; however, Yorkshire won. In 1890 she was third. Then followed two bad years, but in 1893 the big county was at the top, and also in five of the next nine years, her lowest place being fourth in 1897. Surrey has a fine sequence of six headships, beginning with 1886, by far the largest series on the list.

A word may here be added on the connection between the Marylebone Club and the counties. The club has always religiously abstained from interfering in county matters unasked, though reserving to itself the sole right of deciding all questions connected with the game in general. But at times there seem to have been signs of a little petulance on the part of some of the counties, or their representatives, kindly patronage having been mistaken for interference. Nothing, however, could be more satisfactory than the present state of things, the M.C.C. being regarded, as it rightly should be regarded, as the supreme *junta* of cricket, and consequently as the oracle to be consulted in case of difficulty, and the arbiter in the event of difference. The county delegates discuss all county matters, and refer the results of their deliberations to the M.C.C., with a request that the club will duly hall-mark them, and settle any disputes or questions that may arise out of them. A powerful neutral is indeed necessary as arbitrator, seeing that the County Cricket Council, which was born in 1887, proclaimed its own dissolution in 1890, having shown no great capacity for managing its own affairs.

We may now note a few of the more important landmarks in the history of county cricket. The question of qualification, as already stated, was raised as early as in 1868, for it was felt to be an abuse, as well as unfair to certain counties, that men should be allowed to represent two counties in one year; it was, however, an unwritten law that a man did not play against the county of his birth, even if he did not play for it. Thus Howitt, who was practically identified with Middlesex, did not play against his native Notts. Southerton, however, who played regularly for Surrey by the residential qualification, always represented Sussex against Surrey, often to the discomfiture of his foster-county. However, it was not till 1872 that formal legislation took place, when the following arrangements were made:—

(1) No man to play for more than one county in the same year.

(2) Any player with a double qualification to state at the beginning of each season for which of the counties he proposed to play.

(3) Three years' *bona fide* residence to qualify professionals; two years sufficient for amateurs.

These regulations were passed at Lord's, but next year a meeting, held at the Oval, asked that the Lord's authorities would put professionals and amateurs on the same footing, and two years of residence are now required of both alike. It was also enacted that under the term "residence" was included the parental roof, provided that it was open to a man as an occasional home. Lord Harris proposed in 1880 that the two years should be reduced to one, but did not carry his motion, though it was and is felt that in certain cases, *e.g.* in that of an Englishman born in India, or of an officer home on furlough, the rule bears rather hardly. It was further passed in 1898 that a man who had played for a particular county for five years was permanently qualified for it, provided that the series had not been broken by his playing for another.

It seems hardly credible, considering what county cricket has grown to be, to hear that not till 1890 was any real classification of counties undertaken; however, it was at a meeting of the moribund Cricket Council, held at the Oval on 11th August, that eight counties were pronounced to be first-class, and to be the competitors for the championship in 1891. The sacred eight were:—

Notts.	Kent.	Yorkshire.
Lancashire.	Middlesex.	Sussex.
Surrey.	Gloucestershire.	

And these were to play home and home matches with each other. In 1892—prospective legislation this—the lowest of the first-class counties was to play the highest of the second-class for its place, and various details were worked out in connection with this scheme, but when the Council assembled at Lord's on 8th December of the same year, so much difficulty and trouble occurred over the question of classification that it was felt to be a relief when a representative of Middlesex jumped up and proposed that "this Council do adjourn *sine die*." The resolution was accepted with gratitude, and the County Cricket Council was no more.

Next year Somersetshire, having arranged a purely first-class programme, announced the fact at the annual meeting of county secretaries, and was duly recognised as a first-class county. In 1894 the matches played by Warwickshire, Derbyshire, Hampshire, Leicestershire, and Essex were recognised as first-class, though for convenience the counties were considered to be outside the competition for that year. In 1899 Worcestershire made a similar announcement to that of Somerset, and was admitted into the sacred circle, thus making the number of first-class counties up to fifteen. With these increases in the number of competitors, it was clearly impossible to maintain the original principle that each county should play home and home matches with every other, especially in those years when an Australian eleven was in England. Some of the larger and richer counties manage to get through so huge a programme, even with Australian matches thrown in, but in ordinary years the original number of eight is retained as the qualifying number, reducible by decree of the M.C.C. in those years when reduction is necessary. It was in consequence of the increase in the number of the playing counties that the proportional system of 1895 was introduced.

We may now glance at the history of the various first-class counties, taking them seriatim; and I must here express my indebtedness to K. S. Ranjitsinhji's *Jubilee Book of Cricket*, which is a perfect mine of information on the subject.

Derbyshire.—Though the county club only came to its birth in 1870, cricket had long flourished in the land, fostered largely, as one authority tells us, by the clergy. "The game in Derbyshire," he tells us, "owes much at one time and another to the parsons—a fact that is perhaps worthy of more general recognition than is sometimes allowed." The first appearance of the new county was remarkable, as on the Old Trafford ground, in its very first match, it defeated no less a side than Lancashire by an innings and 11 runs, the home county mustering no more than 25 notches in its first innings, when Gregory actually had six wickets for 9 runs. So strong was the county attack in its early days, Gregory being reinforced by Platts and Hickton, Flint, W. Mycroft, and Hay, that the eleven was jestingly described as consisting of ten bowlers and a wicket-keeper, the batting being by no means powerful. Mycroft was one of the most formidable bowlers in England, but with the decadence of himself and the rest of the band, the bowling weakened as the batting improved, though at last the latter, thanks partly to the transfer of good men to other counties, failed so sadly that in 1887 the county was reduced to the second class, only to be restored in 1895, and in that year to reach as high a place as fifth in the championship competition. Fine bowling was again the chief contributory to this success, G. G. Walker, George Davidson, Porter, and Hume, with Storer to keep wicket, being backed by such good batsmen as S. H. Evershed, L. G. Wright, and Chatterton. In Davidson and Storer, indeed, Derbyshire possessed a pair of wonderfully fine all-round men, Davidson's premature death being a grievous loss. Last year (1902) the fortunes of Derbyshire were not particularly brilliant, but the county, always a by-word for bad luck, especially at one period when it seemed impossible for its captain to win the toss, made a good step forward. It is unfortunate for a hard-working and enthusiastic committee that the Derby public gives to cricket but one tithe of the support that it lavishes on football; however, there are plenty of liberal supporters of the club, which has also, in its times of need, proved its ability for raising the necessary funds by means of bazaars and the like. The ground, which is at Derby, has a total extent of eleven acres, with a good pavilion and an excellent pitch.

Essex, founded in 1874, originally settled at Brentwood, but migrated to Leyton, as a more accessible place. The county has had a hard fight in the past to make both ends meet; indeed, at one time the end seemed to be at hand, but kindly friends, chiefly in the persons of C. M. Tebbut and C. E. Green, helped it out of its trouble. To the latter's enthusiasm the very existence of the club is largely due. Created first-class in 1895, Essex has never achieved the championship, though it has more than once knocked possible champions out, especially in its earlier years, when the ground was not all that a batsman could desire; but in 1901, thanks to some of the modern patent "mixtures" used in dressing the pitch, so easy was the wicket that it was impossible, apparently, to get batsmen out, and the scoring was in consequence abnormally large. By way of revenge, when the ground is spoilt by rain, it is absolutely unplayable. In cricketers Essex has been rich: C. J. Kortright is one of the fastest bowlers of this age or any other, and in the days of rough pitches was a terror to the county's opponents; C. M'Gahey and P. Perrin, known as "the Essex twins," have helped to win or save many a match; while in Young, an ex-sailor, the county unearthed a bowler who was good enough to play for England in 1899, but has done little or nothing since. The name of A. P. Lucas must not be omitted, as, though he is now some forty-six years old, he plays cricket in as sound and stylish a fashion as when he was an undergraduate at Cambridge. As before hinted, though Essex has never been close up for the championship, it has always been a factor to be reckoned with.

Gloucestershire is, of course, "the county of the Graces," which is synonymous with stating that its fortunes have been watched and assisted by three of the most talented and experienced cricketers who have ever taken the field. In the early days, it seemed to exist by them and for them; but though professional talent appeared but slowly, a sturdy band of amateurs soon gathered round the brotherhood, and showed that good batting, especially when attended by superb fielding, can compensate for only fair bowling. Such men as W. O. Moberley, F. Townsend, W. Fairbanks, W. R. Gilbert, and J. A. Bush (the wicket-keeper) were both scorers and savers of runs. Of the Graces it is needless to say anything; they were batsmen, bowlers, and fieldsmen, all of different types, but all of one class. E. M.'s fielding at point was only to be matched by G. F.'s at long-leg and W. G.'s anywhere, while it was mainly in county cricket that the Doctor's famous leg-trap was so successful. Pages might be devoted to what the champion did for Gloucestershire, but probably no individual triumph ever delighted him so much as that it should, in 1874, four years after its foundation, be the champion county of England. It was in a Gloucestershire match that Grace scored his hundredth century, completed the 1000 runs that he made in the single month of May 1895, and twice scored a double century, *v.* Kent in 1887 and *v.* Yorkshire in 1888. To pry deeper with the pen into the great man's performance would be to write, what has been written before, a history of modern cricket or his own biography: the works would be almost identical. Woof is undoubtedly the best professional bowler that the county has unearthed, just as Board is the best wicket-keeper, but Midwinter, the Anglo-Australian, Paish, and Roberts have all done good service with the ball. Ferris, however, another Australian who settled in Gloucestershire, quite lost his bowling as his batting improved. Of more recent players the most prominent are undoubtedly Charles Townsend, son of the aforementioned Frank Townsend, and G. L. Jessop. Like Ferris, the former lost a little of his bowling when he became—he has now apparently retired—the best left-handed batsman in England. Of Jessop's hurricane hitting and rapid scoring the whole cricket world has heard and talked. The county ground is at Bristol, and is well equipped for its purpose, but the more famous cricket used to be played on the grounds of Clifton and Cheltenham Colleges, the Cheltenham "Week" being one of the events of the season. One hears, however, that the Clifton cricket ground will be used no more for county matches, owing to the lack of local support. In the early days the matches between Middlesex and Gloucestershire, two teams of powerful amateur batsmen, were famous for the long scoring that prevailed.

Hampshire, as already stated, was the champion county as far back as, roughly speaking, 1780, its famous downs, Windmill Down and Broad Halfpenny Down, having been the scene of many great contests in the days when the Hambledon Club was the champion of England. The history of those days and of the heroes of those days has been so often and so admirably written, besides being somewhat foreign to the scope of this chapter, that one need do little more than record the names of David Harris and William Beldham, as the champion bowler and batsman of their day. But Hampshire found that cricket, like everything else, is transient and ephemeral, and almost a century after the championship days, in 1874, to be accurate, the old Cambridge captain, Clement Booth, worked hard to restore the county's old prestige. Even his energy failed, for, as already noted, it was not till 1894 that the county was recognised as being of first-class merit. Hampshire has naturally been the county of the soldier cricketer, and can boast of E. G. Wynyard and R. M. Poore as being probably the best batsmen that ever wore the King's uniform, J. E. Greig, another soldier, being but little behind them. What the value of these men was to the county is amply demonstrated by the fact that in the absence of the first two Hants won never a match in 1900, but with Greig's appearance next year the county, with six each of wins, losses, and draws, at least gave as good as she got. In E. I. M. Barrett and the professional Barton the army is still further represented in the Hampshire ranks, with a new and valuable civilian recruit in Llewelyn. In fact, now that the piping times of peace have arrived, and the soldier cricketers listen for the pavilion's bell rather than the *réveillé* of the bugle, Hants may well hope to find herself higher up the ladder of cricket. Other good names are those of the two Cantabs, A. J. L. Hill and F. E. Lacey, the present secretary of the M.C.C. The ground, a very fine one, is in, or rather near, Southampton, the club having bought the freehold of it, and it is a great improvement on the classical but unsuitable Antelope ground, situated in the middle of the town.

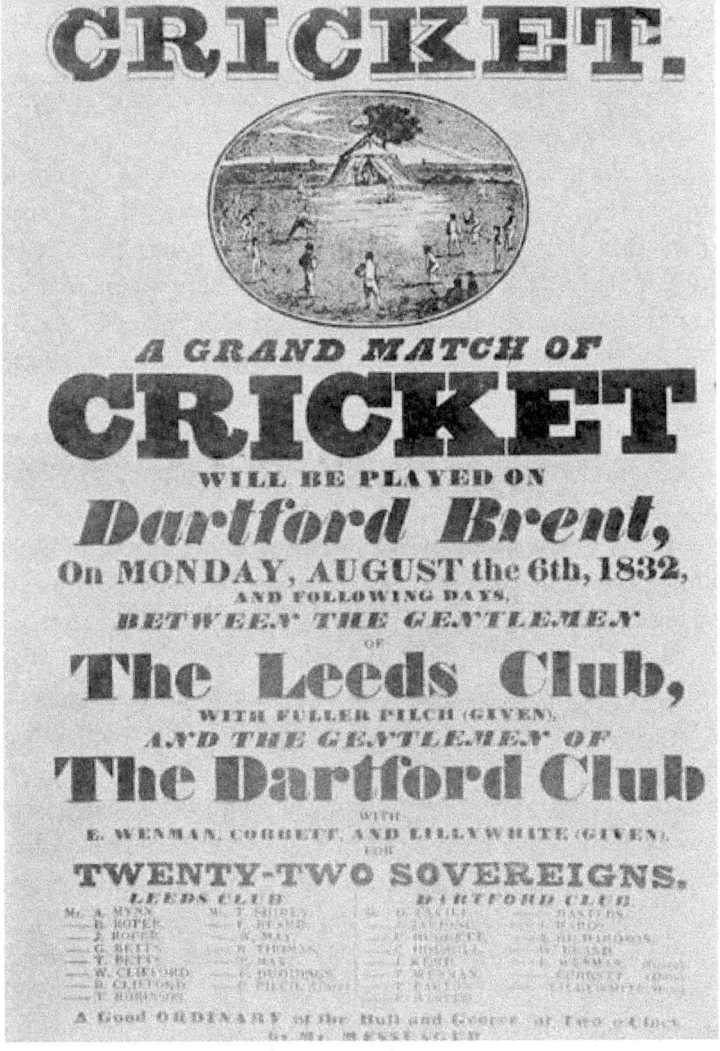

AN OLD "PLAY" BILL.

Kent was one of the pioneers of cricket, the earliest match which she played as a county dating back to 1711, nearly two hundred years ago, when she tackled an eleven of All England. It was, however, a full century later when she was at her prime, supported by such famous performers as Alfred Mynn, Fuller Pilch, Adams, Wenman, "Felix," and others; but of these Pilch was a Suffolk man, who was induced to settle in Kent and give his services to the county. Mynn was probably one of the finest all-round cricketers that ever lived—a fine bat, tremendous hitter, and a grand bowler of the very fast type; yet it is recorded that "off one of Mr. Mynn's tremendous shooters" T. A. Anson, a Cantab wicket-keeper, stumped a man, "using the left hand only"! In later days Kent has continued to flourish exceedingly, but has never achieved champion honours, being, as a rule, like most of the southern counties, deficient in bowling, though Willsher, whose career terminated in the early 'seventies, was a left-handed bowler who was second to none. He was also the hero of the first great no-balling incident. No one has worked harder for Kent cricket, and cricket in general, than Lord Harris, to whose vigour, and to whose enthusiastic efforts to enforce the proper spirit in which the game should be played, the county owes a deep debt of gratitude. The headquarters of the county club, which was established in 1842, the year of the first Canterbury "Week," are at Canterbury, but the executive rightly believes in the distribution of matches throughout the county, and we find that county games have been played, and are still played, not merely at Canterbury, but at Gravesend, Catford Bridge, Beckenham, Tonbridge—where there is also a "week,"—Maidstone, Tunbridge Wells, and Blackheath—truly a goodly list for a county that is not abnormally large. The Mote ground at Maidstone probably possesses a greater slope than any other ground on which great games are played. Among the more famous Kent cricketers we may quote the names of W. Yardley, W. H. Patterson, J. R. Mason, F. Marchant, W. Rashleigh, E. F. S. Tylecote, Stanley Christopherson, the brothers Penn, W. M.

Bradley, C. J. Burnup, and Hearnes innumerable. Than J. R. Mason, the late captain, there are few finer all-round men.

Lancashire dates back to 1864 as a county club, but Liverpool and Manchester had long had strong clubs of their own, and at present the whole county is a perfect hotbed of cricket. Nowhere is a more critical and enthusiastic body of spectators to be found, though cricket "caught on" later in Lancashire, as in other northern counties, than in the south. The bulk of the big matches, including one test match when the Australians are in evidence, are played at the Old Trafford ground in Manchester, where there is huge accommodation and a capital pavilion, a reduced facsimile of that at Lord's; but the wicket, though the turf is excellent, is often on the slow side, as Manchester is a rainy spot. A certain number of big matches are also allotted to the Aigburth ground, Liverpool. It would be hard to say who is the finest player that the county has produced, but it is easy to name the most popular and the most famous, namely, A. N. Hornby, the present president, who played his first county match in 1867, and has only recently retired from county cricket. He was for many years the captain of the team and has probably stolen more runs (and run more partners out) than any other cricketer. From a mere cricket point of view, A. G. Steel is doubtless the greatest of Lancastrians as an all-round player, but his career was all too short, while another equally famous Lancastrian, A. C. Maclaren, holds the record for the highest individual score made in big cricket, to wit, his 424, made against Somerset in 1895. Like Hornby, he is a Harrovian, while Steel, as all the world knows, or ought to know, hails from Marlborough. Among other great amateurs who have played for the county should be mentioned the names of Appleby, Rowley, Makinson, F. W. Wright, Eccles, and Crossfield, while the roll of professionals is equally famous—Barlow, Briggs, Watson, Mold, Crossland, Albert Ward, Tyldesley, Pilling (prince of wicket-keepers), Frank Sugg, and others. It is a curious fact, however, that no less than four of the great Lancashire bowlers have, rightly or wrongly, been severely criticised, and even penalised, for throwing when they were supposed to be bowling.

Leicestershire took to itself a county club in 1878, the very first match being played against the first Australian eleven, and a very fair fight being made against that strong team. Matches had, however, been played under the title of "Leicestershire" between the years 1789 and 1829. Like other counties, Leicestershire has had some hard times, pecuniarily, to pass through, but now that the storm has been safely weathered and a permanent home found, greater prosperity in every sense may be hoped for. It cannot be said that the county has hitherto had great success in the county contests, as eleventh is the highest place it has yet reached; but the 1902 eleven was considered to be much stronger than any other that had represented the county, so that, as there is plenty of fight left in the men, better results may be looked for. Pougher is probably the best all-round man that Leicestershire has produced, the bright, particular star in his career being the bowling down of five Australian wickets for *no* runs. This occurred at Lord's in 1896. In C. E. de Trafford, the present captain, Leicestershire possesses one of the hardest hitters and fastest scorers in England, and in Woodcock one of the fastest bowlers. Among its amateur players have been numbered, or are numbered, R. A. H. Mitchell, T. S. Pearson, H. P. Arnall Thompson, G. S. and C. Marriott, C. J. B. Wood, and Dr. R. Macdonald, and, of professionals, King, Knight, Geeson, Whiteside, Parnham, Rylott, Wheeler, Warren, and Tomlin.

The Middlesex County Club first saw the light in 1864, the year of Lancashire's birth, but, like all other counties, had played matches long anterior to that year under the style and title of "Middlesex"; in fact, in 1802 and 1803, as mentioned before, twenty-two of Middlesex encountered twenty-two of Surrey. Middlesex is as much "the county of the Walkers" as Gloucestershire is "the county of the Graces," for the name of John Walker is identified with the county as closely as are the initials V. E., R. D., and I. D. Indeed, it is to their perseverance and enthusiasm, to say nothing of their unbounded generosity, that the club ever existed or continued to exist. The first home of the club was a ground near the Cattle Market, in Islington. It then migrated to the Athletic Club's ground at Lillie Bridge, and was nearly dissolved for want of funds. A migration to Prince's ground in Chelsea helped to replenish the treasury, and a final resting-place—at least all hope it will prove to be final—was found at Lord's in 1877. It is noteworthy that in 1866, only two years after the club's foundation, Middlesex was the champion county, and was specially invited to play All England next year; but the result was disastrous. The weakness of Middlesex was always due to a dearth of bowling; in amateur batting Gloucestershire itself was hardly its superior; but of late years J. T. Hearne was in the very first flight of bowlers, as also A. E. Trott, the Australian professional. Howitt, of Nottingham, long did good service, as also Burton, Clarke, Phillips, and Rawlin, most of whom—one blushes to say it—were aliens. Several brotherhoods have done good service to Middlesex—in triads, the Walkers, Studds, and Fords, and in pairs, the Lytteltons, Webbes, and Douglases; while of the individuals who have been at the very top of the tree may be mentioned especially the three Walkers, C. T. Studd, A. J. Webbe, Sir T. C. O'Brien, A. W. Ridley, T. S. Pearson, G. F. Vernon, A. E. Stoddart, F. G. J. Ford, S. W. Scott, C. I. Thornton, G. MacGregor, E. A. Nepean, and a host of others who are only in a sense of the word "minor lights." To attempt to single out individuals for comparison would be equally hopeless and invidious; it is only when we recall the weakness of the Middlesex bowling that we appreciate the strength of the batting that has enabled it to hold its own, though since 1866 championship honours have not come the metropolitan county's way. It has, however, till last year, 1902, held a high place. Among its amateur bowlers should be mentioned the Walkers—of course,—J. Robertson, A. F. J. Ford, E. A. Nepean, C. K. Francis, A. W. Ridley, and E. Rutter, while no county has produced such a trio of amateur wicket-keepers as M. Turner, Hon. A. Lyttelton, and Gregor MacGregor, the present captain of the side.

Nottinghamshire played its first match in 1771, but the Trent Bridge ground was not opened till 1839, nor the club formed till 1859 or 1860; but it is safe to say that no club has sent forth such a stream of great cricketers, some to play for their own county, and some to take out naturalisation papers in others, to say nothing of hosts of useful second-class players and practice-bowlers. The Trent Bridge ground, originally opened by the famous slow bowler William Clarke, is rather larger than most grounds, and tries the batsman's powers of endurance rather severely, but the pavilion and the other appointments of the ground are inferior to none, Lord's alone and the Oval being excepted. Of the famous players the name is legion; posterity and contemporaries must settle among themselves as to whether George Parr (the great leg-hitter), Daft (the stylist), Shrewsbury (the all-patient), W. Gunn (the personification of style and patience combined), or Barnes were the greatest, not forgetting that among Notts batsmen were such men as A. O. Jones, J. A. Dixon, and J. G. Beevor, with William Oscroft, Selby, Wild, Summers, Flowers, and Guy, while the bowling names are a dazzling array of talent—Clarke, Tinley, Jackson, Grundy, Alfred Shaw, J. C. Shaw, Morley, Flowers, Martin M'Intyre, Attewell, and John Gunn, with Biddulph, Sherwin, and Wild as wicket-keepers; while to the best of bowlers should be added the name of Lockwood, who, unsuccessful for his native county, has done wonderful work for his adopted county, Surrey. Notts has been champion in no less than thirteen years, and thus heads the list.

Somersetshire can boast of no recorded antiquity as a cricketing society, the county club only being inaugurated in 1875. Curiously enough, the first meeting to consider the proposed club was held at Sidmouth, and the first circular issued from Ilfracombe, both Devonshire towns. It was not till 1891 that Somerset, having defeated all the other second-class counties, passed into the upper ranks, being then almost as strong as it ever has been since. The county ground at Taunton is a gem, but rather a small gem; hence hits into churchyard and river are not infrequent, and scoring rules high. Further, it is a tradition of the county that it generally beats Surrey, and not seldom Yorkshire, in the Taunton match. Of its players, H. T. Hewett was a splendid left-handed forcing player; L. C. H. Palairet is a grand player and a stylist that has no rival; his brother, R. C. N., who has partly retired, was always valuable, but inferior to his elder brother; S. M. J. Woods has lost his wonderful bowling, but is a fine and scoring batsman; V. T. Hill was a wonderful hitter, while J. B. Challen, C. E. Dunlop, W. C. Hadley, and G. Fowler were all useful men. No great professional players have as yet been unearthed, as Braund is a Surrey man who has cast in his lot with the western county, though Tyler, Nicholls, Cranfield, and Gill were, or are, a fairly good quartette of bowlers; but bowling has always been a weak point, ever since Woods strained his side. There has never been a dearth of wicket-keeping, all amateur, such names as A. E. Newton, Rev. A. P. Wickham, and L. H. Gay being famous. It must be admitted, however, that, with its crack players ageing, and new blood not being forthcoming, the prospects of Somersetshire are not at their brightest; but whatever the brilliancy of the prospects, there can be no question as to the brilliancy of the cricket as played both in the present and in the past. No side has been more exhilarating in its methods than the sides captained successively by Hewett and Woods.

Though Surrey has only been champion eleven times to Nottinghamshire's thirteen, yet she might quite fairly assume the words *nulli secunda* as her motto. Not that unbroken success has been the law of her existence, for there were times when Surrey's fortunes were at a very low ebb, but patience and perseverance have enabled the county to win its way upward, while in the list of brilliant cricketers few counties, perhaps none, can claim the right to enrol more names.

CRICKET

From a Drawing by Thos. Rowlandson.
RURAL SPORTS OR A CRICKET MATCH
EXTRAORDINARY AT BALL'S POND, NEWINGTON,
ON OCT. 3rd, 1811.

The foundation of the club dates back to 1845, the first match between Surrey and England to 1747, and by the end of that century, when the dispersion of the Hambledon Club set several Surrey players—Beldham ("Silver Billy") among them—free to return to their native shire, the county was actually strong enough to play fourteen of England, but then almost collapsed, as far as organised cricket was concerned, for over thirty years. With resuscitation came success, and for three consecutive years, 1849-51, Surrey was unbeaten, her successes continuing till the 'seventies, and being due to such fine amateurs as F. P. Miller, C. G. Lane, and F. Burbridge, supported by H. H. Stephenson, Lockyer, Southerton, Griffith, Mortlock, Julius Cæsar, Jupp, the brothers Humphrey, Caffyn, Street, and Pooley. But as these men passed into the veteran stage, no others of equal merit arose to take their place, and with the bowling sadly deteriorated, the position of Surrey was quite unworthy of its name and fame, though by a kind of spurt she was champion county in 1872, Jupp, the Humphreys, Pooley, and Southerton being the chief factors in this success, which was not repeated for fifteen years, when for six consecutive seasons Surrey headed the table. It was mainly the stubborn discipline of John Shuter, the Winchester cricketer, that kept the eleven together during its period of depression, and he had his reward when Lohmann, Bowley, Beaumont, and Sharpe, by their excellent bowling, did much to make their foster-county—none of these were natives of Surrey—forge ahead and stay ahead. In later days Richardson and W. Lockwood (the discarded Nottinghamshire player) bore the brunt of the bowling. It is instructive to note that so many of the Surrey bowlers have been born in other counties, but if even the fact lends itself to criticism from one point of view, it at least throws excellent light on the Surrey system of selection and training where young players are concerned. Surrey's wicket-keepers have been Lockyer, Pooley, and Wood in practically unbroken succession, and all three were of the best, Lockyer's name being worthy of classification with those of Pilling and Blackham. Of her batsmen, the names of some of her professionals have already been mentioned, but there are others who are and will be equally, or more, famous—those, to wit, of Abel and Hayward, Maurice Read and Brockwell, and in a less degree Lockwood and Holland. Among amateur batsmen the name of W. W. Read is a name that will never be forgotten, nor those of the successive captains—J. Shuter, K. J. Key, and D. L. A. Jephson, while we may add those of W. E. Roller, H. D. G. Leveson-Gower, F. H. Boult, C. W. Burls, V. F. S. Crawford, as those of men who have at different periods rendered good service to the county. Though not situated amid picturesque scenery, the Oval is *qua* cricket ground perfect, the accommodation being ample and the wickets superb. The new pavilion alone cost from £25,000 to £30,000. The Prince of Wales is the county's landlord.

Sussex can boast a venerable antiquity and the royal patronage of George IV. when he was Prince of Wales, these being the days of

William Lillywhite, the "Nonpareil," Box and the Broadbridges, to say nothing of C. G. Taylor, the Cantab "crack." The county club was formed in 1839 on Brown's ground, the said Brown being the famous fast bowler, who is said to have bowled through a coat, and to have killed a dog on the other side! But the builder was inexorable in Brighton, and the county was hustled from place to place, till it settled finally—it is hoped—in its present splendid ground at Hove, which is, however, save in the comfort of its appointment, not one whit better for cricket purposes than the Brunswick ground, which the county used between 1847 and 1871. In modern times the names of great Sussex bowlers are few, Southerton playing but rarely, and the others being Tate, the brothers Hide, Parris, and Walter Humphreys, the "Lobster." The earlier names include those of several Lillywhites, Wisden, Brown, and Dean, while of wicket-keepers we may quote those of Box and Ellis, Harry Phillips, and Harry Butt. One is almost bewildered by the dazzling list of great batsmen who have represented Sussex—C. G. Taylor, Wisden, J. M. Cotterill, L. Winslow, R. T. Ellis, W. Newham, G. Brann, F. M. Lucas, Bean, Killick, and Marlow, to say nothing of the great Anglo-Australian player, W. L. Murdoch, who settled in Sussex and was at once invited to captain the eleven. But great as these names are, the names of C. B. Fry and K. S. Ranjitsinhji are perhaps even greater. They are household words at present, as are their wonderful feats with the bat, which—as the tale is not yet complete—may be left to be chronicled by posterity. At the present day, were the Sussex bowling in any sense on a par with its batting, the county would probably carry all before it. One record of Fry's should, however, be recorded, as it is so far ahead of any similar feat. In 1901 he actually scored six successive centuries, the scores being: 106 *v.* Hants, 209 *v.* Yorks, 149 *v.* Middlesex, 105 *v.* Surrey, 140 *v.* Kent, and 105 *v.*Yorkshire. The last of these was made for an Eleven of England, all the others for Sussex. No one else, not even W. G. Grace, has ever made more than three hundreds in succession.

The Warwickshire County C.C. only dates back to 1882, but

it was some years before it "caught on," though it was the energy of William Ansell in pushing the club that led not only to its recognition, but, more or less directly, to the dissolution of the County Cricket Council. Being first of the second-class counties in 1892 and 1893—bracketed with Derbyshire in the latter year—it was duly promoted to higher rank, and opened the 1894 season in sensational fashion by defeating, in rapid succession, Notts, Surrey, and Kent, no other county being successful that year in beating Surrey at the Oval. The county has always held its own well, even though, with the exception of the internationals, Lilley and W. G. Quaife, it has produced no very prominent men: it has won its way by steady and consistent cricket, rather than by brilliancy. The Quaifes—there are two of them—were originally Sussex men, and it is but right to record that a good deal of feeling was caused by the manner of their secession. The present and the only captain of the club is an old Eton and Cambridge captain, H. W. Bainbridge, who has been blessed in having so superlative a wicket-keeper as Lilley, and such prodigies of steadiness as Quaife and Kinneir, to serve under him. L. C. Docker, the brothers Hill, and T. S. Fishwick are the better-known amateurs, with Devey, Charlesworth, Santall, Hargreave, Field, Pallett, Shilton, Diver, and Whitehead among the professionals, few or none of whom have made a great stir in the cricket world. The county ground is at Edgbaston, a suburb of Birmingham, and being well equipped in every way, was selected as the scene of the first test match played in 1902, a match that is dealt with in a later chapter.

The existence of Worcestershire, the latest recruit to the first class, may be considered as due to the superlative excellence of three brothers, the brothers Foster of Malvern College, whose initials, W. L., H. K., and R. E., are as familiar as are those of the Studds, Graces, or Walkers; indeed, some wit, with a keen ear for assonance, has dubbed the county "Fostershire." Splendid batsmen as they all are, no one of them is a bowler, wherein they fall behind the three great fraternities quoted above. The family has, however, a record of its own, as in 1899, playing against Hampshire, R. E. scored 134 and 101 not out, and W. L. 140 and 172 not out; further, R. E. has a private record of *his* own, having made 102 not out and 136 against the Players at Lord's in 1900. In Burrows, Wilson, Arnold, and Bowley, with Straw to keep wicket, Worcestershire has put some useful professionals into the field, while the other better-known amateurs are W. W. Lowe, G. Simpson-Hayward, and the Bromley-Martins. The county ground is to be found at Worcester, and, like most of its sort, is in all respects excellent.

On Yorkshire cricket, and especially on Yorkshire bowlers, volumes might be written, but powerful as the county is now in the present, and has been in the past, it has not been free from the ordinary vicissitudes of life in general and of cricket in particular, to which fact allusion has been made earlier in this chapter. It has also been stated before that Sheffield was the original home of Yorkshire cricket, being a club strong enough to play the rest of the county and beat it, and boasting in Dearman and Marsden, the famous left-hander, two of the great stars of the early nineteenth century. However, the county club was organised in 1862, with the Sheffield ground at Bramall Lane as its headquarters, though the big county is so rich in fine grounds that it distributes its favours among many towns. In the plethora of great professionals the amateur element has always been in a minority in the county eleven, though the names of Lord Hawke, T. L. Taylor, Frank Mitchell, and F. S. Jackson, and in a quieter way of George Savile, Rev. E. S. Carter, A. Sellers, F. W. Milligan, E. T. Hirst, and R. W. Frank, will always be familiar to cricketers, to which may be added that of G. A. B. Leatham, whose wicket-keeping powers would have found him a place in many a good county eleven; but the county of Pinder and the two Hunters has not been hard up for a custodian for many years. Of the amateurs, be it said that no more brilliant all-round cricketer has walked out of a pavilion than F. S. Jackson, and that in Lord Hawke the county found an ideal man, apart from his batting powers, to command its side, a side, too, that has for many years been composed exclusively of Yorkshire-born men. Lord Hawke found the county at a low ebb, shared its struggle upward, and is finally the proud leader of a body of men that lost but two county matches in three years, and he has had the additional satisfaction of helping to raise the county to such admirable financial condition, that it is able to treat its professionals with a liberality that but few other counties can emulate or even approach. It is not unnatural in consequence that the Yorkshire eleven should be practically a band of very happy and contented brothers. The names of the great county bowlers are legion: every one has read of Freeman and Emmett, Ulyett and Bates and Peate, Hirst and Rhodes, Slinn, Atkinson, Allan Hill, Peel, Haigh, Ulyett and Wainwright, but one notes with interest how many of these have been left-handers. Then the batsmen—Stephenson (E.), Rowbotham, Iddison (a lob bowler of much merit), the Greenwoods (Luke and Andrew), Ephraim Lockwood (of wonderful cutting powers), Bates, Louis Hall (the pioneer of stickers), Peel, Brown and Tunnicliffe, Denton and Wainwright, *cum multis aliis*. It is indeed a wonderful list of names, names of cricketers of all sorts and conditions, as versatile as they are numerous. One wonders, considering the years that they cover, that Yorkshire has ever been anything but champion county, especially as the names excluded are only a whit less well known than those that are included.

Such in brief is the history, a mere sketch, of our more important counties, their rise and their fall: a full and complete account of them would fill the whole of a goodly volume, which would be replete with interest and anecdote, but which would require the patience and the genius of a Macaulay or a Froude for its adequate and comprehensive compilation. Cricket may indeed be but a mere pastime, but it is a pastime that has come home to the hearts of Englishmen, or at least to the hearts of a goodly number of Englishmen, during a period of some two hundred years.

CRICKET

THE CRICKET GROUND AT DARNALL, NEAR SHEFFIELD.

He who would write that history must be a man of infinite patience and vast perseverance. He will not find cricket history writ large in columns of big print, but, for the earlier days at least, often packed away in obscure corners of local journals. Thirty years ago there was no daily sporting paper, while the big "dailies" took but little notice of cricket matches. Add a hundred years on to the thirty, and only local papers record a great match. Consequently, he who would write a full and accurate account of the cricket played by the counties, must rummage even more painfully than the recorder of political facts, and in journals that are far less accessible and that give less prominence to the special facts of which the writer is in quest. The great work may yet be written, but the writing thereof will be largely a labour of love, for the divers into cricket lore are but few, and the writer will naturally wonder whether the game will be worth the candle.

CRICKET

From a Painting by J. Lush.
THE EARL OF MARCH.

CHAPTER VII

AMATEURS AND PROFESSIONALS
BY THE HON. R. H. LYTTELTON

It would not appear to be a difficult task to make a clear and accurate definition of the two common words found at the head of this chapter. Forty years ago the making of such a definition would have been easy, and if we could regard things from an ideal point of view, it would be easy now. There are, however, so many difficulties at present in the way, so many changes in the carrying on of the game of cricket, so much acquiesced in which formerly would not have been dreamt of, that the old boundary line has been obliterated—all is confusion, and in too many cases there can hardly be said to be any difference or distinction between the amateur and professional in these days in the world of cricket.

It is strange that such should be the case, and it is also strange that these difficulties should exist so much more in the case of cricket than any other game. Whether this always will be the case appears to be doubtful. In the case of rowing there seem to be dangers ahead, and perhaps in the world of football also. But if I am not misinformed, the rowing authorities are not troubled in the matter as far as this country is concerned. It is owing to the fact that in America there do not appear to be the same regulations on this vexed question as in England—and the American invasion of England includes the chief prizes of Henley as well as the tube railways of London. The rowing authorities have a very difficult task before them. To come to a right decision, and yet not to offend the feelings of a nation we all respect, and have every wish to be, from a sporting point of view, on good terms with, is by no means an easy task, but I can only hope that a satisfactory decision will be attained.

Cricket, however, seems to stand altogether on a different footing to any other game. The boundary line between the two classes of amateurs and professionals has become blurred and indistinct, if indeed it has not entirely disappeared. As far as I know, no such state of things exists in other games, such as golf, tennis, football, or billiards. The reason why this is so seems to be twofold. The first is that if a man wants to play as much cricket as he likes he must practically devote five months of the year to nothing else. A match takes three days to finish, and the whole of each day is taken up by the game, and in this respect cricket stands alone. You may play golf or tennis every day if you have the opportunity; but two or three hours is enough for this, and the rest of the time may be spent in the counting-house. First-class cricket, however, now is of so exacting a nature that it really amounts to this, that nearly half the year must be wholly devoted to the game, and comparatively few amateurs can afford to do this. The other reason is somewhat on a par with the experiences of rowing men, and is because of the Australian invasion. International cricket between this country and Australia has come to stay, and it is much to be hoped this will always remain. Nothing in cricket is so interesting, and no other matches contain so many exciting elements, and in no other class of match is such a high standard of skill shown. In Australia, however, there does not seem to be any very clear distinction between the amateur and professional. In 1878, when they first came to England, the two Bannermans and, I think, Midwinter were classed as professionals, the rest as amateurs. In subsequent years there was no distinction drawn, and without going too minutely into the merits of the case, they are now all called amateurs. It may not be obvious what difference this makes to English cricket, but nevertheless on more than one occasion there has been friction, and it is notorious that the bone of contention is to be found in the fact that the English professionals have a somewhat well-founded idea in their minds that the Australian cricketers are really professionals like themselves, and they should in both countries stand on the same footing.

It is necessary, however, that some comparison be made of the conditions that existed thirty years ago, with the state of things now. This is a delicate and thorny subject, and it is almost, if not quite, impossible to avoid treading on corns; but the matter is a critical one for the welfare of the great game, and some clear understanding should be arrived at, and to attain this the public should know all the facts, that they may come to a right opinion.

It has been said that a definition of the words amateur and professional forty years ago would have been easy, and this is true. The question of money for the amateur was purely a personal one for himself. He played cricket according to his means. If he was of a sufficiently high class, and was qualified to play for a leading county, he played on the home ground if his business, if he had one, allowed him, and if he could not afford railway and hotel fares, he did not play the return match, it may be two hundred miles away. No doubt there were far fewer matches in those days, for Surrey, the chief county in the 'sixties, only played on an average ten or eleven matches a year. For an amateur of Surrey to have played in all these matches was no doubt a tolerably arduous task, but it was not an impossible one. If the first-class amateur could not afford to play away from the neighbourhood of his home, he simply declined to play. The reason was obvious, but tact forbade the cause being inquired into, and the amateur was not thought any the worse of on this account. No doubt cricket was not in one sense the serious thing it is now. There were no carefully compiled and intolerably wearisome tables of statistics that drown one in these days; nevertheless there was just as much keenness for success, but championships and records did not constitute the *summum bonum*; it was the genuine sport that was chiefly considered. In other words, the game was generally carried on, in the best sense, in more of the amateur spirit than now, and this notwithstanding the fact that far more so-called amateurs play first-class cricket now than formerly. There was more cricket in matches of the class of Gentlemen of Worcestershire against Gentlemen of Warwickshire; the famous touring pure amateur clubs, such as Quidnuncs, Harlequins, I Zingari, and Free Foresters, played as they do now; and there were as many club matches played by the M.C.C. and Surrey clubs as were in those days wanted, and in these the amateur was able to take his part.

The ambition of every player in these days is to reach such a measure of skill as to earn him a place in the picked eleven of England against Australia, and very properly is this the case. To represent the Gentlemen against the Players at Lord's is still the goal of many, but not so much now as it was. For a University man a place in his University eleven is as keen an object of ambition now as it used to be, and though the bowling may be weak and the fielding not so good as it ought to be, still University cricket is the same as it always has been—the embodiment of the purest amateur spirit of the game. But forty years ago, to be selected to represent the Gentlemen or the Players, as the case might be, set the seal on both amateurs and professionals, in the same way as to be selected to play for England against Australia does now. The amateur came up cheerfully to share in the annual defeat that almost invariably awaited him; the bowling for most of them was too good, and his record, speaking generally, at Lord's at any rate, would be laughed at by the modern critic, stuffed out as he is with centuries, statistics, and comparisons, but to be selected made him happy.

The reader may now naturally ask, When and how does the amateur of forty years ago differ from the amateur of the present day? The question will be discussed more fully later on, but the answer is simply this, that in former times no amateur ever received one penny for his services, whether disguised under the name of expenses or by the receipts of a benefit match, euphemistically called a complimentary match. Here at once is the difference, and for the present it is sufficient merely to state the fact, and file it, as it were, for future reference.

The professional of old was drawn from the same sources as he is now. He comes from the shop, from the factory, from the pit, and from the slum. He had by no means so much cricket as he has now in the way of first-class county matches, but he filled up his time, if he arrived at a certain height of skill, by playing a series of touring matches against local twenty-twos, and these matches, if they did nothing else, gave an impetus to local cricket. There can be no doubt, however, that an enormous change has taken place in the type of professional cricketer. The first-class modern player moves altogether in a higher plane. He earns far more money in populous centres, such as Bradford, London, and Manchester. He has been known to clear £2000 and more by a benefit match. A spectator coming on to Lord's at five o'clock in the afternoon, during the annual match between Gentlemen and Players, might easily for a moment be uncertain which side were fielding. There could have been no mistake in old days. Older cricketers well remember Jemmy Grundy in an old velvet cap more fitted for the North Pole than an English cricket ground, such a cap as a poacher would wear. You can see prints of Hayward and Carpenter in spotted shirts and large belts and ties, and Jemmy Shaw bowling his hardest in a yellow shirt that did duty apparently for the whole summer. Now, without any disrespect to the amateurs, the professional is as smartly dressed as his opponents. He is clad in spotless white; he is smart; and, in fact, as far as appearance goes, he is an amateur, and good at that. Two reasons may be given for this. In the first place, he is more highly paid; in the next place, the great number of county matches brings him more frequently into contact with amateurs; and it is also true that county committees look more closely after the players than they did. The life of a professional is a very hard life in the way of work, and though a sound batsman, who is of steady habits, like poor Shrewsbury, can play for a long while, the fast bowlers are overweighted with the constant labour of bowling on too perfect wickets, and they cannot keep their pace and skill for much more than six or seven years.

The professionals who are not good enough to play for a first-class county have by no means so good a time. They get engaged by clubs such as are found all over South Lancashire and in the West Riding of York, and they bowl for several hours all the week to members of the club at the nets, and on Saturdays play for the club in league matches. The results of these matches are tabulated in the local newspapers and in the sporting papers published on Sundays, and in their own district cause no end of excitement. The end of the season finds one of these clubs champion of the local league; and cricket is carried on very much like football in this respect. There are senior and junior leagues, there are Pleasant Sunday afternoon leagues, and in each of them there exists a carefully considered system of tables and elaborately calculated records of averages, and the leading cricketers, like the leading football players, are heroes. The game, however, as played in such matches, is of a distinctly lower type, and if report speaks truly, the umpires have often more than their proper share in determining the issue of the match. The professional supplements his income in other ways. He generally supplies bats and balls and other cricket materials, and sometimes, if he is a man of business, he establishes himself finally in a shop, more frequently in a public-house, and settles down for life.

CRICKET

MR. J. H. DARK .(Proprietor of Lords)
GWM. HILLYER , THE UMPIRE.(Wm. Caldecourt)
WM. MARTINGELL

CRICKET

FULLER PILCH,
Who was considered, till the days of Dr. W. G. Grace, the best Batsman that had ever appeared

The descriptions of the amateur and professional as given above are accurate enough, and many of us who can remember the former state of things probably think that, in comparing the epoch of 1860 to 1870 with that of 1892 to 1902, the condition of things was better, as far as the amateur is concerned, in the 'sixties, and worse for the professional, and that now the position is exactly reversed. An amateur should be either one thing or the other, but nobody can say in these days what he is. The change has taken place gradually, and began from causes that sprang into existence perhaps thirty years ago, and these we will now try to explain.

Nobody who has watched the game carefully can fail to be struck with the wonderful development of county cricket. The ideal county cricket really exists, speaking of first-class counties alone, in the three counties of Nottingham, Yorkshire, and, we think, Derbyshire. Regarded impartially, a county ought to be represented solely by county players, but as a matter of fact this is not the case anywhere but in Nottingham and Yorkshire. But in many counties are to be found gentlemen who like to have first-class cricket in their county, and a county cricket club is founded. The financial prosperity of the club depends in a great measure on the success of the county eleven, and if a county has three or four amateurs who materially strengthen the side, the committee make great efforts to secure their services all through the season. The natural result follows. The amateur is driven to confess that he cannot afford the expenses of travelling and living at hotels, and he must decline to play. The winning of matches being the golden key to financial prosperity, the committees have been driven to adopt a system of paying the amateur money, that their counties may play their best elevens, and the first step in obliterating the boundary line that should exist between the amateur and professional has been taken, and what thirty years ago was done in one or two instances is now a matter of universal practice.

I am now for the moment making no comment; only stating a

fact. As far as the balance-sheet of the county club is concerned, you cannot assume that the club can run its eleven cheaply by playing amateurs, who in truth cost the committee as much per head as the professionals. It would involve too much worrying into detail, and might lead to other harmful consequences, to get exact statements of the cost of railway tickets, etc.; so there is a fixed payment in a majority of cases given to every amateur, and this fixed payment is on a sufficiently generous scale to enable many an impecunious amateur to devote his services to his county. Nor is this the only way of providing livelihoods for skilful amateurs. There has to be, of course, a secretary, and you can either appoint a cricketer to this post, and provide him with a clerk who can do the work while his employer is playing cricket, or else make the cricketer an under-secretary, both posts, of course, having a salary attached. It is also, if report speaks truly, a matter of fairly common practice for employers somehow or other to find some employment for cricketers during the winter, of course at a salary, and it has therefore come to this, that many an amateur has found in the game of cricket a means of access to a livelihood. No distinction has yet been given between a complimentary match and a benefit; the result is much the same in both instances; the proceeds of gate-money, after deduction of expenses, are handed to the player for whom the match is played.

A short time ago there was a proposal, emanating, if I am not mistaken, from the Australian authorities, that the M.C.C. should undertake the arranging and selection of an English eleven to represent this country in a series of matches in Australia. The committee of the M.C.C. undertook the task, though not, it must be confessed, in a very sanguine spirit. Their labours did not last long. Difficulties met them on the very threshold, and these difficulties were entirely on the ground of the amateurs' expenses. Now it must be assumed that, if the principle of paying amateurs' expenses be allowed, there ought to be no difficulty in the way of settling with amateurs. A manager has to go out; why should not he take all the tickets, pay the coaching and railway expenses and hotel bills, receive the proper share of the gate-money, and deliver the amateur safe back in his own country without the payment to the amateur of a penny? The word expenses has a well-defined and proper meaning, known to everybody. It represents the actual cost to a player of living, travelling, and playing, from the moment he leaves this country to the moment he sets foot in it again; but it is perfectly certain that, if left to the amateur to make a sort of private bargain, other and improper developments will take place, and it is notorious that they do.

Now let us consider for a moment the position of affairs, as far as this question of amateurs and professionals is concerned, in the case of Australia. As was said before, there was some sort of discrimination between the two in the first Colonial eleven in 1878. Both the Bannermans, as noted above, were avowedly professionals, and Midwinter also, if I remember rightly, and perhaps one or two others. But the bulk were amateurs, and the mystic sign "Mr." was placed before their names. If no authoritative statement is made, and no balance-sheet made public, nobody can be surprised if the facts are more or less conjectural. But for all that, rumour in this instance is no lying jade, and without fear of contradiction, I assert that many of the so-called Australian "amateurs" who have been to this country have made money over and above their expenses. Let nobody be misled, or assume from this that any stigma attaches to any of these Australian players; it is not their fault, but some may complain of the system. The profession of a cricketer, the calling of a professional, is in every way an honourable and good one. What puzzles so many of us is that, this being the case, so many should adopt the profession, but deny the name. They seem to prefer the ambiguous position of a so-called amateur to the straightforward, far more honourable one of a professional. This is not the case in other professions. Take the case of the dramatic career. There are many actors and actresses of more or less high social standing who have been driven by their love of the work and skill to adopt the calling of an actor. There is no ambiguity about it. They become what they are. They do not call themselves amateurs and receive salaries under the guise of expenses, which is exactly what cricketers do; and many of us ask ourselves, what is the reason of this?

To this question all that can be said is that circumstances have so changed that what was easy to define formerly is difficult now. It may be impossible to have the same rules and regulations now that used to exist forty years ago. But even if this is true, there can be no doubt that in these days a most unhealthy state of things prevails. It is bad for the nominal amateur, it is bad for the game, and it is bad for the country. Cricket is the finest game ever invented, but it is after all only a game, and it is wrong that things should have developed in such a way that amateurs become professionals in all but the name, and that gate-money should be the real moving spirit and ideal of all county clubs. To be prosperous financially a county must win matches, to win matches you must get the best possible county eleven, therefore the best amateurs as well as professionals must be played; and if these amateurs cannot afford the time and the money to play, why, then, they must be paid, and paid accordingly they are. That this is the case now everybody knows, and it seems strange that the greatest game of the world should be the one game where such things occur. No complaint need be made of the Australian system, except in this, that players who are in fact professionals should be treated as such. We are always glad to give them every welcome and show them every hospitality; nevertheless, they should have the same treatment and stand on the same footing that our professionals do when they visit Australia. In the same way, if any player feels himself unable, at the invitation of the M.C.C., to go out to Australia, because he is only offered the payment of the actual cost of travelling and living, and afterwards goes out under some private arrangement, he should be treated and recognised as a professional. It is an old proverb that you cannot eat your cake and have it, and if the modern amateur does not care, on social grounds, to become a professional, then let him honestly refuse to play cricket if he cannot afford to play on receipt of his bare expenses only. Richard Daft, in old days, found himself in the same dilemma, and grasped the nettle and became a professional, and justly earned the respect of all for so doing.

Put briefly, in these days the state of things is this. A large number of amateurs directly and indirectly make something of a livelihood by cricket, and yet they are recognised as amateurs. Such cricketers are those who, under the guise of expenses, get such a sum that after paying these expenses leaves something to be carried over, as Mr. Jorrocks called it. A few others do things on a far more lordly scale. They have complimentary matches given them by their counties; in other words, they have benefits like many of the leading and deserving professionals, but still they are called amateurs; and whether it is correct to call a class of men one name, when they are obviously and openly something different, is perhaps a matter of opinion, but for my part I do not hesitate to say it is neither right nor straightforward.

Further trouble arises from the curse of gate-money. This hangs like a blight over everything. County clubs dare not take a decided line about cricket reform, lest a shortening of the game might diminish the gate-money, and professionals do not speak out because they are forced to bow the knee to Baal. County clubs are therefore in this position: they must attract gates; to do this they must have a fine eleven; to get a fine eleven they must have amateurs, and these amateurs cannot play regularly without being paid, and so paid they are. The expenses of running a first-class county eleven are therefore very great—so great, in fact, that few can stand the strain. Some years ago we used to have three or four wet seasons running occasionally. If ever this occurs again, bankruptcy awaits several county committees, as Warwickshire and Worcestershire have some reason from last season's experience to dread. It now costs as much to run a team of amateurs as professionals, as all have to be paid. Perhaps some day, when the public get tired of seeing match after match unfinished, and refuse to pay their entrance money, and the cricket world find out that some reform is necessary, and the duration of a match is two days and not three, county clubs will find out that they cannot pay these wages for amateurs, and a remedy will be found from an unlooked-for cause.

Having thus given vent to a growl on an unpleasant subject, the features of professional and amateur play may now be discussed. There used to be great differences in old days, far more than there is now, but in one respect there is a great difference still, and that is in bowling. We all know what sort of bowling will be seen in a University match, or in Free Forester and Quidnunc matches. There will be one or two fair slow bowlers, but that is all. Good fast bowling has not been seen for some years in amateur elevens, but for this the amateurs are hardly to blame. The modern wicket, shaved and heavy rolled, has made it practically impossible for any really fast bowler to do any good, unless he is one of the shining lights, like Richardson or Lockwood. Amateurs like Messrs. Jessop, Kortright, and Bradley have an occasional day of success, but these bowlers, being naturally fast, depend mainly for their success on the agility of the field in the slips, and on their capacity to make the ball bump. To attain this they generally have but a short career.

They take out of themselves by adopting a gigantic long run and banging the ball down from straight over their head at a terrific pace. Flesh and blood cannot stand this for more than a short time. A human being is but human after all; he is not a machine built to order like a steam engine, and work like what he has to undergo knocks him up.

CRICKET

Attributed to Thos. Gainsborough, R.A.
PORTRAIT OF A YOUTH.
(Said to be of George, Prince of Wales, afterwards George IV.)

WILLIAM DORRINTON.

The professionals have always had much the best of it as regards bowling, and they have so still; but why this is so is not easy to see. Between the ages of twelve and eighteen there is no reason to suppose that the professional practises more at bowling than the amateur; the probability is the other way. A young amateur is at school during this period, where cricket is more systematically carried on than at the board school, which the professional leaves at thirteen and exchanges for a shop or a factory. But the tendency in amateur bowlers is to promise well as a boy, and not to come up to expectations as a man, and especially is this the case when, as so often happens, there is a corresponding improvement in batting.

In my experience of more than thirty years, the only instance I can call to mind of an amateur who bowled above medium pace like a professional—that is to say, with a professional's accuracy and method—was Mr. Appleby, who died last year. Mr. Appleby had a beautiful easy action, and was always to be relied on to keep a length and direction, as J. T. Hearne did for many years. Mr. Jackson is still in the middle of his career, and next to Mr. Appleby, bowls more nearly approaching to the professional standpoint; but, good bowler as he is, he does not strike one as quite like a professional bowler. Slow bowlers are not quite in the same class. Here the amateur is more at home. Mr. W. G. Grace and the late Mr. David Buchanan were worthy of being classed with Alfred Shaw, Peate, and Rhodes. Mr. Grace must be so much used to hearing his merits discussed entirely from the batting point of view, and has done so little bowling as compared with batting, that it may interest the present generation that for some years as a bowler he was as effective as the best professional. His method, however, was very different. At a time when a wicket was supposed to be worth only ten runs, and when nearly every bowler bowled more for maidens than they do now, Mr. Grace was the first to show the way of a deliberate system of getting wickets by getting men out, other than by merely bowling them. He habitually placed a deep square leg in the right place, and tempted men like Oscroft, Charlwood, and many more to send chances there, and many a time and oft has the trick come off. He frequently bowled in a way that showed what idea was in his head. A very common device of his was in regard to l.b.w. He never objected to being hit over the ropes, as he would silently argue that an ordinary batsman, having once tasted the sweets of a mighty leg hit over the ropes, would very much like to repeat the feat, and Mr. Grace would drop down a tempting ball on the leg stump, and if, as often happened, the batsman did hit at it and did miss it, he was out l.b.w. To this day, to batsmen like those who come from Australia for the first time, and have therefore never seen Mr. Grace bowl, I would as soon put on Mr. Grace to bowl for a few overs as any man in England. He is and always has been quite unlike any other bowler, both in the way he delivered the ball and the strange way he placed his field.

Mr. Buchanan was another bowler who copied Mr. Grace in one sense, for though he did not bowl for catches to leg, he carried out the theory of bowling for catches on the off side more than any bowler before or since. A bold hitter might hit Mr. Buchanan, if he was quick on his feet and had a good eye, but for all that there were few bowlers who so rarely bowled a bad-length ball. Neither were there many bowlers who made such absolute fools of batsmen as Mr. Buchanan did. The picked professionals who played against him in Gentlemen and Players matches at Lord's and the Oval as a rule displayed all the feebleness that was possible. Daft, Lockwood, and Oscroft were exceptions to this. Lockwood, who had a wonderful cut, more than any other, realised the danger of hitting at the pitch of Mr. Buchanan's off ball. Instead of doing this, he got back and cut the ball behind the wicket for three runs—it might have been four, but Lockwood was a slow runner. Mr. Buchanan did not like to have a third man, and his nervous system was seriously insulted at Lockwood's method, which forced him to change the disposition of his field in a way he did not like. Mr. Grace and Mr. Buchanan were two amateur slow bowlers who really studied the art of bowling, and both of them, Mr. Grace in particular, studied the play of their batting opponents; but when you have mentioned Messrs. Appleby, Grace, and Buchanan, and for a short time Mr. Steel, you have nearly exhausted the list of bowlers who during the last thirty years may be said to have challenged comparison with the best professionals.

In batting it is very different. Mr. Grace, of course, must be left out of any calculation. Apart from him, however, the amateurs can quite hold their own in batting. It is not fair to take as an illustration the performances of each in Gentlemen *v.* Players matches, because the bowling on one side is so superior to the other. But in international test matches, both here and in Australia, Messrs. Stoddart, Ranjitsinhji, Maclaren, Jackson, and Steel have been fully as good and successful as Shrewsbury, Barnes, Gunn, Hayward, and Tyldesley. As far as style is concerned, the older professionals, such as Shrewsbury and Barnes, had a more distinctive difference of method than their modern successors. Hayward and Tyldesley far more closely resembled the amateur method of Messrs. Jackson and Palairet than Shrewsbury and Barnes did that of Messrs. Steel and Stoddart. It is not easy to explain on paper the difference, but every decent judge of the game could see that a difference was there. Some of the players, like Ulyett and Bates, could and did hit as hard and as often as the amateur, but in the professional there was little real grace of style. It is strange that this is so, for grace and ease are qualities that must be born, not made, but it is true, nevertheless, speaking of the older cricketers. Nowadays it would seem that Tyldesley and Hayward have nothing to fear, as far as style is concerned, from any amateur, always excepting Mr. Palairet. As far as mere run-getting is the point of discussion, there would seem to be very little in it one way or the other. In the great series of test matches, both here and in Australia, during the last ten years there have been Stoddart, Maclaren, Ranjitsinhji, and Jackson, as there have been Shrewsbury, Hayward, Tyldesley, and Gunn, the amateurs perhaps having a shade the better of it.

The fielding also is and always has been tolerably even. In this, however, there is a great difference now as compared with old times. Thirty years ago the professional wicket-keeper was a class, even two classes, above the amateur. Lockyer, Pooley, Plumb, and Pinder formed a class that the amateurs could not show any comparison with. Possibly the rougher wicket and the, generally speaking, faster bowling made the position more unpleasant than it is now, but undoubtedly the amateur has improved beyond all knowledge in wicket-keeping, and there is not much to choose now. In other respects also the quality seems tolerably equal. The observer will undoubtedly notice a change in the figure of the ordinary professional now. The old Yorkshire eleven, with the well-known figures of Roger Iddison, Luke Greenwood, and Rowbotham, and the Nottingham eleven with Bignall and Wild, seem quite out of date now, though Hirst looks promising in this respect. But Gunn, Maurice Read, Tyldesley, Wainwright, Hirst, Braund, and several others were and are fully equal in fielding to any that the amateurs can bring to compare with them.

It would appear, then, that in batting and fielding there is little to choose between amateurs and professionals, but in bowling there is great superiority among the professionals. Of course this superiority, *cæteris paribus*, is so important that as long as it exists the professional must win the vast majority of matches. As a general rule this has been the case, but when Mr. Grace was in his prime, that is, between 1869 and about 1887, his tremendous skill gave the amateurs the predominance that, as far as appearances go, does not look likely to occur again.

Some good judges of the game have maintained that the common practice, which has prevailed for some time, of engaging professional bowlers to bowl to boys at school and undergraduates at the universities, and to the amateurs generally belonging to clubs, is a bad one, and that amateur inferiority in bowling is to be traced to this custom. Something no doubt may be done by practising bowling, but it is probable that the bowler even more than the batsman is *nascitur non fit*. Unless there is a natural break and some spin or mysterious quality which makes the ball hang or kick in a bowler, he can hardly acquire it. The utmost he can attain to, if he does not possess these virtues, is experience in estimating the quality of his opponents, and a modicum of skill in varying length and pace. But these will not avail him much if the natural gifts of a bowler are not in him by nature. Even these will go if, as frequently happens in these days of easy wickets, the bowler gets too much work thrown on him, for the cricket life of a very fast bowler is not more than six years on the average.

In the matter of generalship, or the managing of a side, professionals have hitherto shown very little skill. The professionals themselves would probably prefer to be led by an amateur. George Parr, Daft, Emmett, Alfred Shaw, and Abel have at different times acted as captains, but none are to be compared to Messrs. V. E. Walker, A. N. Hornby, J. Shuter, and Maclaren. A professional who is captain seems always to think it proper to give every bowler a chance, whether a change of bowling is wanted or not, and a natural bias towards members of his own county is not always successfully resisted.

CRICKET

From a Painting by W. Bromley.
GEORGE PARR.

From what has been said in this chapter, the reader will be able to learn that, as far as England is concerned, the relations between amateurs and professionals stand on an altogether different footing in cricket from what they do in other games. In

Australia, unless we have been misinformed, most if not all the players who come to this country earn, on an average of years, a fairly substantial sum by cricket played over here. They are really professionals, and it is probable that in their own country they are so regarded. If this is so, we have the curious fact of a totally different standard prevailing in the two countries. But this, as far as England is concerned, is not important. What is important is that there should be some distinct understanding on the subject, and the present nebulous state of things put an end to. If it is necessary to have something paid to amateurs, the greatest care should be taken that nothing beyond *bona fide* expenses are paid, and we believe that by the Surrey club this is done now. Not until there is established some clear and understood principle under which a true definition of the word "amateur" is arrived at, will the present unsatisfactory state of things be put an end to, and it is earnestly to be hoped that some day this will be done.

CHAPTER VIII

EARLIER AUSTRALIAN CRICKET
BY THE EARL OF DARNLEY

The rivalry between English and Australian cricketers, which has been productive in recent times of so many splendid matches, can now look back to its starting-point through quite a respectably large number of years.

In the year 1861 H. H. Stephenson captained the first English team of cricketers which visited Australia, and it was seventeen years later before the seeds then sown had sufficiently matured to allow the Australians to feel full confidence in their powers to return the compliment, and to try conclusions with English players on their own grounds.

Between these dates, 1861 and 1878, three other English elevens visited Australia—G. Parr's in 1863, W. G. Grace's in 1873, and J. Lillywhite's in 1876. Of these four elevens, three were almost wholly made up of professional players, and the fourth, that captained by "W. G.," included five amateurs. Amongst their numbers, however, they included most of the great players of the day, and the first and second elevens in point of date each left behind in Australia one of its members, whose coaching was invaluable to the rising generation of Colonial players: these two instructors were C. Lawrence, who remained from the first English eleven, and W. Caffyn, about the best all-round man of his time, from the second. Many times has the writer heard striking testimony offered in Australia to the invaluable help given by these two cricketers in those early days, and certainly they might well have felt proud of the aptitude of such of their pupils as have come to us from 1878 onwards.

The matches in these first four English visits have no very special points of interest, as they were almost invariably played against considerable odds. It was, however, plain to all that the standard of cricket in Australia was greatly improving year by year, and no one was surprised when it was announced in 1878 that our friends felt themselves strong enough to send their first eleven to England, to try their fortunes on level terms. So many Australian elevens have come and gone since then, that it is difficult now to imagine the intense interest and excitement which was felt in English cricket circles at this epoch-making event. The arrival of an eleven which might hold its own against our best men was up to this time so wildly improbable an eventuality, that the majority of the English cricketing public could hardly be brought to believe in its possibility.

A very short time sufficed to show that there was no mistake about the capacity of our visitors for holding their own with our best men on even terms. After a moderate start at Nottingham, where the county won by one innings and a few runs, came perhaps the most startlingly dramatic match ever played by an Australian eleven in England, against a strong selection of the Marylebone Club, including such well-known performers as W. G. Grace, Hornby, Ridley, A. J. Webbe, A. Shaw, and Morley. To dispose of such a side for 33 and 19, and win the match by nine wickets in one day, was a feat that even the warmest admirers of the Australians had hardly imagined, and from that memorable day may be said to have begun that intensely keen and interesting rivalry that has lasted right up to the present day.

It may be worth while to attempt some slight personal sketch of this remarkable 1878 Australian eleven, which included several players who were to be the backbone of future elevens, and which achieved its successes in some measure by methods to which we in England were as yet strangers.

On looking through their batting list, there are names which suggest plentiful run-getting capabilities. As a matter of fact, however, at that time the batting was, with one exception, C. Bannerman, of the most rugged and unfinished description. The above-named exception, Bannerman, might well have been given a high place among contemporary batsmen as a fierce-hitting, powerful player, worthy of any eleven for batting alone, but Blackham, Midwinter, Horan, Murdoch, A. Bannerman, and Garrett had none of them yet acquired the powers which in after years were to be theirs in such abundant measure, and the batting of the whole side, after C. Bannerman, was distinctly of the rough, useful order. In this connection it may be noticed, however, that although finish was to be looked for in vain, even at this early stage was evident that fearless and dogged resistance to adverse circumstances which has since then successfully extricated many an Australian side from a tight place, and has always given their adversaries that uncomfortable feeling of never being quite certain that they have really got them safely beaten. What an invaluable asset is a reputation of this sort, and how well and consistently have our Australian friends sustained this hardly-earned character!

Emphatically this was a bowling and fielding eleven. In nineteen eleven-a-side matches, only twice was the 250 exceeded by their opponents, a convincing record that speaks for itself. Of the four bowlers, one great name stands out supreme, and who is there that remembers that year and the ten or twelve that succeeded it, but must confess that his whole ideas of bowling were revolutionised by what he saw of Spofforth in the prime of his powers? With physical qualifications admirably adapted to fast bowling, very tall, long-limbed, active, wiry, and impossible to tire, Spofforth had scientifically studied the art of bowling to a most unusual degree. The hard, true wickets in Australia had even then begun to exercise a decisive influence on the characteristics of bowling in that country, and unless a bowler could develop quite exceptional powers of deception, spin, and break, he was soon reduced to absolute helplessness. This difference in climate may be said to be the one element which makes a distinction between cricket as played in the Colonies and cricket as played in England, and, while its influence has been decisive in keeping up the standard of Australian bowling to a very high pitch of excellence, it has been at the same time hardly less favourable to the formation of a free and good style of batting, a style far more difficult to acquire when the ground is unreliable and the climate variable.

At that time Spofforth's methods varied considerably from those which he afterwards employed. He was then as a rule a fast, sometimes terrifically fast, bowler, with occasional slow ones, the change of pace being most admirably masked in the delivery. In after years his average pace was rather over medium, with an unusually big break back for that pace, while the very fast or very slow ones were the exception and not the rule. In addition to these types of ball, no man ever bowled a more dangerous fast yorker than Spofforth, and his armoury may well be said to have contained as damaging a collection of weapons as ever taxed the powers of an opposing batsman. Boyle, Allan, and Garrett made up the bowling strength. Of these Allan, partly probably through being the possessor of a constitution which suffered greatly from the severities of our summer climate, never came out in his true form; his bowling had a fine natural break, and swerved considerably in the air, and, although not on the whole very successful, he occasionally showed quite enough of his powers to warrant the great reputation enjoyed by him in the Colonies. Both Boyle and Garrett were extremely useful bowlers of the good-length-lasting style, which carried them through many subsequent years of good performance.

In wicket-keeping again did English cricketers find that there was something new to be learnt. Both Blackham and Murdoch showed for the first time how perfectly possible it was to stand up to the fastest bowling without a long-stop; and Blackham especially gave promise of powers that were to make him for some years perhaps the most brilliant wicket-keeper ever seen.

The fielding all round and throwing were unusually good,

and climate again may probably be answerable for the fact that Australian elevens, taken all through, could almost invariably out-throw any English eleven man for man.

From this short description it will easily be seen that they were a team to be seriously reckoned with, whoever their opponents might be, and when we look to the completed records of their matches, the result must be held to be decidedly creditable. By comparison with the programmes of after years, the relative test of their powers can hardly be said to be so severe. No really representative English eleven was encountered, although the full strength of both the amateurs and the professionals was played separately. At the hands of the Gentlemen they met with one of their heaviest reverses, but the professionals were narrowly defeated once, while the other game ended in a fairly even draw.

Nineteen matches played, of which the Australians won ten and lost four, made up a highly satisfactory total, and, in addition, only three out of twenty-one matches against odds were lost by them.

It was not a batsman's year, 1878, but even taking that fact into consideration, only one innings of over 100 hit against Australian bowling shows unmistakably wherein lay the chief strength of the eleven. Mention has already been made of the remarkable wicket-keeping of Murdoch and Blackham, who for the first time in English cricket performed their duties without the aid of a long-stop. We think we are right in saying that Murdoch was at first looked upon as the regular wicket-keeper of the team, but from that time onward the wonderful talent of Blackham gained for him the superior position, and his wicket-keeping for several years was at least the equal of that of any other competitor that could be brought against him. Standing very close to the wicket, and of marvellous quickness, he had the happy knack of invariably showing at his best on great occasions; a batsman too of a resolute, fearless description, and a very quick runner between wickets, his play in Australian elevens for many years was no small factor in their success.

THOMAS BOX.

The composition of this eleven is of especial interest, not merely because it was the first of the series to come to us, but by reason of its including some prominent names of men who were to be the nucleus and backbone of those that were to follow. Blackham, Murdoch, A. Bannerman, Garrett, Boyle, and Spofforth are names that will frequently recur in following years, and we shall see how, with their help, the standard of success rose consistently through the tours of 1880 and 1882, and then, after a slight falling-off in 1884, for reasons which will afterwards be alluded to, fell gradually away until a revival set in about the time of Stoddart's first tour in Australia in 1894.

The next event of any prominence to be noticed is the visit of Lord Harris's eleven to Australia in the winter of this same year 1878. A fine batting and fielding eleven, but hardly strong enough in bowling to be really representative of English cricket at its best. Emmett and Ulyett were the only two professionals included, and for a side so weak in bowling, they may be said to have made an excellent appearance. One match only was played against the returned Australian eleven, who were successful by ten wickets. Four new names appear amongst those chosen to represent the various Australian sides, all more or less successful, Palmer, Macdonnell, Massie, and Evans. The last-named cricketer was about that time at his best, and many and outspoken have been the regrets that this fine cricketer could never spare the time to appear much in English *v.* Australian cricket until he was well past his prime. In both appearance and performance he was thoroughly typical of the highest class of colonial cricketer. His tall, unusually active, well-built figure, bearded, bronzed bushman's face, presented the most perfect example of the Australian athlete, while his overhand accurate bowling and really splendid fielding and steady batting made him a worthy addition to any eleven.

Against the representatives of the individual colonies the Englishmen more than held their own, and six matches won to three lost make up a highly creditable record.

In the summer of 1880 appeared the second Australian eleven, and amongst their number several additional names to those who were with us in 1878.

Palmer, whose performance against Lord Harris's eleven

made his inclusion a certainty, appears for the first time, and he has more than justified his selection by coming out top of the bowling averages in eleven-a-side matches, according to number of wickets taken, although Spofforth, who was unable to play in several matches, has the lesser average of runs per wicket. No prettier bowler to look at than Palmer ever bowled a ball; a style of delivery that apparently cost its owner no effort whatever, and, as usual with great Australian bowlers, a much greater break than the pace of the ball would lead you to suspect. Strong and sturdily built, his power of bowling a very fast yorker was unusually great, and was frequently used early in a batsman's innings with deadly effect. With such an easy delivery, it is not easy to see why Palmer's successes did not continue for much longer than they actually did, but we may probably look for the explanation in a too great fondness which he subsequently developed for the fast leg breaks, which first destroyed the excellent length for which he was famous, and finally lowered the standard of his bowling altogether. The great improvement in his batting powers may possibly also in his case, as in that of many other bowlers, have had something to do with it. His style in batting was almost as attractively graceful as that of his bowling, but lacked something of that tenacity which must be added to style to bring about the real power over the bowlers characteristic of a great batsman.

The name of Macdonnell recalls many a dashing, vigorous innings, perhaps some of the most fascinating displays of hard, but not usually high, hitting ever seen. This season of 1880 saw him already among the leading batsmen, with an average in eleven-a-side matches second only to Murdoch, whose immense improvement as a bat deserves separate mention. Macdonnell belongs to that small circle of Australian players who were able by the fierceness of their hitting to practically win a match by their own unaided efforts when their companions were comparatively helpless, and this type of batsman, which was one of the chief features of every Australian eleven up to 1893, seems, curiously enough, to have almost disappeared. We may not improbably be able to trace this to the great predominant influence which has altered the whole character of modern cricket, and, in the judgment of many, brought about a dull level of too easily performed feats of run-getting, that only drastic legislation can alter, viz. the increasing excellence of the artificially prepared wickets. The value of an exceptional hitter, such as any member of the little band above alluded to, is far greater when the conditions are difficult. He alone perhaps can offer any effective resistance when the bowler is revelling in favourable conditions; but, if the ball comes along easily and well, it pays far better to determine at all costs to keep up the wicket, to abandon the more attractive methods of the hitter, and let the runs come, as they almost inevitably will come under such circumstances.

A great feature of the cricket of this year was the immense improvement noticeable in Murdoch's play; from this time forward he took rank as one of the greatest batsmen of the time, and perhaps the best of all the Australian players that have come to us. It is gratifying to see that, as in the case of our own champion, the ever-vigorous "W. G.," Murdoch's perfect upright style has enabled him to keep up a more than respectable proportion of his best form through at least twenty-five years of first-class cricket. This very day in April 1903, the morning paper tells us that, snow-showers and north winds notwithstanding, these two grand old cricketers are once more making an excellent appearance, going in first together at Kennington Oval. Long may they flourish! Another name that strikes us as appearing for the first time in these matches is that of G. Bonnor. We have already noticed the athletic and powerful frames that help our Australian friends so frequently to distinction in cricket, but how can we sufficiently admire the really magnificent physique of this giant among cricketers! 6 feet 6 inches in height and between 16 and 17 stones in weight, a very fast runner and prodigious thrower, we might well search the country through before we find his match as a splendid specimen of humanity. Let the reader think over all the men of at all similar proportions that he has ever met with, and see which of them could run at full speed and pick up a ball in the long field as he could. In so big a man this great activity implies a perfection of muscular development and proportion that is very rarely met with, and to see Bonnor hit and field at cricket may without exaggeration be described as the realisation of an almost ideal athletic experience.

There have been endless discussions as to who has been actually the biggest hitter at cricket within living memory, but in the writer's mind there is no doubt that Bonnor's extra power gave him the first place for distance, although C. I. Thornton's much more perfect swing made the competition a closer race than their relative physical powers would lead one to expect. Bonnor, Macdonnell, Massie, Lyons—what prodigious smacks to the unfortunate ball do these names bring to our recollection! It will be indeed a bad day for the old game when the conditions do not give reasonable encouragement to this heroic type of batsman, and, at all events while Jessop continues to play, we may well hope that there is no immediate danger of the race becoming extinct.

Taken as a whole, the team showed a decided advance on their predecessors, and Murdoch and Macdonnell in particular gave many fine displays of batting. The bowling suffered from the absence of Garrett, and the failure of any adequate substitute to take his place, and also from Spofforth's absence in half the eleven-a-side matches. When he was able to play, however, his bowling was as irresistible as ever, while Palmer at once worked his way into the front rank of bowlers.

From a Painting by A. S. Wortley.
DR. W. G. GRACE.

A new departure in the programme was made in the match against a picked England eleven played rather too late in the year, on 6th September. The weather, however, was all that could be wished at that time, and a great match resulted in a well-deserved win for England by five wickets. Murdoch and W.

G. Grace were fittingly the batting heroes of the match, and the time was evidently at hand when the best English eleven would find its equal in our rapidly improving Australian friends. Only four matches lost out of thirty-seven played was the final result, although only eleven of these were eleven-a-side matches, and the programme did not provide the sterner test of later tours.

In the winter of 1881 a very strong professional eleven under the captaincy of Alfred Shaw played a short round of first-class matches in Australia, and amongst these were two matches against Australia and two against the Australian eleven which was to come to England in 1882. The two Australian sides consisted of practically the same players, except that Evans was not included in the team to visit England. So strong, however, was that team that it is difficult to say who could have been advisedly left out to make a place for him.

The results of these four matches clearly indicated the great strength of Australian cricket at this time. Two wins and two drawn games against a side which had Barlow, Ulyett, Selby, Bates, Shrewsbury, Midwinter, and Scotton to bat, and Peate, A. Shaw, Barlow, Bates, Ulyett, and Emmett to bowl, was a thoroughly unmistakable performance, and added immensely to the interest with which the arrival of the 1882 Australian eleven was anticipated. No absolutely new names had appeared on the colonial side, but the standard of play had everywhere made a distinct upward movement, and almost every man of the eleven had reached the prime of his powers. An opportune alteration of the match list for that year provided eleven-a-side matches throughout the tour, a better test, and one likely to keep up the interest and play of the men more efficiently than a number of matches against odds, which are no particular honour to win or disgrace to lose.

A glance at the composition of this famous eleven shows a collection of very well distributed powers. For batting, Murdoch, now at his best—and that means no small praise; Horan, a talented, correct player, who, although not very successful with the first eleven, was now one of the best in Australia; Massie, Bannerman, Bonnor, Giffen, greatly improved, and soon to be one of the best all-round players of the day; Macdonnell, Blackham, and S. Jones. In bowling, Spofforth, Palmer, Boyle, Garrett, and Giffen—probably as good a company as ever bowled together in one eleven. Blackham to keep wicket. No wonder that the cricket critics, whose numbers were rapidly increasing, have never ceased to dispute whether this eleven or one of those that have come to us since 1896 was the stronger.

Unquestionably from 1884 to 1894 the Australian form steadily declined, but whether the improvement that has since set in has reached or passed the level of 1882 and 1884, is a question of considerable difficulty to tackle, and has moreover this recommendation, so thoroughly favourable to the pronouncement of varied and strongly-laid-down opinions, that from the conditions of the problem it is impossible that the issue can ever be really conclusive. Whatever may be the reader's verdict on this vexed point, no one can deny that few elevens have ever contained so many brilliant performers in their own departments of the game.

The days of a series of test matches had not yet arrived, although efforts were even then made by those arranging matters to fix dates for them. Some more years of hammering against the gates of cricket conservatism were necessary before this most palpably necessary improvement was instituted.

The one England match was as usual fixed very late in the season, 28th August, and for the first time an ever-memorable contest resulted in a narrow win for Australia by 7 runs. Two very fine elevens fought it out on difficult wickets, and in the end England failed to score the 84 that was required of them by the above-mentioned small margin. Spofforth's bowling fourteen wickets for 90 runs stands out conspicuously, but, for so important a trial of strength, what a pity that wicket conditions should have rendered such figures possible!

It was curious that, out of four matches lost during the whole tour, two were against Cambridge University and Cambridge Past and Present. The other two defeats were at the hands of the Players and the North of England, and these four defeats make a very small total when placed against twenty-three victories out of a long series of thirty-eight matches, while the average strength of the opposing elevens was far in excess of anything previously met with.

The winter of 1882 saw a mixed team of amateurs and professionals, under captaincy of the present writer, start for a tour in Australia. The all-round strength of the side was very considerable, but only four of their number had been chosen to represent England in the previous summer. However, as the remainder included Morley, Bates, W. W. Read, and Tylecote, the paper form was undoubtedly strong, and had not illness and accident, especially the unfortunate mishap which more or less crippled Morley, their only first-class fast bowler, been unfortunately frequent, an even better record than the respectable results achieved might have been realised. A rubber of three matches was played with the victorious 1882 Australian eleven, and after each had easily won a match, the decisive game ended at Sydney in the victory of England by 69 runs.

Cricket enthusiasm was at a very high pitch in Australia at this time, the first victory of Australia over England having greatly excited the public mind, and the attendance at the test matches exceeded all previous records.

The rubber having now been won by England, a suggestion was made that another match should be arranged, and one or two players included in the Australian side who had not been to England with Murdoch. Evans and Midwinter were accordingly chosen to take the places of Garrett and Macdonnell, and, although it seemed highly doubtful if this change was calculated to be for the better, its advocates would doubtless claim the justification of their choice in the Australian victory which resulted by four wickets. Fifty-five thousand people were supposed to have witnessed the play during the four days that the match occupied, and a new plan was adopted of having a fresh wicket for each of the four innings. This was necessitated by the peculiar nature of the Sydney turf, a thick-bladed, flat-growing grass, which looked perfectly smooth, but wore very badly.

These four matches showed the Australians hardly perhaps in their best form, but Bonnor, Bannerman, and, in the last match, Blackham, did some excellent service in batting, especially the first-named. His hitting in three out of the four matches was terrific, and most difficult to deal with, as our English eyes were not so well able, in the very clear atmosphere of these latitudes, to judge the many high twisting catches which he impartially presented to various fieldsmen. In an innings of 87 in the fourth match he was supposed to have been missed eight or ten times, and several of these misses were to be laid to the charge of a usually very safe fieldsman who shall be nameless. The demoralising effect of such a succession of disasters on our bowlers and fieldsmen may be well imagined, and the problem of how long a bowler should be kept on who is having a chance missed off him nearly every over presented itself in its most perplexing form to our captain.

The Australian bowling as usual found itself in safe and capable hands, in the persons of Spofforth, Palmer, Boyle, etc., while the Australian summer supplied us with an unusual number of wet wickets, much to the delight of the sheep-farmers who came from all parts of Australia to see the games.

On the English side Steel proved a tower of strength in both bowling and batting, and Leslie, Barlow, Bates, and Read all well upheld their batting reputations. Of the bowlers, Barlow and Bates did about the best work, and the latter performed one or two notable feats in this line. The want of a reliable fast bowler was many a time sorely felt, poor Morley, who attempted to play several matches with a broken rib, breaking down time after time.

For the first time Queensland was visited by an English eleven, but the experience, in spite of the extraordinary hospitality and kindness of the Queenslanders, was not altogether encouraging.

The semi-tropical heat caused several slight cases of sun effects amongst our players, and the drenching thundershowers necessitated, in one case, small drains being dug quite near the pitch to allow the water to subside quickly after the storms.

Cricket touring in Australia in those days differed from more modern experiences in several respects. The railways between Adelaide and Melbourne and Melbourne and Queensland had not yet been completed, so that most disturbing little sea journeys, lasting about thirty-six hours, on small and not overclean steamers, had to be undertaken on several occasions. Nothing more calculated to temporarily disarrange the health and form of a travelling cricket eleven could be well imagined, and the railway journeys which have now been substituted must be far preferable, from the player's point of view.

The cricket grounds in the chief capitals were already very good, but in Adelaide the turf had been too recently laid to have nearly reached the perfection to which it afterwards attained. In Sydney, the species of grass which has been before alluded to has now, we believe, been altered to English grass, then supposed to be quite unsuited to the climate, with the best possible results.

No new players of any prominence appeared among the Australians, unless we make an exception in the case of W. H. Cooper, the Victorian. He had already played in first-class cricket for some years, and had made a considerable reputation by his wonderful leg breaks. The usual penalty attaching to this great power of twist, viz. loss of pitch, always made him a very doubtful quantity, and he was liable to be ruinously expensive in the matter of runs.

The arrival of an Australian eleven in England every second year had now become quite an established custom, and 1884 saw a strong selection of players once more with us. The changes in the personnel proved to be the substitution of Scott, Midwinter, Alexander, and Cooper for Horan, Massie, S. Jones, and Garrett, and there can hardly be a contrary opinion that this change was slightly for the worse. Scott certainly sustained his own part with considerable success, but the displaced four names proved in the long run to be very difficult to replace adequately.

Three matches with England produced the not very satisfactory result of two drawn games and one win for England, a foretaste of the indecisive sequences which have stirred up the attempts at legislative interference in later times. Although unable to win one of the three matches, the Australians had certainly rather the best of the two that were undecided. In the first match, at Manchester, England was only 93 runs on with one wicket to fall, after a first innings of 182; and in the third match, at the Oval, they gave us a very fine display of batting, winning the toss and making 551, the largest total yet recorded in these matches.

Murdoch, true to his character of leading batsman, headed the list with 211, Macdonnell 103, and Scott 102, while the English bowling was reduced to such straits that Alfred Lyttelton's lobs were afforded the chance of a lifetime, and actually captured the last four wickets for 19 runs!

When in the first innings eight English wickets had fallen for 181 runs on a good wicket, the match looked almost over, but with W. W. Read's appearance began a notable partnership, which was not broken before 151 runs had been added to the score. Read's 117 ranks very high indeed among the great innings of great matches, and his mastery of the varied and excellent bowling brought against him was complete. Two wickets down for 85 runs represented England's second innings, and Australia could claim an immense advantage on the match as far as it went.

The third match, at Lord's, ended in quite another fashion with a one-innings defeat for Australia, principally due to a very fine 148 by A. G. Steel for England, and some excellent bowling by the two Yorkshiremen, Peate and Ulyett.

YOUTH WITH A CRICKET BAT
(Supposed to have been Painted about 1780).

The English representative eleven of the day showed a very high standard of play, especially in batting. When one finds A. Lyttelton going in ninth on the list of batsmen, and W. W. Read tenth, the side may be safely estimated to be as strong in batting as any that has ever played together. The bowling, on the other hand, did not stand out in quite such overwhelming strength, although Peate, Ulyett, A. G. Steel, Barnes, and Barlow are a by no means contemptible selection. On the whole year's performances in batting, Murdoch once more emphasised his superiority, with an average of 30 per innings, 1.7 in advance of his next competitor, while most of the older hands, in addition to Scott, came out on the list with good figures.

Spofforth's bowling was if possible even more successful than before—216 wickets, with an average of 12 runs per wicket; with Palmer second, with 132 wickets for an average of 16 runs. These two, with Boyle and Giffen, made up an attack strong at all points.

Eighteen matches won and seven lost does not compare too favourably with the figures of the 1882 eleven, and this difference was, we think, exactly to be accounted for by the slight change for the worse in the alteration made in the old eleven by the substitution of the four new men before alluded to.

Although their successes had possibly not quite equalled those of 1882, the four players who had not been able to come to England were still in as good form as ever, and Australian cricket at this time was still at about its highest point. No real symptoms of that gradual decline which lasted up to 1894 had commenced to show themselves before about 1885-86.

In the winter of 1884 another strong lot of professionals under Alfred Shaw visited Australia, and an unfortunate dispute with the lately-returned Australian eleven deprived most of the chief matches of their representative character, as the members of the Australian eleven refused to play in them. However, towards the end of the tour matters were smoothed over, and three matches were played against Australia's full strength. The first, a very fine struggle, was won by Australia by 7 runs, the second by the same side by eight wickets, and the third by the Englishmen by an innings and 98 runs. The professionals were a very strong side at all points of the game, and Barnes greatly distinguished himself by heading both batting and bowling averages, sharing the batting honours with Shrewsbury and Bates, while the bowling was very equally distributed among six well-known names, Barnes, Bates, Flowers, Attewell, Ulyett, and Peel.

The 1886 Australian eleven in England furnished some names new to English grounds, and for the first time Evans was able to find the time for the journey. As it turned out, however, his great reputation would have been better cared for if he had not been brought over for the first time when his powers were decidedly on the wane, and both in batting and bowling he was practically a failure. Jarvis appears as a wicket-keeper, and a very able colleague to Blackham he has always proved himself, besides being at times useful with the bat. J. Trumble, W. Bruce, and M'Ilwraith are the other new names, and of these, Bruce alone has made much mark in first-class cricket,—a beautiful fieldsman and thrower, and a pretty, hard-hitting, left-handed batsman, but one who has never quite succeeded in doing himself full justice on English grounds.

The same signs of deterioration that were observable in the 1884 eleven, as compared with that of 1882, were now more strongly pronounced. The new men were quite unable to adequately replace Murdoch, Macdonnell, Bannerman, Massie, Horan, and Boyle, while, to add to their misfortunes, Spofforth met with a severe accident which crippled him for some time, and never allowed him to again reach his proper form during the tour. On the other hand, their English opponents could command a very strong side, and in place of the dearth of fine new players which the Australians were experiencing, found ready to hand several younger players of great promise. The days of Lohmann, Briggs, and Stoddart were commencing, names that were destined to furnish a difficult nut for Australians to crack for many a day. The older men too on the English side were all at the best period of their play, and Grace, Shrewsbury, Read, and Steel could hardly fail to put up a big score among them on any given occasion. The only cheerful feature of a dismal record, in which the nine victories could only claim a narrow lead of one over the eight defeats, was the fine all-round form of Giffen. This great player, now at the top of his game, headed both batting and bowling averages, and was to be from this time a tower of strength to Australian cricket. Spofforth's unfortunate accident came at a time when there seemed every likelihood of his being quite as successful as ever, but from that time to the end of the tour his bowling powers seemed to have temporarily deserted him, and that alone was a disaster to the side of the very first magnitude. Garrett and Palmer still continued to do yeoman service in bowling, although rather more expensive than formerly, and both S. Jones and Scott gave some fine batting displays.

Of the three matches against England, the first was won by England by the small margin of four wickets, and each of the other two in one innings. Fortune had indeed deserted our Australian friends for the moment, and, worst of all, the absence of promising young players gave no hope for the immediate future. Yet, if we consider for a moment how comparatively small had been the amount of first-class cricket hitherto played in Australia, we may well rather wonder at the remarkable brilliancy of the players sent to us up to this time, than that they should now find some difficulty in replacing them.

Without making invidious distinctions, it may be safely asserted that in these last two Australian elevens of 1884 and 1886, the loss of Murdoch's captaincy was severely felt, as he always seemed to have the happy knack of keeping his team well in hand and up to the highest standard of their play.

Once more in 1886 did a strong team of professionals go to Australia under the indefatigable Shaw and Shrewsbury. Although beaten twice by New South Wales, they won four matches out of five against representative Australian elevens, the other being drawn, no mean achievement. The days of Turner and Ferris were beginning, and the former was now rapidly becoming one of the great bowlers of the day. A beautifully easy delivery and great power of pace, combined with a quickness of break back that baffled the strongest defence, were the characteristics of this fine cricketer's style. Ferris, although not so attractive in his methods, made an excellent colleague in their bowling partnership, with his steady left-handed deliveries.

Lyons for the first time appears among the representative Australian players. Very big and powerful, he proved a worthy successor to the great hitters of the earlier Australian elevens, and some of his hitting, performed with little apparent effort and without moving the feet, was a wonderful exhibition of sheer muscular force of arm. Giffen's loss from illness was a great blow to the Australians, and some of the older bowlers were now losing something of their skill. On the other side, the English bowling was very strong, with Lohmann and Briggs to lead it, and Shrewsbury at the top of his form in batting.

So popular had these Australian tours now become that in the winter of 1887-88 two separate English elevens visited Australia, one under G. F. Vernon, and the other under Shrewsbury. This division of forces, which was for many reasons to be regretted, did not appear to materially affect their chances of success, as the teams lost only two or three matches between them. H. Trott and H. Trumble were prominently seen for the first time this season, and were both destined to take a very leading part in the games of the next few years. Trumble as a bowler is probably now second to none, making admirable use of his great height, and exercising the best of judgment in his admixture of different paces and flights. Trott, an excellent batsman and useful change bowler, was always a useful man on the side, but it has been his fine judgment as captain that has proved him to be so invaluable a member of it.

The representatives of Australia were met three times by Shrewsbury's eleven, and twice by Vernon's, and all these five matches ended in English success—crushing evidence of the now seriously deteriorated form of the Australians. Shrewsbury and W. W. Read gave many fine exhibitions of batting, and came out more than 25 points ahead of their nearest competitors in the batting list. Lohmann and Briggs for Shrewsbury's side, and Attewell and Peel for Vernon's, did most of the bowling with conspicuous success.

The 1890 Australian eleven for England furnished a surprise in the return of Murdoch to the headship of affairs, and, in spite of some obvious disadvantages of increasing age and weight, his form was once more able to place him at the head of the batting averages. First of a rather moderate lot must be the estimate of this performance, and only Barrett besides himself was able to claim an average of over 20, his and Barrett's being 23 and 22 respectively. Barrett, here for the first time, was a left-handed bat with dogged powers of defence, highly uninteresting to watch. Burn, the Tasmanian, a batsman of some reputation, did not show to much advantage over here, and Walters, a powerful Victorian, who had proved a great run-getter in Australia for some years, seemed quite unable to accommodate himself to altered conditions. S. E. Gregory appears for the first time, and at once made a name for himself by his wonderful fielding and throwing in from cover-point or mid-off. The powers of batting which were to make him so useful a member of most of the Australian elevens of the next few years were not yet much in evidence. The most of the bowling was as before entirely thrown on the shoulders of the undaunted pair, Turner and Ferris, and most admirably did they acquit themselves. 215 wickets for an average of 12 and 215 wickets for an average of 13 are figures that speak eloquently of a hard season's work well performed. Charlton and Trumble were their assistants nearest in point of performance, but Trumble, although at that time a steady persevering bowler, had not yet acquired sufficient mastery of break and pace to be really dangerous. For the first time the losses of the team, sixteen, exceed the victories, thirteen, a terrible falling-off from the successes of ten years ago. Three matches were arranged against the full strength of England, but only the first two were played, both won by England, by seven wickets and two wickets respectively, the third match being abandoned through rain. It was said, not untruthfully, that these two narrow defeats against strong English sides, especially the latter of the two, conferred more credit on the Australians than any other of their performances, but an eleven can hardly be congratulated that has such a criticism as its chief recommendation.

In the winter of 1891-92 quite a new plan was carried out, Lord Sheffield collecting and taking out a strong English eleven, including once more the veteran "W. G.," Stoddart, and other fine players. The eleven, to be really representative of England's strength, would have required some additions to the batting, but Grace, Stoddart, M. Read, and Abel made at all events a strong backbone to the defence, and the bowling was well up to the highest mark in the hands of Briggs, Lohmann, Attewell, and Peel. Three matches were played against combined Australia, the first two being lost by 55 and 72 runs, and the third won easily in one innings. Of this last match, however, it should be said that the two sides batted under quite unequal conditions, the English on a hard dry wicket, and the Australians on one spoilt by rain. Lyons, Bannerman, and Bruce all did excellent service in batting, and Lyons' second innings of 134 in the Sydney match was a very fine display of hitting. Australian bowling had suffered considerably from the absence in England of Ferris, and Turner, although still about the best Australian bowler, was hardly so deadly as formerly. Grace was able to show his Australian admirers that the eighteen years that had elapsed since his last visit had little diminished his marvellous skill, and his average of 44 in eleven-a-side matches brought him easily to the top, Abel, Stoddart, and M. Read all coming out with good figures.

The improved form of the Australians this season added much to the interest which was felt in the 1893 Australian eleven, who came, moreover, as a thoroughly representative side, no other Australian cricketer, except possibly Moses, having any real claim for selection. An advance on the form of the last few years they certainly exhibited, but, although the quality of the cricket opposed to them was certainly of great merit, the summed-up results of the tour, eighteen matches won to ten lost, cannot be said to show conclusively that all the lost ground had yet been made up.

The season of 1893 was exceptionally sunny and fine, so that many more hard wickets were played on than in an average English summer. The strain on the bowlers of a travelling eleven was accordingly severe, and Turner was not able to preserve the unassailed position of superiority hitherto held by him. On the hard wickets G. Giffen was perhaps the best bowler of the side, and he is said to have not unreasonably complained of the invariable regularity with which his bowling was made use of on the hard wickets, while, on the more difficult wickets, the other bowlers were able to dispose of their more easily conquered victims.

A great improvement is to observed in Trumble both in batting and bowling, and he had now reached a formidable degree of power in both departments of the game. Graham made a most promising *début* as a bat and fine out-field; indeed, his batting was quite one of the features of the tour. Another pair of batsmen of most unequal appearance and batting methods were also very successful, Lyons and A. Bannerman, who generally went in first together. Some of Lyons' hitting ranks high among the recorded feats of big hitting, and Bannerman's dogged defence was never more usefully employed during his long career. G. H. Trott, too, and G. Giffen were both generally useful with the bat, and the eleven throughout showed a higher level of batting power than had been seen for some years.

If we compare this eleven with the strong years of 1882 and 1884, we should say that the 1893 team would naturally suffer in the absence of Murdoch at his best, and in the bowling falling somewhat below the standard of that of the four great bowlers of that day, Turner not being at his best and Trumble not quite attained to his full powers.

The English representatives of this year were of great strength. Grace, Shrewsbury, Stoddart, Gunn, Jackson, A. Ward, W. W. Read, all in fine form, made an immensely strong batting combination, while an era of great fast bowlers was arising, with Richardson, Mold, and Lockwood all now coming to the full possession of their great powers, and the slow bowling in the safe and capable hands of Briggs and Peel. It is doubtful if in the whole history of English cricket three such exceptionally fine fast bowlers as these ever flourished at the same time, and the bowling of one or other of them influenced the play of most of the great matches for some years at this time.

Only one of the three matches against England was played to a finish, and that resulted in a one-innings victory for England. The other two both ended in draws none too favourable to the chances of an Australian victory.

Many fine innings were played by the chief English players during these matches, while Graham with 107 at Lord's and Trott with 92 at the Oval did great things for the Australians.

A great drawback to Australian success in a summer so favourable to hard wickets was the absence of a reliable fast bowler. The days of E. Jones were now soon to begin, and had he been available at this time, a great addition to the all-round strength would have been realised. The unusual wealth of bowlers of this description in the English elevens at this time made this weakness especially noticeable.

AN ELEVEN OF MISS WICKETS.

And now, having traced in somewhat cursory fashion the ups and downs of Australian *v.* English cricket through some thirty-two years of its earlier existence, we leave the history of its further development at a time when the present generation of Australian players are beginning to make their appearance. The process of development between the days of 1861 and the date of the first Australian eleven, 1878, seems to have been gradual and steady. With the arrival of that notable eleven were apparent great possibilities in the future, and, quicker even than could have been thought possible, came the rapid progress, until the culminating point of 1882 and 1884 was reached. From that time came the curiously steady and disappointing decline, till, as we have lately seen, the 1893 team once more gave promise that the ten lean years were over, and a new era of prosperity about to begin. Right up to the present day Australians were now to show themselves fully equal to meeting our very best on even terms both here and in the Colonies.

How profoundly this interchange of cricketing visits has influenced the course of cricket in England can hardly be too much insisted upon. Without them a representative English eleven would have never been seen in the field at all, and how great a loss this fact alone would have been to the cricketing world, both of players and spectators, can hardly be overstated.

That our Australian cousins should so soon have been able to tackle us on even terms, in spite of their vastly smaller population and their comparatively small number of first-class matches, must always be a somewhat humbling problem for our cricketing philosophers. Certainly they have the advantage of a longer cricketing season, and a greater likelihood of finding the weather sufficiently fine to ensure their cricket being played on good wickets. In this last factor we may probably find the key to the whole matter, and, favourable conditions being their normal experience, we may always look with confidence to them for a very high level of play, and one that will tax to the utmost the capacity of our best players.

CHAPTER IX

ENGLISH AND AUSTRALIAN CRICKET FROM 1894 TO 1902 BY A. C. MACLAREN

In the autumn of 1894 Mr. A. E. Stoddart, acting upon the invitation from the New South Wales and Victorian Cricket Association, sailed for Australia, with a side composed of the following players: A. E. Stoddart, F. G. J. Ford, H. Philipson, L. H. Gay, A. C. Maclaren, T. Richardson, W. Brockwell, W. Lockwood, A. Ward, J. Briggs, R. Peel, J. T. Brown, and W. Humphreys. In the selection of his team Mr. Stoddart gave general satisfaction, although some well-known names were missing, which was not surprising, since it is impossible for all who are invited to see their way to leave home for seven months of the year. If there was a weak spot in the team, it was generally admitted to lie in the batting; yet, as events proved, the bowling was the more unreliable of the two. It should not be forgotten, however, that bowlers cannot possibly be expected to come out with the same figures as on our English wickets; and in the same way, it is only reasonable to expect our batsmen to do even better than on our home wickets, which certainly do not come up to those of Australia, where the climate can be depended upon. L. H. Gay, whose performances at Cambridge were of such excellence that the English skipper invited him without ever having had the opportunity of seeing him perform behind the wickets, kept so much below his form, at the outset of the tour, that the second string, H. Philipson, took his place, and with such excellent results that the old Cantab never secured a place in the team at all. The wicket-keeping of H. Philipson had not a little to do with our winning the rubber. The tour opened none too auspiciously, since we went down before South Australia, our first big engagement; but too much importance ought never to be attached to the opening game, owing to those who have not previously visited Australia being wholly unaccustomed to the great glare of Adelaide, and to the fast pace of the wicket. Again, it should not be forgotten that the captain, without wishing to jeopardise his chance of a win, distributes his bowling as equally as he can, since there are but two matches before the first test match takes place, and the men who are not bowling their length in these early games are given longer turns with the ball than they would have in a test match. Thus, when a man is found to be in form, not much use is made of him, unless the game appears to take a turn against his side; and the necessary amount of trundling meted out to those out of form may have been the means of keeping off the star bowler too long. The Australians, when touring in England, work on very similar lines, to enable them to get the side as well balanced as possible for the test matches, which is sufficient to prevent them from quite winning one or two of the early games. In our first innings at Adelaide, no fault could be found with our batting, since Lockwood, Ford, Ward, Stoddart, Briggs, and Gay all scored from 38 to 66, whilst Brown scored 113 out of a total of 477. Our opponents replied with 338, Darling, whose first big match it was, contributing a fine innings of 117, whilst Clem Hill also made his bow to the public, being sent in to bat No. 10, and scoring 20 runs. Richardson, who never got his length, since he kept over-pitching the ball, was bowled a great deal, which was only natural, his one wicket costing 83 runs, whilst Peel, as a contrast, took five wickets for 69; Lockwood had 70 knocked off him without taking a wicket, and Briggs 74 for two wickets, whilst Humphreys took two for 62. But in regard to the last-named, it was apparent to all that he would do little or no good in the first-class matches, since the Australians treated him with the greatest respect, refusing absolutely to be drawn; thus the out-fields had little or nothing to do, and singles and twos, chiefly by placing, were the result. It caused us no surprise when our captain decided to leave him out in the eleven-a-side matches. That Humphreys was past his prime, I for one will not admit, for his bowling was as good as anything he showed us at home; but, with only three days to finish a game, it is not surprising that our players, for the most part, played a free game when pitted against him, whilst the Australians preferred to take no liberties when such were unnecessary, owing to the games being played to a finish in their own country. To these altered conditions of the game do I attribute the failure of the lob bowler, for he used his head well, and his fieldsmen, upon whom a lob bowler must depend, were all that he could have wished. During our tour it was very evident that our opponents intended to do little or no hitting, with one or two exceptions, and I am of opinion that their policy is the best; indeed, with the exception of hitting in the air for the purpose of keeping a man in the out-field, I would have none of it, and would never wish to see any member of my side attempt the same, excepting always the hitter of the Jessop or Ford type. It had very nearly escaped my memory that Humphreys carried all before him in the up-country or picnic matches, the locals for the most part attempting to hit him out of the ground, with disastrous results so far as they were concerned. To return to the Adelaide match, our batting failed hopelessly in the second innings, although the wicket played well right up to the finish, our opponents being left with 226 to win, and obtaining the same for the loss of four men, Reedman, of somewhat awkward style, scoring 83 of the number. Journeying on to Melbourne, we were more successful, for, always having a bit the best of matters, we eventually won by 145. The batting was rather uneven, for Stoddart, Peel, and myself scored no fewer than 350 out of 416. A. E. Trott bowled far and away the best of our opponents, taking six for 103; whereas C. M'Leod, of whom much was expected, could claim but two victims for 89 runs. Beyond his length, there was little in his deliveries, although later in the tour he bowled a ball which went away with his arm, and which required very careful watching. Our opponents replied with a total of 306, Harry Trott coming out best with a score of 70; but there was nothing which struck us very much in regard to the batting of our opponents in this innings. Peel did what little he had to do with the ball very well, taking three for 27, and Briggs, who had a long turn, came out with the satisfactory analysis of five for 97. Richardson, however, was far from himself yet, so far as his bowling was concerned, but I can well remember dropping two easy catches off his bowling at cover-point, and I was not the only culprit. The fast bowler's later successes only gave us a further proof, if any was needed, of what determination and stamina he was possessed. In our second innings, Stoddart, 78, again was seen at his best, with Briggs 43, and Peel 165. C. M'Leod came out with the best bowling figures, taking four for 71. When the Victorians went in to bat, Peel, five for 73, and Briggs, three for 95, were too much for them. H. Trott, 63, and R. M'Leod, 62, did best. Our first match with New South Wales resulted in a very easy win for us, after Iredale, in the first innings, proved himself well worthy of a place in the forthcoming test match, by scoring 133 in his best style. The batting of our opponents was very laborious, the total of 293 taking a long time to compile, Peel bowling no fewer than forty-seven overs for 75 runs and three wickets. Humphreys had one more trial, but without success. Our total of 394 was made up of three big innings from Brown, 117, Stoddart, 79, and Brockwell, 81 run out, the latter playing a beautiful innings. In this match Howell astonished all by taking five wickets for 44, a very fine performance, on that excellent wicket at Sydney. C. T. B. Turner, on the other hand, was far from successful, taking but one wicket for 100 runs, and on the face of this performance it would have been better to have played the younger man in the following week, as events proved. On going in a second time, Gregory was the only one who was able to do himself justice, Peel accounting for the dismissal of our opponents, his five wickets costing 64, whilst Briggs took three for 19. Left with 81 to make, Ford soon knocked up 39, and we eventually won with eight wickets to spare.

Prior to the first test, we played one more game, and that against a very poor team representing Queensland, the chief features of the match being the return to form of T. Richardson, who had the satisfaction of taking eight wickets for 52 in the first innings and three for 11 in the second, whilst in the batting, Stoddart, 149, Ward, 107, each topped the century. The time had now arrived for the first test at Sydney, with both sides in fairly good form. Stoddart lost the toss to Trott, but so well did Richardson bowl that three wickets had fallen for 21 before the game had been in progress half an hour, Trott, Lyons, and Darling all being clean bowled by the fast bowler. On Iredale and Giffen becoming associated, the game underwent a remarkable change, no fewer than 171 being added for the fourth wicket; but had our wicket-keeper, who was standing back to the fast bowling, been in anything approaching form, no such stand for the fourth or for the ninth wicket could possibly have been made. Owing to more than one life, Giffen was batting for some four and a quarter hours, his cricket being marked by stolid defence. Iredale played a far more attractive game, his cutting and driving on the off side being excellent. After Giffen's departure, wickets fell with fair regularity until Blackham joined Gregory, whose cricket throughout was of very high order, his cutting, glancing to leg, and hooking of any short ball being a treat to witness. For an innings of 201, the chances were few and far between, and it will always stand out as one of the best innings ever played in a test match. Blackham too played a great game for his 74, which went a long way towards the making up of so big a total as 586. Of our bowlers, Richardson did really well in taking five wickets for 181, considering how many catches were dropped off his bowling. Peel, without bowling badly, certainly was disappointing, his two wickets costing 140 runs. Against the huge total of our opponents, we replied with 325, Ward 75, Briggs 57, Brockwell 49, and Gay 33, being our chief scorers, whilst Giffen certainly bowled best of our opponents, keeping a perfect length throughout and using his head well. His four wickets cost 75 runs only, and bowling, as he did, forty-three overs after scoring 161, the performance was all the more remarkable. Following on, as so often happens, we did better at the second attempt, Ward again playing a splendid innings of 117, and being well backed up by Brown, Briggs, Ford, and Stoddart. Our total of 437 was a good performance under the circumstances. Giffen, acting captain in the absence of Blackham, who had unfortunately damaged his thumb at the close of our innings of 325, had a very long bowl, his analysis reading, 75 overs, 25 maidens, 164 runs, 4 wickets; yet it could not be urged that he bowled himself too much, since he always looked more like wickets than any other bowler. If any one might have been used a little more, that man was H. Trott, whose style was so different from that of the other bowlers. With 177 left to get to win, it was expected that our opponents would knock off the runs on the evening of the fifth day, but so slowly did they play that 64 were still required when stumps were pulled up for the day. Considering that heavy clouds were seen on the horizon and that Richardson had to leave the field after bowling a few overs, owing to having contracted a chill, it was all the more surprising that Giffen and Trott should have played in such pottering fashion on the fifth evening; and, without any exaggeration, no forcing tactics were necessary to enable the Australians to get the runs that evening. At the close of play on the fifth day, 113 runs had been scored for the loss of but two wickets; then, owing to very heavy rains in the night, the wicket was wellnigh unplayable on the last morning, with the result that Peel and Briggs were too much for our opponents, the last eight men being sent back for 53, leaving us with a margin of 10 runs. Peel and Briggs were seen at their very best at the close, when the fates favoured us; but small as the total was, it would have been still less had not I, and later Brown, each missed a catch. Against these mistakes, however, there was an exceptionally fine catch by Brockwell, which sent back Darling, and which had as much as anything to do with our victory.

The second test match at Melbourne resulted in another victory for us by a majority of 94 runs, after our opponents had won the toss and decided to put us in to bat. With such bowlers as Turner and Trumble against us, on a difficult wicket, it was not surprising that our total was a poor one, the whole side being sent back for 75. Turner took five wickets for 32, whilst Trumble secured three for 17, after Coningham had commenced the attack and had quickly got rid of two of the first batsmen. As often happens, the wicket dried at a great pace, with the result that we were bound to get wickets quickly on the afternoon of the first day's play, if we were to hold any chance of winning, since it was patent to all that the wicket would be perfect on the following morning. Tom Richardson, thoroughly grasping the situation, fairly revelled in the importance of the occasion, taking five wickets for 57, and those good wickets were captured on a much-improved pitch. This fine performance on the part of the fast bowler enabled us, in the place of our opponents, to bat on a good wicket next day, with the result that our captain fairly excelled himself by scoring the huge total of 173, exercising much self-restraint throughout his long stay at the crease; and thanks to this fine display, and to the general consistency of the batting, we totalled 475. When our opponents went to the wickets for the last time, so well did Trott and Giffen play that 190 was on the board for the loss of but one batsman. At this stage of the game a wise move on the part of Stoddart, in handing the ball to Brockwell, brought about an extraordinary change, Giffen being easily taken at point in attempting to play a ball to leg which went away with the bowler's arm, and immediately afterwards Trott, who had played capital cricket for 95, being very well caught and bowled low down by the same bowler, Brockwell. With the exception of Bruce, who hit freely for 54, no other batsman withstood the attack of Peel and Brockwell, a victory for us resulting. In regard to this match, I have always thought that for downright good cricket it was not to be beaten. The wonderful bowling of Richardson in the first innings, together with that short, sharp piece of work on the part of Brockwell, will ever be dear to our memory, when the fine batting of Trott and Giffen seemed almost certain to reap the reward of a win for the Colonials; nor will it be possible to forget the great effort on the part of our captain, whose long innings never lacked sparkle, even if the importance of the occasion demanded all his patience.

The third test match, at Adelaide, was disappointing from a spectator's point of view, since on a perfect wicket our opponents were dismissed for 238, of which number no fewer than 79 were made by the last two men, A. Trott and Galloway, whilst our effort resulted in the paltry total of 124, the wicket for both teams being in a good run-getting condition. On going to the wickets a second time, our opponents played in something approaching their proper form, scoring 411, Iredale claiming 140, a very fine innings, whilst A. Trott again carried his bat for 72. Our second venture proved no better than the first, the whole side being sent back for 143, A. Trott meeting with extraordinary success in taking eight wickets for 43; and seldom, if ever, has any one met with such success as did the younger Trott with bat and ball in this test match. Our failure was due, to a very great extent, to the excessive heat, which deprived us of all chance of a good night's rest throughout the match, but at the time the match was played I have no hesitation in giving it as my opinion that our opponents were considerably the better team, and thoroughly deserved their victory.

Curiously enough, the fourth test match, at Sydney, like the first game, was spoilt by rain, and on this occasion the Australians extricated themselves from a very awkward position as only good men can.

From a Drawing by N. Wanostrocht.
THE HON. SPENCER PONSONBY.
(Right Hon. Sir Spencer Ponsonby-Fane, G.C.B.)

On winning the toss, Stoddart decided to put his opponents in first, a move which we, to a man, considered the right one, and up to a certain point all went very well, six of our opponents having been sent back for 51. Then, however, an extraordinary exhibition of forcing tactics at the outset, to be followed by more careful play, on the part of Graham, entirely altered the aspect of affairs, no fewer than 284 being on the board at the close of the innings, A. Trott once again playing admirable cricket for 86 not out. When the game was resumed on Monday, there had been so much rain overnight that the wicket was quite unplayable, and instead of having the firm wicket we had expected to bat upon, we found the pitch to be impossible, with the result that we were dismissed twice for the small totals of 65 and 72, Turner and Giffen doing what they liked with the ball. Had Graham been dismissed cheaply, we would undoubtedly have batted for the last two hours of the first day, the only occasion of the wicket being in favour of run-getting throughout the match. In that case we should very likely have won, since our opponents would have had a bad wicket for their second strike. In my opinion, Graham's performance in scoring 105 was one of the finest things that have ever happened in test matches, coming in as he did when the wicket was at its worst, and going right out to the bowling from the commencement of his innings, hitting to all parts of the ground, until the wicket gradually improved, when he settled down to a sounder game; nor should A. Trott's fine score be overlooked, although the wicket then had improved.

The final test game, at Melbourne, which was to decide the rubber, was one of the very best fights in which I have taken part. On winning the toss the Australians certainly gained an advantage, for the wicket was in perfect condition for long scores, and thanks to consistent scoring throughout the team, the good total of 434 was run up against us, to which number Darling 74, Gregory 70, and Giffen 57, were the chief contributors. Considering that H. Trott also made 42, and that several others got going, it was perhaps astonishing that more runs were not obtained, but Peel, Richardson, and Briggs all kept pegging away in their best style, and few runs were given away. Our start was not too good, four wickets being down for some 120 runs; Stoddart alone, in scoring 68, playing up to form. On Peel joining me, 162 were added for the fifth wicket, a stand which caused it to be anybody's game. Unfortunately, the tail end did little, and we finished the innings 29 runs to the bad. Of the Australian bowling, H. Trott did far better than any other bowler, his four wickets costing 71 runs only, and I have always thought that had he bowled more in the tests there would have been a different tale to tell about these games. Turner might have been very useful, and his exclusion caused a lot of criticism at the time, and rightly so, too, we having the greatest respect for him as a bowler. Still, it is very easy to be wise after the event. In our opponents' second innings, wickets were always falling with fair regularity, thanks to Richardson putting in some sterling work, whilst Peel kept them playing. Darling, Giffen, and H. Trott, all of whom had done very well in the first innings, again played well, but the rest were very disappointing from a Colonial point of view, and the fact that a dust-storm made itself felt was scarcely a good enough excuse to account for the want of success on the part of so many. Richardson's performance in taking six wickets for 104 was one of which he might well feel proud, but to thoroughly appreciate such work one should be on the spot, for there is a certain indescribable charm in watching such a man. C. T. B. Turner and J. T. Hearne, in the same manner, have always had their admirers. With 297 left for us to get to win, our task was no light one for a fourth innings, and it became no easier when Brockwell was sent back after scoring 5. Next morning H. Trott succeeded in getting the skipper out l.b.w. from the first ball bowled, and our position became desperate. As all the cricketing world knows, Brown and Ward now made their never-to-be-forgotten stand, the first-named from the commencement of his innings going for the bowling in a manner which had seldom, if ever, been seen before on the Melbourne ground. Driving along the ground and over the in-fields' heads, together with the short-arm hook of any ball at all on the short side, were his chief methods of scoring, and he treated all bowlers alike. Ward in the meantime was playing his usual patient game, without failing to score whenever opportunity presented itself, and his effort was second only to Brown's. Not until he had scored 140 was Brown sent back, and, disappointed as the spectators must have been, yet they could not resist giving him a splendid reception on his return to the pavilion. Ward, too, was equally well received when he had the misfortune to be sent back only 7 short of the century. With 30 odd runs only left to get to win, Peel and myself were together when the number had been scored. This was certainly one of the grandest matches ever witnessed, and for downright good cricket from both teams I place it in front of all the test matches in which I have taken part. If we had any luck in the game, it was in the Scotch mist on the last day of the match, which helped to put the dust together on the pitch, and enabled the wicket to play as well as it did on the first morning of the game. It was remarked by not a few at the time that seldom did the best batsmen all come so well out of the bag together on such an important occasion, and it certainly was exceptional that the five men in form should have scored as follows—the two innings being added together: Ward 125, Brown 170, Stoddart 79, Peel 88 for once out, and myself 140 once out.

I have gone rather fully into details in regard to the 1894-95 tour in Australia, for the purpose of laying the foundation of my work. In 1896 it was the turn of our opponents to visit our shores, and H. Trott brought over a far better combination than many expected after reading the criticisms of some of the experts in Australia. It has always remained a mystery to me and many others why A. E. Trott was left behind, after all his good work against us in the Colonies, for he was in those days unquestionably a greater player than in any one of his English seasons' cricket. The team did a great deal better than expected, for not a single county defeated them, although two out of the three test matches went against them. In H. Trott they had as fine a leader as ever captained an Australian, or, for that matter, any other team; never missing an opportunity throughout the many phases of the game, he had his men well in hand from the commencement of the tour, and his quiet manner, together with a never-ruffled temper, won him the esteem and respect of opponents and comrades alike; indeed, it is no exaggeration to say that no team from Australia ever pulled quite so well together as did that of H. Trott. Possibly Trott's excellence as a captain lay in the fact that he always appeared to know exactly what bowler to use against each batsman, added to which, he never gave batsmen any presents of runs by having a fieldsman in a useless position. Although there was nothing very startling about the batting, yet it was very well balanced, no fewer than seven of the side obtaining over 1000 runs, in a season when the wickets in August were most difficult. Gregory, Darling, Hill, Iredale, Trott, and Giffen all had their admirers, whilst Kelly kept wicket in his best form throughout a long and trying tour; and but for coming immediately after such an artist as Blackham, more notice might have been taken of his excellent work. The variety of the bowling had not a little to do with the success of the team, always remembering how well it was handled, whilst we must not lose sight of the fact that each fieldsman had every confidence in the bowler, occupying at times the most daring positions under the very nose of the batsman, which often resulted in the downfall of a wicket, without the said fieldsman ever running much risk of an accident. The simple reason was that the bowler always knew what his men were working for, and never gave them away by an overtossed or by a short-pitched ball. The Australians, generally speaking, have always appeared to me to know better than we do how a batsman is the most likely to be defeated, and on their side there is more of that mutual understanding between bowler and fieldsmen that is so valuable. M'Kibbin, Trumble, Jones, and Giffen all took over 100 wickets, and if the first-named came out with the best analysis, Trumble took far more wickets, and could boast of never having a bad day, for if the wicket was suitable for small scoring, he never failed to do all that was asked of him, and if I had to name one for excellence of length, I should without hesitation name Trumble of all bowlers it has been my pleasure to see or play against. Jones's pace secured for him many wickets, and if some expressed a view that his action was, to say the least, doubtful, there were others who considered his bowling on this tour fair, and I certainly never saw anything wrong on the occasions on which I played against him in England. Giffen had the distinction of scoring 1000 runs and taking 117 wickets, a great achievement, considering the many times he has visited us. In fielding the team more than held their own, for Gregory at cover was always a treat to watch, whilst Iredale at the time had no superior in the out-field, and Hill and Darling possessed the safest of safe hands, in whatsoever position they were fielding. Added to this list of honour must be the name of Jones, who did many brilliant things at mid-off. In regard to returning the ball to the wicket from any part of the field, the Australians have always, since I have known them, given us a long start, the ball being returned more accurately and, what is equally important, more swiftly. We naturally have our shining lights in this respect, but as a team the Colonials show themselves off far better than do we in the field. In regard to the test matches, the first of the series, which was played at Lord's, was rather peculiar, since our visitors, playing a long way below their proper form, were dismissed for 53 on a wicket which could have had little the matter with it, after the total of 292 made against them. Richardson and Lohmann were the two bowlers to carry all before them, but the aversion the Australians have always had to the ground at headquarters may have had not a little to do with the poor display of their batsmen. On our batsmen going to the wickets, those two sterling veterans, W. G. Grace and Robert Abel, after the dismissal of Stoddart, played so finely that the game appeared to be at our mercy; but the tail end did not do quite so well as expected, and the total of 292 was the result.

There was nothing in the bowling of the Australians worth commenting upon. It was in the second innings that our visitors showed such good form, when the game appeared too far gone to give them any chance of a win. All the more credit then to the captain and Gregory for their great stand of 221, which caused their side to have a lead of 44 runs with six wickets to fall after the dismissal of Gregory; and had the end batsmen taken as much getting out as usual, it is quite possible that they would have won, since there was a lot of rain on the second evening of the match. As it was, many of our supporters were dubious as to the result when we were set 111 to get to win, on a wicket which had been affected by rain. The runs, however, were hit off for the loss of four batsmen, thanks chiefly to Stoddart and Brown; but had all the chances been accepted, there is no doubt that the game would have been closer. Every one was delighted with the fine batting of Trott and Gregory, many being of opinion that it was the finest exhibition ever witnessed in a test match; the Englishmen, however, were very confident that Trott was caught by Hayward with his score at 61. This was the occasion of the crowd encroaching on the field of play, which handicapped our opponents not a little. The second test, at Manchester, resulted in a meritorious win for the Australians, after they had won the toss, and always appeared to hold the trump card in a game which was played throughout on a perfect wicket—in fact, a wicket after the heart of the Colonials. Thanks to Iredale, who started very shakily, but later played a beautiful innings, and Giffen, who played his usual game of soundness, a total of 412 was run up against us. Iredale played a fine game for his side in compiling 108, most of his runs being obtained by crisp cutting and driving on the off side. With the exception of Trott, no one else bothered us much, in spite of the big total made against us. Richardson put in some of his best work in obtaining seven wickets for 168, bowling as he did no fewer than sixty-eight overs. Our batting in the first innings was as feeble as that of our opponents had been excellent, for with the exception of K. S.

Ranjitsinhji and Lilley, who scored 62 and 65 respectively, no one showed any form at all. The wickets were very equally divided amongst our opponents, of whom possibly M'Kibbin, who was left out at Lord's, bowled best. Following on, the batting of the side again failed most ignominiously, with one exception, and that was the wonderful display of K. S. Ranjitsinhji, who scored no fewer than 154, and at the finish was not out. His performance was without doubt the finest in the match, playing as he was throughout his long stay at the wicket a losing game—and every cricketer knows what that means. His cutting and leg-glancing will never be forgotten by those who were lucky enough to be there. The miserable failure of all others, excepting Stoddart, was inexplicable, since the wicket remained true throughout the game. M'Kibbin again came out with the best analysis, and had he played at Lord's, we might not have won so easily as we did. On the Australians going in to get 125 to win, so well did Richardson bowl that the runs were not hit off until seven wickets had fallen, and when No. 9 batsman, in the shape of J. Kelly, joined Trumble, 25 runs were still required to win. One cannot speak too highly of the coolness exhibited by both men, who came through the trying ordeal most creditably. Richardson's bowling performance in this innings will be remembered by all who can appreciate fine bowling, for, working his utmost for three solid hours, he took six wickets for 76 runs, on a wicket which remained good up to the finish, and I have always thought that this was one of the best things ever done by a bowler in a test match—all the more the pity that the combined effort of K. S. Ranjitsinhji and the Surrey express did not meet with its just reward of a win for the Old Country. The decider at the Oval naturally aroused a lot of enthusiasm, but unfortunately the weather was not propitious, a commencement not being possible until five o'clock on the first day. Our winning of the toss meant practically the winning of the game, for the pitch was in such a state of wet that it was all in favour of the batsmen, and when stumps were pulled up for the day 69 runs were on the board for the loss of W. G. Grace. Next morning the wicket was unplayable, with the result that Trumble carried all before him, taking six wickets for 59, the majority of which were made on the previous evening, when the wicket was all against bowling and fielding, and I consider our opponents were justified in criticising the action of the umpires in commencing on the first evening. So badly did our men bowl on the treacherous wicket before lunch that 70 went up with Darling and Iredale unseparated. Afterwards Jack Hearne went right through the side, taking six wickets for 41, keeping an impossible length, and making the ball do just enough without too much. Peel really was the culprit before lunch, it being the only occasion on which I ever remember him failing to do well when all was in favour of the bowler. Darling played a fine game for his score of 47, and, thanks to his and Iredale's effort, the Australians finished off their innings but 26 behind us. In our second innings Trumble again did what he liked, taking six wickets for 30, the whole side being out for 84. On the last morning of the match, with our opponents left with 111 to get to win, the pitch had dried considerably, but Hearne was always able to get enough spin on the ball to beat the bat, and the quick break was too much for the Australians. As Peel also bowled in his very best form, the result was one of the most extraordinary processions to and from the wicket by the batsmen, nine wickets being down with 17 only on the board. M'Kibbin, the last man, hit up 16, so that the total realised 44—and yet we are told that wickets are not broad enough! This match was the occasion of the professionals holding out for higher payment than £10, and then withdrawing from their position. That they had right on their side was proved by the increase of pay from that date in the test encounters, and it is not generally known that their request for higher payment was not sprung upon the Surrey committee at the very last moment. Considering the strain of these big matches upon the players, it cannot be said that they do not deserve the £20 now given to the professionals.

A CRICKET SONG.

A LYRIC OF THE CRICKET FIELD.

The second team that A. E. Stoddart took to Australia consisted of the following: A. E. Stoddart, K. S. Ranjitsinhji, J. R. Mason, N. F. Druce, A. C. Maclaren, T. Hayward, T. Richardson, J. Briggs, W. Storer, E. Wainwright, G. Hirst, J. H. Board, J. T. Hearne. On the eve of the first test, at Sydney, our troubles commenced, the trustees taking it upon themselves to postpone the match until Saturday, from Friday, the original date of the fixture. This, of course, they had no right whatsoever to do; in fact, the Melbourne Club telegraphed to the Sydney trustees that the game must take place on the original date fixed. Their sole reason for the postponement was to prevent disappointment to the up-country people, since there had been a lot of rain. We naturally were indignant at the decision, since it was made without any one being consulted on our side, and the first we heard of the postponement was during dinner on Thursday night, when one of us saw an announcement outside a public-house, to the effect that the match was put off. By putting the match off until Saturday, the trustees were making it absolutely a game of chance, just what they said they were trying to avoid, since the captain who won the toss on Saturday would undoubtedly have put his opponents in first, and, with fine weather, the wicket on Monday would have been perfect for batting, after the Sunday intervening. As it happened, the pitch was quite fit to commence at twelve o'clock on Friday, the umpires being of that opinion. There is no doubt that the alteration was made solely for the purpose of the gate, and with no intention of doing us a bad turn. Still, it would have been better had those responsible for the blunder admitted their mistake at once, instead of trying to make stupid excuses, and giving ideas to the press which were scarcely complimentary to us. Owing to a merciful providence, it rained all Saturday, and consequently got the trustees out of a mess, the match being started on Monday on a perfect batsman's wicket. Unfortunately our captain had the sad misfortune to receive a cable from home announcing the death of his mother on the Friday morning, which kept him out of all the test games, and naturally caused him to be unable to show anything approaching the brilliant form of his previous tour. The first test was an extraordinary walk-over for us, and yet we never looked like winning another game, so far as the tests were concerned, afterwards, unless we except the last game at Sydney. After Mason had been sent back cheaply, Hayward and myself stayed some considerable time together, and our stand was well followed up by Ranjitsinhji, 175, and Hirst, so much so that we totalled 551. On getting our opponents in for the last one and a half hours on the second day, Richardson and Hearne bowled so well that, after the cheap dismissal of their best batsmen, they were never able to recover their lost ground, although Trumble and M'Leod made a magnificent effort at the finish of the first innings. Following on, 314 to the bad, the Australians did far better, Darling playing a grand innings of 101, whilst Clem Hill put together 86 in his best style. The remaining batsmen played very disappointingly, with the exception of Kelly, the score reaching 408, leaving us 96 to win, which were hit off for the loss of Mason's wicket. Ranjitsinhji played a wonderful innings, considering how ill he had been, only having got out of bed on the Sunday morning, when he went for a drive. He was just able to last out the hour's batting he had on the Monday evening, and next morning played, especially towards the close of his innings, when his strength was leaving him, a regular forcing game. In the second test, at Melbourne, owing to the game being played on a new piece of turf, which the groundsman was most anxious to avoid, whatever chance we might have had was taken from us. The wicket opened out to such an extent that one could put one's fingers into the cracks on the pitch, which meant that the ball was always doing something which it had no right to do, getting up or keeping low according to the angle at which it struck the crack. The Australians were very fortunate, under the circumstances, in winning the toss and batting on a perfect wicket on the Saturday. They made such good use of their luck that 520 were scored, of which number C. M'Leod made 112, whilst Hill, Gregory, Iredale, and Trott all showed excellent form, scoring 58, 71, 89, and 79 respectively. Our bowling was thoroughly collared, and even had the wicket remained good, I do not for a moment consider we were good enough to win, after the excellent start of our opponents. Our score of 315 was very creditable. As previously explained, the heat of the sun on Saturday and Sunday caused the ground to crack, the wicket previous to the test match having been covered up from the sun's rays for a fortnight. Ranjitsinhji, Hirst, Storer, Druce, and Briggs all played well for their runs, although the ball kept getting past their defence occasionally, as was only natural. On our following on, with the wicket getting worse, we were all dismissed for 150, a small score for which we were prepared, Noble and Trumble only having to keep a length, whilst the wicket did the rest for them.

At Adelaide, the strong light of which city our men dislike as much as the Australians take exception to the bad light of Lord's, we went down before our opponents most decisively, they thoroughly outplaying us. Joe Darling opened the ball with a clipping innings of 178, his driving being very powerful throughout, and, as Hill scored 81 with him, the Adelaide people were rightly delighted with the success of their two men, the score eventually reaching 573, of which Iredale again took 84 in his approved style. Hayward and Hirst alone of our men played good cricket, the total being 278 when all were sent back, Howell doing most of the damage on an excellent pitch. Following on, we did no better, Ranjitsinhji and myself being the only two to bother our opponents, who gained a meritorious win by an innings and 13 runs, proving beyond all doubt that we beat them at Sydney before the eleven had struck form, our first test in the Colonies generally being the least difficult to win, for this reason. Noble and M'Leod divided the wickets, and in the former our opponents had unearthed a bowler of the first order. It was very evident that they were now on the top of their form, and our chances of another win in the tests were not too rosy. At Melbourne the fourth test resulted in a further easy win for our opponents, after they had commenced their innings very inauspiciously, losing six wickets for 57, when Hill and Trumble dug their side out of a nasty hole, 165 being put on for the seventh wicket. Hill played his finest innings of the season; the fact that the total reached only 323, of which his contribution was 188, speaks for itself, and it is quite possible that the South Australian was at his very best about this time. Trumble once again came to the rescue, and I cannot bring to mind any player who has so often come off at a pinch. Richardson and Hearne divided the wickets practically, and our bowlers did all that could have been expected of them. When it came to our turn to bat, every one appeared to be out of form, the total reaching 174 only. Whoever was put on to bowl, a wicket resulted, the batting being feeble in the extreme. Following on, we did very little better, as those who appeared to get going were sent back when we were commencing to hope for better things, and our opponents had no difficulty in obtaining the required number, 115, to win, losing two wickets in the process. In this match we were completely outplayed, after we had obtained a flattering start, and I have not the slightest hesitation in saying that this combination was well in front of any other against which I had played in the past, even as it was in front of the team that we met in 1901-2. Sydney appeared more to our liking than did other places, if our cricket was any criterion, for we certainly did better on this ground, which has not quite the same fiery life possessed by other Colonial grounds. In the last test our form was better, since, on winning the toss, we put together 335, and then dismissed our opponents for 96 less, Richardson putting up a capital performance by obtaining eight wickets for 94 runs. We completely broke down in our second innings, being all disposed of for 178, Trumble and Jones doing the mischief. As our opponents had 276 to get to win, the match was by no means lost, so far as we were concerned, and as we got M'Leod and Hill out at once, our hopes were raised, but Darling soon put the issue beyond doubt, hitting out most viciously from the commencement of his innings, although it should be mentioned that, with his score at 40, our fast bowler, as well as the wicket-keeper, was confident he was out l.b.w. But the umpire thought otherwise. On the other hand, Ranjitsinhji was given out l.b.w. for an appeal from point, when he was most confident he played the ball—a misfortune which, coming as it did immediately after my dismissal, had a great bearing on the result of the game. But I in no manner wish to insinuate that the umpire made a mistake in either case. At the finish our opponents won handsomely by six wickets, a very meritorious victory, once more proving, if any proof was required, that they could extricate themselves from any position, however difficult; and only a really great side is able to do such a thing with consistency. Their performances of this tour in Australia were so full of merit that I, for one, began to doubt our ability to beat this little lot in our own country, and was not slow to communicate my fears to better men than myself on my return; so that the result of the next Australian tour in England came as no surprise to most of us.

When Darling brought over the same team which defeated us in Australia, a good time, so far as their cricket was concerned, was predicted by all of us who had knowledge of their excellence in their own country; and after the first test match, played at Birmingham, it was admitted on all sides that we had not exaggerated their merits. On winning the toss in the first game, it took them a whole day to compile 252, which slow and over-careful play just cost them the match. Hill, Darling, Noble, and Gregory all played well against a not very powerful bowling combination, and more runs ought to have been made. Of our lot, Ranjitsinhji and Fry alone played good cricket, and our opponents were able to claim a lead of 55. On going to the wickets a second time, they put together 230 for eight wickets, when they declared; and but for Ranjitsinhji, who played a perfect innings in his own inimitable style, the Australians would have won, the Sussex amateur carrying his bat for 93. At Lord's there were many changes—too many, I should say; for Jessop, Townsend, Lilley, Mead, and myself took the places of W. Gunn, Storer, Hirst, J. T.

Hearne, and W. G. Grace, the latter having telegraphed for me. On winning the toss on a fast wicket, we were all out to Jones before we could turn round, with the exception of Jessop and Jackson, who made 51 and 73 respectively, the total reaching 206, a poor one on that fast wicket. Owing to Hill and Trumper, who fairly collared our bowling, our opponents collected the big total of 421 against us, the two named scoring 135 each, Trumper being left to carry his bat. Both played magnificent cricket, and with the exception of Noble, 54, no one else did anything. In our second venture we did little better, scoring 240, Hayward, Jackson, and myself alone doing anything, the wickets being divided up amongst five bowlers, thus showing the variety of attack at Darling's disposal. The 28 required to win were hit off without loss, and from this point onwards to the end of the tour our opponents preferred to play not to be beaten rather than to lay themselves out for a win, and under the existing conditions one could scarcely blame them. At Leeds, on a wet wicket, the Australians were disposed of for 172, Young bowling extremely well, but with provoking bad luck, since he beat the bat times without number without hitting the wickets. Worrall hit well for his 76, but the boundary was far too short a one, some of his mis-hits going over the heads of our out-fields. Briggs was seized with an attack after the first day's play which unfortunately kept him out of the field for more than a season, and we were much handicapped in the second innings of our opponents, when our first two bowlers required a rest. They were unable to get it, however, and Trumble and Laver pulled the match out of the fire; and if both were in difficulties at times, they played a fine game for their side. Hearne bowled in magnificent form, as also did Young. Owing to rain, there was no play on the last day, when we required 158 to win, with all our wickets to go down. Hill was unable to play any more cricket after this match, being in the hands of the doctor. At Manchester—thanks to a wonderfully sound innings on the part of Hayward, who scored 130 when things were not looking too rosy for us, an effort that was well backed up by Jackson and Lilley—we scored 372, and on our opponents going to the wickets, owing to Bradley bowling with much fire, they were cheaply dismissed for 196. Young, who was suffering from a bad knee, took four of the remaining wickets. Following on, with our bowlers literally fagged out, it was not surprising to find our opponents masters of the situation, scoring 346 for seven wickets, when they declared. Worrall, Darling, Trumper, and Noble played in their best form, the latter in particular playing a great game for his side, but a game which, owing to its slowness, was not appreciated by the large crowd, disappointed with the turn the match took. With an hour left for play, our batsmen went in to have a hit, for the sake of giving the crowd a change, and it was surprising to find so many people weighing up our chances on what took place in that last hour's play, which ought to have been ignored. This was the third drawn game out of the four matches played, and those of us who knew the manner in which that Oval wicket had been pampered with patent stuffs, etc., thought it the last ground in the world to finish a test match on in three days, with one side laying itself out not to be beaten. We compiled the huge total of 576, and as the last six men had instructions to be out in less than an hour, one might well have wondered what the score would have been had all got as many runs as possible. Hayward again played a fine innings of 137, and Jackson was at his best for 118, 185 being put up for one wicket, a record by 15 for a first-wicket stand in a test match, W. G. Grace and Scotton having held it up to that time. At the end of the day's play 435 appeared on the board for the loss of but four batsmen. Next morning, however, each player had to get out to give our bowlers a chance, if we were to win the match. Our opponents did well in scoring 352, after their somewhat trying experiences of the day previous. Gregory played a masterly innings of 117, and with his captain, who made 71, saved his side from a defeat, when nothing better than a drawn game awaited them. Lockwood, who had been more or less a cripple throughout the season, showed us all what we had missed by our inability to play him by taking seven wickets for 71 on this perfect pitch, bowling no fewer than fifty overs, a performance which caused his leg to give way again, and which prevented him from letting himself go in the second innings, when our opponents always appeared to have the game saved. But had Worrall been caught early on, it is possible we might just have got home. In the last half-hour the wicket commenced to go, but it was too late for our chance, although Rhodes in that time bowled beautifully, taking three wickets in very quick succession. At the drawing of stumps our opponents had four wickets still to fall, and were 30 runs on. So ended the tour, and out of five test matches no fewer than four were left drawn. It is not astonishing to find so many who are to-day playing for England wishing for fewer test games, and to have them played out; and yet the same order of things continues, gate-money alone, so far as can be gathered, standing in the way of a much-needed alteration in the test games.

In the autumn of 1901 the Australians honoured me with an invitation to collect a team, but owing to the action of the Yorkshire committee in not allowing their professionals to accept my invitation, the bowling question was made a most difficult one for me to tackle. Thanks to all other county committees giving me all assistance possible, a side was collected, and had one of our bowlers, in whom I had every confidence, only remained sound, it is quite possible that we might have come back victorious, for, after winning the first test at Sydney, we had the match at Adelaide three parts won when Barnes broke down at a time when the wicket had crumbled badly at one end, and when he was the only one who could hit the spot. On that occasion the two left-handers, who made all the runs, if we except a fine innings of Trumble, were the only two who could have put us down, owing to this spot being, of course, on the wrong side of the wicket for their batting, looking at it from a bowler's point of view. At Sydney we headed our opponents on the first innings in the fourth test, and in the last match, at Melbourne, we only went down by 32 runs, after having to bat on a wet wicket. That we were unable to stay our games out, especially in the later stages of the tour, was scarcely surprising, since we were practically without two of our bowlers for more than half of the time, which meant that those who were left had far more trundling than was conducive to their strength. In the first of the tests, at Sydney, thanks to a good start on our part, we ran up a total of 464, Hayward, Lilley, Braund, and myself all getting going. On our opponents going to the wickets, so well did Barnes bowl, as also Braund and Blythe, that only 168 runs were on the board when the last man was sent back. Following on, our opponents scored but 4 more than in the first innings, and we were left easy winners, Braund and Blythe bowling as well as they ever did in their lives. Before the match at Sydney commenced, Blythe unfortunately sprained his hand, but it was not until that game was finished that he really felt any pain. The leading surgeon in Australia advised rest for some considerable time, but the Kent professional thought that the hand would not suffer much, especially taking into consideration the fact that the wicket was all against long scores, so he took his chance in the second test at Melbourne. On winning the toss, I decided to put our opponents in, and had Barnes been able to bowl in the mud only half as well as he had previously done on the fast wickets, our opponents would not have scored 100. As it was, they only put together 112, but Blythe found that spinning the ball gave him all the pain which the doctor had predicted he would suffer, and Barnes bowled very short throughout, notwithstanding the fact that he took six wickets for 42, which really was not a great performance on that unplayable wicket. When our turn came to bat, our effort resulted in 61, of which Jessop claimed 27. Before the day was finished we got rid of five of our opponents in their second innings for 48, and had none the worst of the match. Next morning, however, with some of the best batsmen still to come in, Hill played on the top of his form on what was now a batsman's wicket, scoring 99 before Braund beat him, whilst Duff, who had batted out and out the best in the first innings, went one better by scoring 104 in his first test match, both players being seen quite at their top game. Had a chance been accepted, Armstrong, who helped Duff to add 120 for the last wicket, would not have received a ball. After our early wickets fell, rain made it impossible for the remaining batsmen to make a fight of it, although Tyldesley played fine cricket for his 66. It is only fair to state that, rain or no rain, our opponents always appeared to have the game safe after luncheon on the second day. Noble in our first innings took seven wickets for 17, making the ball do everything but talk, whilst his performance in the second innings was very little inferior, when he captured six for 60. Trumble, who bowled an excellent length, took the remaining wickets in both innings. In the third test, at Adelaide, a lot of runs were obtained, considering the wicket was by no means perfect; but the bowlers on both sides were not seen at their best, from various causes. Noble was suffering from a strain, and Trumble was far from himself, which had a good deal to do with our total reaching 388, out of which number Braund, who played a beautiful innings, scored 103, whilst Hayward was also at his best in compiling 90, and Quaife chipped in with a very useful 68. Our opponents replied with 321, Hill coming out best with 98, being well backed up by Trumper 65 and Gregory 55. Of our bowlers, Barnes broke down, after bowling seven overs, at a time when he looked very dangerous; but Gunn came along in great style, taking five for 76, and Braund also did well. After obtaining 200 for five wickets in our second innings, a dust-storm, which did us no good, but which brought enough rain to eventually do the wicket good, stopped play for the day. Continuing, we added another 40, Barnes being unable to bat and Trumble bowling in good form. Wanting 315 to win, our opponents, thanks to the two left-handers, who made 166 between them, and a fine effort on the part of Trumble, claimed a great victory by four wickets; but we were very unlucky in losing the services of Barnes, who on that wicket could not have helped bowling well. It should not be overlooked that the left-handers were batting on a good wicket, whereas right-handers had to face a crumbled spot outside the off stump. At Sydney we again claimed a lead on the first innings, Hayward, Tyldesley, Lilley, and myself all getting runs, whilst Saunders, Trumble, and Noble divided the wickets. On the second day Jessop, bowling at a great rate, succeeded in getting four good men caught in the slips; but Noble and Armstrong mended matters next morning. In our second innings, with a lead of 18, we went out one after the other in most surprising fashion before the bowling of Saunders, who carried all before him on a perfect pitch, our effort resulting in the paltry total of 99. Our opponents had no difficulty in making 121 for the loss of three wickets. In the last match, at Melbourne, on a difficult pitch, we disposed of our opponents for 144, Hayward and Gunn meeting with success. We replied with 189, thanks to Jessop, Braund, and Lilley, but Trumble was too much for most of us. In their second innings our opponents pulled themselves together, and with Hill and Gregory in form the total reached 255; and as more rain fell on our going to the wickets, our task was a difficult one. In the end we had to put up with a defeat by 32 runs, our total of 178 being very creditable under the circumstances, since we had much the worst of the wicket, on which Noble was seen at his best. Thus ended a tour which was not too successful from our point of view; but with the exception of one match, all the test games were very close ones, and it was admitted on all sides that no team ever fielded in more brilliant style than did ours. Jessop did some marvellous bits of work in every match, whilst Jones, Braund, Tyldesley, and Quaife all were at their best. Lilley did his work well behind the wickets, but was unfortunate in this respect, that if he made a mistake, which wicket-keepers are bound to do, it was generally a costly one.

The team which Joe Darling brought over in 1902 was, in my opinion, not quite so strong as some of us thought, although nothing like so weak as some people in Australia tried to make us believe. Possibly they had the best of the luck in regard to the weather in the big matches; but there was no getting away from the fact that whatever the fates gave them they made the very most of, never allowing a chance to slip through their fingers in any of the games in which I played against them. There was no fortune in losing the services of Trumble for the first six weeks or so of the tour, in consequence of an accident at the nets, which necessitated a free use of Noble in the bowling department in the early matches. At Lord's, too, during what little took place, they were far from themselves, as far as their health was concerned; but from that match to the finish of the tour they never looked back, and it is quite possible that the reappearance of their reliable bowler, Trumble, was a far better tonic than any of the medicines they were taking for influenza. In regard to the bowling, Darling may not have had too much, but the variety, together with the consistent good form of those bowlers at his disposal on the wet wickets, was quite sufficient to dispose of the best batsmen playing against them in all the matches of the tour. Jones could scarcely be expected to do well on the wet wickets, and naturally his figures are nothing like so good as on previous occasions. Trumble always made it as near a certainty as possible that few runs would be made against him, provided the wicket gave him the slightest assistance, thanks to his accuracy of length, together with his wonderful knowledge of each batsman pitted against him, which he used to the full, and to me he appeared to bowl almost better than ever. If Noble was not quite so consistent as previously, he can excuse himself on the ground of the extra effort required at the commencement of the tour in the absence of Trumble; but when he was to be caught at his best, as in the test at Sheffield, he carried all before him, and I still think he bowls a more difficult ball than any other bowler to-day. That Saunders was included was a very good thing for our opponents, since his great break from leg on the wet wickets made it very difficult for the batsmen to score off him, even if his length was indifferent, as was the case at Manchester in the test game, when it was impossible to get him away on the leg side of the wicket. In his case it was a triumph for the selectors, since, with one exception, his performances in Australia scarcely led one to believe that he would do so well as was the case. Howell was far from well, added to which he was the recipient of most painful news from his home, which was quite sufficient to prevent him from showing any of his old brilliance. The fielding of the team was of the greatest use to the bowlers, since mistakes were few and far between. Hill, Hopkins, and Duff, in the out-field, were very safe, whilst their return of the ball to the wicket was, as usual, most accurate and far ahead of our style. Of the others, Noble at point was very clever, and Gregory was as neat and clean in the picking up and return of the ball as ever. Joe Darling handled his team admirably throughout, whilst the entire absence of discord, together with the many denials of pleasures which one and all underwent, proved how well he was fitted for his post. Of the batsmen, Trumper stands right out by himself, and I can pay him no higher compliment than saying he has only done what I have always thought he was good enough to do. His cutting of the ball, which was always placed to beat the fieldsman at third man, was admirable, as was his hooking, chiefly by wrist work, of the short ball. His driving, too, was not the least conspicuous feature of his batting. The pace he always went at at the very start of his innings frequently demoralised the bowler, and to his rapid commencements, especially at Manchester and Sheffield, in the second innings, do I ascribe the poorness of our attack in the majority of the test games. Hill played many fine innings, but I thought he was a great deal more aggressive, for which his defence had to suffer, causing the bowlers less difficulty than used to be the case in obtaining his wicket, although I do not wish to insinuate that he is not now one of the world's greatest batsmen. Darling lost a little of his old form, although he gave us flashes of his former brilliance, as in the test match at Manchester. May be the cares of captaincy told on him slightly, at which I do not wonder. Noble was only just beginning to enjoy himself with the bat when the tour was at an end, although he made 284 against Sussex, the highest score of the season. Of the new men,

Duff proved himself to be a capital man to accompany Trumper to the wickets, being possessed of excellent defence, with a slicing sort of cut which brought him in many runs. Hopkins takes all the risks of an Englishman, being specially fond of the hook stroke, and it is safe to predict that he will continue to improve, although he would be the first to admit that, if he is to bowl, it must not be until several others have failed first. Armstrong did well all round, adopting a somewhat defensive game, with an occasional straight drive, very powerfully executed, and if he has a weak stroke it is the ball between his legs and the leg stump that he does not care about. Kelly was really excellent behind the stumps, and if occasion arose he was generally good for some runs. A great feature of his wicket-keeping was his absolute fairness of appeal; and this remark applies to the whole team. In regard to the test games I do not intend to write much, since they are all still fresh in our memory. The weather was very unsatisfactory, the two first games being drawn, whilst in the three finished games, at Sheffield, Manchester, and the Oval, rain was of no use to our chances of a win, generally managing to come at the wrong time for us; but this is all in the game. Had it remained fine, I feel very confident that three days would not have been sufficient to finish the matches; and in my opinion the addition of half an hour, which necessitated the luncheon interval being taken at 1.30, handicapped the bowler, since 4-1/4 hours were left for play afterwards—a very long spell when no interval for refreshments was allowed. A rest, however, was agreed upon later, with good results too, as the bowler generally obtained his wicket after the interval. The first test, at Birmingham, ended disappointingly, for after a very poor start on our part, which Tyldesley and the Hon. F. S. Jackson set right, we scored 376 for nine wickets, when we declared our innings closed. Tyldesley played a fine forcing game for 138, and from the time when the Hon. F. S. Jackson and he got together, everything went right for us, Hirst, Lockwood, and Rhodes all playing excellent cricket. Owing to the rain which followed our innings, our opponents had very little chance of drawing level, but no one was prepared for the poor display of their batsmen, the whole side being sent back for 36. Rhodes did what he liked with his opponents, although the ball was not turning to any great extent, as the wicket was quite on the wet side, and by no means unplayable. The Australians adopted a hitting game, but the first attempt at a drive, no matter whose it was, ended disastrously, without exception. Hirst also did well, his three wickets costing 15. Rhodes had the excellent analysis of seven wickets for 17, his bowling being very accurate, whilst he suited his pace to the wicket admirably. Owing to more rain, only half an hour more play took place, the Australians losing two wickets for 46. There is no doubt in my mind that our opponents were nowhere near their proper form at this time, and that the team without Trumble was something like cod-fish without oyster sauce. At Lord's there was another disastrous start, which righted itself, when copious rain put an end to further play. At Sheffield we had a great game. Our opponents, winning the toss, did fairly well in compiling 194, Noble making the highest score, 47, whilst Barnes, who came in for Lockwood, bowled best of our men on a wicket possessed of considerable life. It suited his style of bowling admirably, and he took six wickets for 49. Braund did what little he had to do very well, commencing by clean bowling Trumper for 1. It has been stated that a grave mistake was made in leaving Lockwood out; with those of that opinion I do not agree—and no one has a higher opinion of the Surrey bowler than myself. In the week before the test match he secured but two wickets, and one of those occasions was the match against Lancashire, whilst the other game was that against Yorkshire. It was not Lockwood at all who bowled at Old Trafford. At the end of the first day's play we had scored 102 for five wickets, but owing to a sharp shower in the night, the wicket was soft on the top the next morning, and our last five men added but 43. After the heavy roller had been over the pitch it played beautifully, all devil having been taken out of it, which made the one man Barnes, who had been so successful in the first innings, practically harmless, since he has never been seen to advantage, in big cricket, with the fire out of the wicket. Hill and Trumper went along at a great pace, all our bowlers catching it, F. S. Jackson securing both their wickets, but not until Trumper had made 62 and Hill 119. Well as both men played, the bowling in this innings, as in the first innings at Manchester, was, to say the least, very moderate. With the exception of Hopkins, no one of the remaining players caused much trouble, Rhodes finishing up by taking four wickets in 19 balls. But those of us near the wickets knew why, for F. S. Jackson, who had kept an excellent length for some time at that end, suddenly made two balls nip back very quickly, and then the left-hander was immediately brought on. In fact, the moment the wicket broke up at that end, Rhodes made full use of his opportunity, as did the Australians when they got us at the wickets, Noble on the last day, from the end which Rhodes had bowled, being every bit as difficult, and taking six wickets for 52. It was only due to Jessop's hitting that we scored 195. As I had the luck to stay there as long as any one, I know what I am writing about, and I have no hesitation in saying that the wicket suddenly went all to pieces from the moment that Jackson made the ball turn quickly. Noble also did this to some purpose, making it kick up, too, very sharply, as on the occasion when Jackson was bowled off his chest. In our second innings I do not blame our batsmen in the least. Noble was seen at his best in both innings, whilst Saunders did as well as he in the first innings.

CHAPTER X

UNIVERSITY CRICKET BY HOME GORDON AND H. D. G. LEVESON-GOWER

To thousands who have never been near the banks of the Cam or the Isis, "the 'Varsity match" forms one of the episodes of each recurring year. It is a social festival; perhaps, also, it is the last great manifestation of cricket as a game, and not as a money-making business, which is to be found among first-class fixtures. But the University match is more than this, for it is the Mecca of all who have gone down from Oxford or Cambridge, the opportunity for the renewal of former acquaintances, possibly the only occasion when you come across those who were amongst your greatest friends in the day of *arcades ambo*. It is good to meet old comrades, good to hear the ring of the old jests, good to see how time is treating those who are your own contemporaries—ay, and good to give one kindly thought to those who have drifted to all the quarters of the Empire, and to remember those who have been removed from us by Death.

The University match is, however, more than an excuse for reunion. It is the battle of the "Blues," the struggle between eleven picked representatives of Oxford and the eleven contemporary delegates of Cambridge. All old University men, and all the undergraduates of to-day, with their families, relations, and friends, young and old, unite in shouting for their own side. It is as cheery a display of enthusiasm as one could care to show to that hypothetical individual, "the intelligent foreigner"—the foreigner one really encounters being "a chiel amang us takin' notes" for hostile purposes. But little care we for international complications when Blue meets Blue. It is a grim, grand struggle for mastery, and some illustration of the evenness of the fight can be gathered from the fact that after sixty-eight contests Cambridge should only lead by four.

But the value of the University match exceeds all yet indicated, for it is the supreme and unsullied manifestation of genuine amateurism. When cricket is degenerating into a business, when too many eke out a pseudo-amateurism in unsatisfactory ways, when individuals play for their averages and sides play against the clock, we hail the University match as the recurrent triumph of the true amateur, the keenest, manliest, most entrancing, and most spirited match of the year—and likewise the one haloed by the richest traditions. All these views are apt to be forgotten when county committees are clamouring for valuable Blues to neglect their University trial matches in order to help their shires in championship fixtures. That is why this article is heralded by a pæan of genuine enthusiasm, and it is this that we would say to undergraduates in years to come—you may represent your county as long as your purse and your skill permit, but no living man can participate in thirty-six matches for Oxford or for Cambridge, nor more than four times meet the opposing Blues. Therefore, take University cricket as the happy fruit of early manhood, and believe that nothing in after years is quite equal, quite identical with its delightful experiences.

With these preliminary observations concluded, let us first see where the game is played. Of course the University struggle is at Lord's, and probably every one who reads the present volume, even if he has not been himself to headquarters, has a pretty good idea of what the ground is like. Even in the last twenty years it has undergone a number of changes in order to bring it to the level of latter-day requirements. Of course the original picturesqueness of the surroundings has been impaired. The present pavilion has been ingloriously compared to a railway station. The extension of the grand stand has rendered all the north side unsightly, and the huge mound at the south-east corner looks like part of the auditorium at Earl's Court. Even the tennis-court has been shifted. But all said and done, 15,000 people can get a decent view of the game at Lord's, and the turf itself has been improved beyond measure. Time was when the pitch at Lord's was proverbially treacherous, and old scores bear eloquent testimony to this. To-day a superb wicket can be provided for a big match, one equal to any in England, despite the fact that comparatively few drawn games take place at St. John's Wood.

From a Aquatint by Francis Jukes.
SALVADORE HOUSE, TOOTING, SURREY.
(After a Drawing by John Walker, end 18th Century).

From a Drawing by Crowhurst.
CRICKET GROUND, TODMORDEN.

So much for the meeting-place. Now for the trial-grounds of the rival Blues. In this respect, Oxford had far more difficulty than their rivals. The earliest grounds used by the Dark Blues were those of the Bullingdon Club and of the Magdalen College School. The Bullingdon ground, on the site of the present barracks, was at a goodly distance from the town, but possessed some of the finest turf in the kingdom. The Magdalen ground was a part of Cowley Common, and this was the first enclosure ever leased to the Oxford University Cricket Club. With a few individual digressions, there the bulk of the home fixtures were contested until, in 1881, the University settled down on its own admirable ground in the University Parks. A hard, fast pitch could be obtained, in a central situation, with an excellent practice-ground always available, while a commodious pavilion, exactly behind the wicket, affords those in authority, and the legion who love to give gratuitous advice, an admirable position from which to watch the trial matches. Though not as yet dealing with the fixtures, it may be broadly stated—without fear of contradiction—that the Oxford eleven has displayed far more cohesiveness since it has acquired a permanent establishment. Of course the fact that no gate-money can be taken militates against the quality of the professionals engaged on the ground-staff. It is a rule that only one home fixture shall have a charge for admission, and then the match is played on one of the College grounds, generally Christ Church, which affords the greatest accommodation. When the Australians come, their game is invariably the one selected. In other seasons it is usually a county match.

Cambridge have been far more fortunate in the matter of a ground. The University originally played on Parker's Piece—a huge village green; but in 1848, at the instigation of Lord Stamford and Lord Darnley, who considered the ground too public, as well as the tradition that the M.C.C. refused to appear again, because of the ill-mannered chaff of the spectators, F. P. Fenner induced the University to move to his spacious ground. The original pavilion, not built until 1856—and then at the trifling cost of £300—was replaced in 1875 by a handsome structure on which over £4000 has been expended. The University eventually obtained Fenner's on an admirable lease, and the ground can be regarded as one of the finest in the country. Level and true, the pitch does not take the heart out of a batsman, while a bowler obtains all reasonable assistance. In estimating modern University cricket, it may be fairly considered that all undergraduates have every opportunity to train up to the best possible standard to which they can attain, and that, so far as expenses and wickets are concerned, they have, in the phrase of Mr. W. S. Gilbert, "nothing whatever to grumble at," either at Oxford or Cambridge.

In the view of the writers of the present section, there is no need to dilate at great length on the earlier history of the cricket at the two Universities. The old matches have been replayed by a score of pens since the stumps were originally drawn. I am not saying they were not as admirable as those of later years—indeed, I would at a pinch rather argue on the other side. But I do believe that those who will read the present volume take more interest in the cricket of the last twenty-five years than they feel in that of previous generations. Therefore it is not from want of appreciation that I deliberately incur the charge of treating in a condensed form the early battles of the Blues. Were a volume at my disposal, instead of a chapter, I would gladly act in a very different fashion.

The University match was at first a friendly game rather than a serious contest. Numbers of people would be surprised at being told that Oxford had not always met Cambridge at Lord's. But though the first match took place at St. John's Wood in 1827, no less than five have been fought out at Oxford, either on the Magdalen, Bullingdon, or Cowley Marsh grounds, four of which were won by the home side. To this may be appended the following indications of the haphazard nature of the game. In 1836, when there had been no University match for six years, Cambridge lost by 121 runs, with two men absent; why, no contemporary troubled to set forth. In 1838 began the regular succession of annual encounters, but in a game won easily by Oxford there was one man absent in three out of the four innings. Next year, when

Cambridge won by an innings and 125 runs—the top score in an aggregate of 287 being 70 by Mr. Extras, followed by 65 by Mr. C. G. Taylor—the losers not only played one short throughout the match, but history does not even give a reason, nor does tradition state who the eleventh man should have been. Of the 46 wides sent down by Oxford, it was said, "the bowlers evidently at times lost their temper at not being enabled to disturb the wickets of their opponents." But the greatest proportion of extras had been in 1836, when these amounted to 63 in Oxford's second total of 200, and 55 in Cambridge's first of 127, with 149 extras in an aggregate of 479. Against this must be set only 24 extras in an aggregate of 751, a creditable feature of the game of 1885.

Among the early giants for Oxford may be cited Mr. Charles Wordsworth, subsequently Bishop of St. Andrews, who bowled fast left-hand lobs twisting in from the off. To him appears to have been due much of the organisation of the big match. The earliest cricketer from Oxford chosen to play for the Gentlemen was Mr. H. E. Knatchbull. A good many of the Dark Blue triumphs mid-way in the 'forties were ascribed to the very fast round-arm bowling of Mr. G. E. Yonge, who, in five matches *v.* Cambridge, removed the bails thirty times, in all capturing forty-three opponents. This is the parallel of the terrific devastation wrought by that very fine bowler, Mr. A. H. Evans, who sent back thirty-six Cantabs for 13 runs apiece, twenty-two being clean bowled. Admit, too, the prowess of Mr. G. B. Lee, who in 1839 took nine of the ten wickets and scored a fifth of the Oxford aggregate. He was for many years Warden of Winchester College, and his death, which occurred on 29th January last, was deeply lamented by a great host of friends. The first of the cricket "families" who have made immortal names in University cricket was the Riddings. When two of the brothers played for Gentlemen *v.* Players in 1849, the elder long-stopping and the younger wicket-keeping to such tremendous bowling as that of Mr. G. E. Yonge and Mr. Harvey Fellowes, tradition says that nothing was seen like it until Mr. Gregor MacGregor put on the gloves to take the bowling of

Mr. S. M. J. Woods. In 1849 the Gentlemen won by an innings and 40 runs, the biggest victory until 1878, and one mainly due to the Oxonian combination.

The next family was that of the Marshams, a triumvirate whose achievements have been mentioned by every successive generation of Oxonians, and to which Cambridge could offer no parallel until the era of the Studds. Mr. A. Payne was a very fast bowler; so was Mr. Walter Fellowes. Among batsmen come Messrs. Reginald Hankey and W. H. Bullock, but towering above them stands Mr. C. G. Lane, whose name is enshrined among the pristine heroes of the Oval. Nor prior to 1860 must the prowess of Mr. Chandos Leigh, Mr. Arthur Cazenove, and Mr. W. F. Traill be forgotten.

CRICKET AT RUGBY IN 1837.

CAMBRIDGE UNIVERSITY STUDENTS PLAYING CRICKET IN 1842.

The Light Blue giants up to this time had also been notable. The earliest of great fame is Mr. C. G. Taylor, a batsman of great repute, an old Etonian, who was an adept at nearly every sport. With him must be associated Mr. J. H. Kirwan, a very fast amateur bowler, "with a low delivery which approached a jerk, but was allowed." No matter how he was hit, he persisted in keeping his fieldsmen behind the wicket, ready for catches. Mr. T. A. Anson appears to have been the earliest of the famous Cambridge stumpers, but his renown pales before that of Mr. E. S. Hartopp, "the only man who could stop the famous fast deliveries of Mr. Harvey Fellowes with any degree of certainty." What that meant on the old-time bad wickets may be estimated by the fact that, when there was some discussion about pace, it was the unanimous consensus of those old enough to judge that Mr. Fellowes had never been equalled for lightning speed. Eton provided the next Cambridge bowler of importance, Mr. E. W. Blore, whose pace was slow, with an excellent length. More famous, of course, is Mr. David Buchanan, who in his University days was a fast left-handed bowler. By the way, he himself confessed that he would not remain a fortnight "kicking his heels about" in order to play in the University match of 1851. His marvellous prowess with the ball was altogether apart from his undergraduate career, though he captured six Oxonian wickets in 1850. Mr. Mat Kempson, who hailed from Cheltenham, was a clever fast bowler, with so much spin on his ball that he was the only cricketer George Parr could not hit to leg. It is said that while he and Canon J. M'Cormick were together, they never lost an eleven-a-side match at Cambridge. The feat of Mr. M. Kempson and Sir Francis Bathurst, bowling unchanged for the Gentlemen against the Players, has only been equalled by the two Cantabs, Messrs. S. M. J. Woods and F. S. Jackson, in 1894, and by A. H. Evans and A. G. Steel, who, in the Gentlemen v. Players match in 1879, dismissed a strong side of players for 73 and 48, both being then in residence at their Universities. Mr. E. T. Drake, with bat and lob bowling, was esteemed by his contemporaries as only second to Mr. V. E. Walker.

The name with which Cambridge cricket will be historically associated in the nineteenth century is that of Mr. Arthur Ward. He weighed 20 stones when he played for Cambridge, and was so much chaffed by the crowd at Lord's that in 1854 he managed the match from the pavilion. But to him is due the acquisition of Fenner's, where he reigned as an autocrat, despotic but delightful. He has been even as much to his old University as Mr. Thomas Case, wise, vigilant, and full of foresight, has been to Oxford cricket. The twain will never be forgotten, and unborn generations should breathe benedictions upon them.

Two successive secretaries of M.C.C. represented Cambridge in 1854. One was that delightful personality and sturdy hitter, Mr. R. Fitzgerald. The team he took to America in 1872 was the parent of many tours in many climes, all enjoyable, if not of such public importance as the great expeditions to Australia. He was succeeded at Lord's by his friend of many years' standing, Mr. Henry Perkins, who is to-day cheery in his honoured retirement after twenty-one years' work, the full value of which was not entirely appreciated by the younger generations of M.C.C. until afterwards. In his day he must have been a keen good cricketer, and, considering how little he watched the modern game, and then always behind the pavilion windows, it is marvellous how he could so skilfully diagnose the skill of players. His kindness to quite young fellows fond of the game is one of those traits to which enough justice was not done at his retirement, possibly because the tributes came from older friends. It may be noted that Mr. T. W. Wills, who represented Cambridge *v.* Oxford in 1856, was never in residence. The group of cricketers who went up from Brighton College will always be memorable. In 1860 for Cambridge appeared Messrs. G. E. Cotterill, Denzil Onslow, A. E. Bateman, and E. B. Fawcett, as formidable a quartet as could be desired. Mainly owing to the spinning slow bowling of Mr. H. M. Plowden, the Cantabs won by three wickets on a soaking ground, with two of the best Oxford men too unwell to play.

The next eighteen years can be regarded as the mid-Victorian section of University cricket. Preeminent from 1862 to 1865 was Mr. R. A. H. Mitchell, then absolutely the finest amateur bat in the country. He averaged 42 in seven innings against Cambridge, though his highest innings was only 57. He was a wonderful bat, timing the ball with something of the judgment of "W. G.," though, like the champion, he was *never* quite happy facing Alfred Shaw. Possibly no other amateur ever hit so well to leg, and he has the distinction of being the earliest of the great captains who developed the game according to our modern ideas. It was he, too, who gave Oxford four successive victories after four previous reverses. After he went down, Oxford had no star for some seasons, except that Sir Robert Reid proved as nimble behind the sticks as he has since been successful at the Bar and in Parliament.

Cambridge in the same period had more men of mark. At the outset there were the erratic but devastating deliveries of Mr. T. Lang, who captured in all fifteen Oxford wickets for 84 runs, and for his University has the magnificent figures of forty-six wickets at a cost of 5.54 apiece. Then too flourished Lord Cobham, of whom Mr. Clement Booth—a veteran not given to rash assertions—states, "He was absolutely the best all-round cricketer I ever played with." Note that Mr. Booth actually participated in first-class cricket—fine steady bat that he was—until 1887, and still keeps up his interest in the game. To collaborate with these three were Messrs. H. M. Marshall, A. W. T. Daniel, H. M. Plowden, an excellent slow bowler, and W. Bury, "who never missed a catch." Truly was it said that the 1862 eleven was not surpassed until that of 1878. It will be noted that Cambridge was now enjoying the era of the Lytteltons, G. S., the second brother to Lord Cobham, coming up in 1866, and showing wonderful nerve in a trying finish in the following year. It was then the turn of the Light Blues to win for four successive encounters. Much of this was due to the great command of that eccentric free-lance Mr. C. A. Absalom over the ball. He was outside all laws of cricket convention, among other ethics of his being that a half-volley on the leg stump was the best delivery with which to attack a fresh batsman. Altogether he took one hundred wickets for 14 runs each as an undergraduate, and twenty-two wickets for 247 runs in his three encounters with Oxford. Of course he was utterly unorthodox as a bat too, but his hard hitting produced quite a respectable figure in the average-sheet of the Light Blues. Of his acrobatic agility in the field, it is safe to say that never will its like be seen again.

Slightly senior to him was Mr. C. E. Green, the father of Essex cricket, and hardly had he gone down than Cambridge possessed one of the most remarkable groups of attractive players to be noted in our annals. This was in 1869—known, by the way, as the University wicket-keepers' match, as the two stumpers, H. A. Richardson and W. A. Stewart, between them annexed fourteen out of the forty wickets. In that year Messrs. C. I. Thornton, W. Yardley, J. W. Dale, W. B. Money, H. A. Richardson, and C. A. Absalom all played for the Gentlemen. Of these, the repute of Mr. C. I. Thornton as a stupendous hitter has not even been dimmed by that of Mr. G. L. Jessop himself. For about thirty years "Buns" went in to slog, and undoubtedly succeeded. Some day, perhaps, when feats of hard hitting are collected, an adequate catalogue of his amazing feats may be presented. They will certainly prove unparalleled, and if others have hit as hard, possibly no one ever *drove* with such mighty impetus. Nor, in even this brief allusion to his connection with University cricket, must it be forgotten what service he annually rendered in collecting strong scratch teams for his visits. It should be put on record that his two fine scores of 50 and 36 were made against Oxford in 1869 by steady defensive cricket.

Of "Bill of the Play," it is difficult for us, who never saw him bat, to adequately write, when so many of our readers have been more fortunate. A very eminent judge, however, supplies this note:—"Yardley comes next to 'W. G.' among amateurs. Ranji may have produced new strokes, notably that astounding 'hook,' but his physique never gave him that impressive *command* over the ball which was the characteristic of the elder Cantab. Yardley possessed all the grace of Palairet, with a strength equal to that of Ulyett. I should regard him as the perfection of really beautiful batting accompanied with remarkable power. He played all round the wicket, but he was stronger on the leg side than modern bats."

To Mr. Yardley belongs the unique distinction of having made two centuries in the University match, 100 in 1870 and 130 in 1872, the former being the first made in the game—oddly enough, at a time when he was supposed to be out of form—and the latter the highest, until Mr. K. J. Key passed it with his 143 in 1886. Mr. J. W. Dale was a stylish, pretty bat, while Mr. W. B. Money, besides being a clever lob bowler, was a good and often aggressive bat, though from nervousness he failed to do himself justice against the rival Blues. To all generations of cricketers, the Oxford and Cambridge match of 1870 will be known as "Cobden's game," despite the first recorded century. It was also true that the hat trick had also never been performed in the match, and Mr. F.

C. Cobden now achieved it under almost miraculous conditions. Mr. Cobden bowled a good fast ball of the average type, nothing marvellous, and it is this one feat which has immortalised him. Oxford had a fine eleven, the match being a genuine battle with giants on both sides. The Dark Blues, to begin with, possessed in Mr. C. J. Ottaway one of the coolest and most skilled of defensive batsman. He belonged to the race of University stonewallers (the apotheosis of which was Mr. Eustace Crawley, who was an hour at the wicket without scoring, and in his second innings was another hour before he "broke his specs," amid stentorian applause, only to be out with the very next ball, though the year before he had scored a century). Mr. A. T. Fortescue was an excellent, watchful bat, Messrs. Pauncefote and Townshend were useful, Mr. Walter Hadow a dangerous run-getter, and Mr. E. F. S. Tylecote a sound, clever batsman, and so fine a wicket-keeper that he has put on the gloves creditably in test matches. Moreover, that good bowler, Mr. C. K. Francis, was a bat that had to be reckoned with. On fourth hands Oxford needed 179 to win, and with Messrs. Fortescue and Ottaway scoring steadily, and Mr. Tylecote playing good cricket, the match looked a very hollow affair, despite the excellent bowling of Mr. E. E. Harrison-Ward.

Over the concluding incidents there is some conflict of evidence, but it seems probable that the fact of an extension of the playing time having been agreed to affected the finish, the light becoming bad. When Mr. Ottaway was dismissed, Oxford needed 19 to win, with five wickets to fall. Subsequently Messrs. Townshend and Francis were sent back, but only 4 runs were required, with three wickets to fall. Then came Mr. Cobden's sensational and renowned over. Off the first ball, Mr. F. H. Hill, who was well set, made a vigorous stroke which was so well fielded by Mr. A. Bourne that only a single was scored. Off the second ball Mr. S. E. Butler was sharply annexed by the same opponent. Mr. T. H. Belcher was bowled by the next delivery, and it is even now controversial whether clean or off his pads. Finally, in came Mr. W. A. Stewart, who was, under the circumstances, naturally extremely nervous, and the victorious bowler at once removed his bail, amid a scene of frantic excitement.

Wonders now come in battalions, for in the very next University encounter was performed another feat never again or before achieved in this especial match. This was the capture of all ten wickets on a side. Whether much of the success was due to the ground is beside the question. The fact remains that Mr. S. E. Butler took all the ten Cantab wickets at a cost of 38 runs, and then claimed five more for 57. He was a fast bowler, who on this occasion found a spot which made the ball keep very low, and on a difficult pitch he was absolutely unplayable. Oxford this season had the benefit of the fine batting of Lord Harris, the man who, next to Lord Hawke, has probably done more for cricket than any one else. He was a stylish, attractive bat, with brilliant strokes and great driving power. Few batsmen have performed better against fast bowling; but his prowess ripened by his association with Kent rather than in his University days. Still, the Cantabs possessed the bulk of the new cricketers. Mr. W. N. Powys, a rather fast left-handed bowler, had the splendid figures of twenty-four wickets for 153 runs, while the two Etonians, Messrs. George Longman and A. S. Tabor, acquired high repute as batsmen. The former was the more attractive, comparable in a later generation to Mr. Norman Druce, while the latter, though more cramped, also might have been the more difficult to dislodge. In 1872, both being freshmen, they were the earliest who ever put up a century for the first wicket in the University match.

The next triumph of Oxford came in 1875. This was due to Mr. A. W. Ridley, whose lobs were preternaturally successful at the crisis. Both sides carried men famed in the game. Mr. A. J. Webbe has in some measure occupied a unique position. Apart from his high repute as a batsman, he has devoted himself with assiduity to cricket at both Oxford and Harrow, in many ways materially influencing cricket, apart from his illustrious connection with Middlesex. Others to be noted were Mr. Vernon Royle, possibly the grandest field who ever donned flannels, Mr. W. H. Game, a big hitter, apt to prove disappointing, and Mr. T. W. Lang, who, besides being an admirable bowler, had trained into a very useful bat. Mr. Ridley as a bat, too, was a delightful exponent of the best Etonian traditions. Cambridge, however, enjoyed the services of some wonderful cricketers. In his quiet, patient, yet admirable method, how few can have excelled Mr. A. P. Lucas! Seven-and-twenty years after the match in question, a junior among the last Australian team expressed his opinion that Mr. Lucas was among the first flight of English batsmen of to-day. One critic has judiciously remarked that he never attempts to place a ball, or he would have scored three times as many runs, but for sheer accuracy who can ever have surpassed him? A colleague was Mr. Edward Lyttelton, most famous but one of all the family—a fine bat, remarkably free, a magnificent field anywhere, with heart and soul in the game. Mr. F. F. J. Greenfield, unorthodox but capable, was another useful man, and the bowling rested mainly on W. S. Patterson.

The sensation of the match in which all these participated was in the close finish. Cambridge, needing 174 to win, had reached 161 for seven wickets, everything having gone in their favour until Mr. Webbe caught out Mr. Lyttelton in the country, a catch which many judges still watching the game think was the finest they ever witnessed. Mr. W. H. Game persuaded his captain, Mr. A. W. Ridley, to go on with lobs at this crisis. "It was much against my own judgment. My first ball got rid of W. S. Patterson; then Macan came in and made a single off the next. This brought Sims to my end, and he hit my third ball clean over my head for four. Lang then bowled against Macan, who kicked a leg-bye, and afterwards a no-ball made it seven to win. It was now that Sims was caught, and Arthur Smith came in. He looked rather shaky, and no wonder. He managed to keep his wicket intact for two balls, but my third bowled him, amid terrific excitement." Thus Mr. A. W. Ridley himself, in reply to the request for his own reminiscence for an article in the *Badminton Magazine*. His modest impression deserves to be resurrected here. Mr. Edward

Lyttelton has stated that the ball with which the victorious lob bowler dismissed each of his victims was "a straight low one on the leg stump which did not turn an inch." Of the match in 1876 it may be stated that Mr. W. S. Patterson was the first "centurion" to be undefeated, and Mr. W. H. Game, the first Oxonian to run into three figures against Cambridge, though in the following year his example was followed by Mr. F. M. Buckland. It may be pointed out that Oxford from 1871 to 1875 and Cambridge from 1876 to 1880 each won four victories, interrupted by one defeat. In 1876 each University had won an equal number of matches. 1878 was the first year of modern cricket as generally accepted, but it was hardly more notable for the first visit of the Australians than for the unrivalled ability of the Cambridge eleven. They played eight matches, and won them all, a result as much due to magnificent fielding as to any other cause. Of course the phenomenal agency was the marvellous skill of Mr. A. G. Steel, but this great exponent of every department of the game was admirably backed up by the whole side. They opened by defeating Mr. C. I. Thornton's eleven, which included Dr. W. G. Grace and his younger brother, as well as Mycroft and Midwinter, by 79 runs, though 90 runs behind on first hands. Single-innings victories were gained over M.C.C. and the Gentlemen, while Yorkshire was disposed of by a margin of ten wickets. Migrating to the Oval, Surrey fell to the tune of an innings and 112, while M.C.C., strongly represented at Lord's, were left in a minority of 106. Although Messrs. A. J. Webbe and A. H. Evans appeared for Oxford, the University match was felt to be one-sided, and so it proved. Mr. A. D. Greene took four hours and ten minutes to get 35 runs, while in the second effort Messrs. A. G. Steel and P. H. Morton sent the whole side back for 32. Finally the Cantabs, though deprived of the great services of Mr. A. P. Lucas, beat the Australians before lunch on the second day by an innings and 72 runs. In emphasising this startling succession of victories, it ought to be pointed out that only once did opponents exceed a total of 127, and then the aggregate was only 193, while six sides were dismissed for less than 70 runs apiece.

Now for the doughty team which Mr. Edward Lyttelton led so admirably. Be it noted that he was the only Englishman who in 1878 scored a century against the Australians. To him, and to Mr. A. P. Lucas, allusion has already been made. To do adequate justice to the great game always played by Mr. A. G. Steel is beyond our pens. Suffice it to say that the true panegyric lies in his magnificent record. In connection with Cambridge in 1878, he headed both tables, taking seventy-five wickets for 7 runs apiece, and averaging 37 for an aggregate of 339. At that time his bowling was incomparably difficult, mainly because of the way he used to vary his "pitch and break." Never did any attack need such careful watching. His batting, of course, reached its climax in that superb 148 *v.* Australians at Lord's in 1884, and its most brilliant piece of fireworks when he went in ninth at Scarborough, and scored a century while the others made 7. But it was not even his skill which made Mr. A. G. Steel so great. It was his masterly and inspiring confidence, together with an unparalleled grasp of the game, which made him the greatest amateur after "W. G." that we have looked on.

Following him must come Mr. Alfred Lyttelton, a great wicket-keeper, who would have been greater still, had he not appeared in the transition stage between long-stopping and standing up to the bowlers. He was also a really free and attractive bat, who could force the game well. Mr. P. H. Morton would nowadays be regarded as only a medium-paced bowler, whose difficulty arose from the speed at which his ball came off the pitch, whilst it was doing a great deal. His career in cricket was practically bounded by his time at Cambridge, in connection with which his bowling will always be worthily remembered. Mr. Herbert Whitfeld proved somewhat of a stonewaller type, shaping with admirable correctness, and in the field has known no superior. Hon. Ivo Bligh (now Lord Darnley) only lacked good health. As a bat he was an almost perfect exponent of Etonian traditions, so long as he could play forward. We are of opinion that his cutting was at times harder than that of any other amateur. Mr. D. Q. Steel had his days; batsmen of his reckless temperament must have a heavy percentage of failures. But for fine play all round the wicket, when he was in the vein, he could be commended as a positive peril to any opponents. Mr. A. F. J. Ford could hit "high, hard, and often," bowl a useful change, and catch opponents in the slips with the facility and length of reach subsequently displayed by Tunnicliffe. Mr. L. K. Jarvis was an attractive bat, but was a good deal more dangerous on a fast wicket than a slow. Finally, Mr. F. W. Kingston, who could put on the gloves with considerable credit, was a sound, careful bat, who used to play the old "draw" stroke with notable ability. But after all, it was the cohesion and the fielding which made 1878 *the* Cambridge eleven *par excellence.*

Not much noteworthy happened in 1879, a season that maintained its unpleasant record for wetness and chilliness until 1902 relegated all previous experiences into mere episodes. But 1880 saw the Studds following the Steels and Lytteltons into the Cambridge eleven. There was always an element of uncertainty about Mr. G. B. Studd, but he was often a really brilliant bat and brilliant field at cover-point. As for Mr. C. T. Studd, he is the greatest amateur between Mr. A. G. Steel and Mr. S. M. J. Woods. Few men have ever played cricket with such accuracy. Those who have seen J. T. Hearne pitch ball after ball with mechanical precision at Lord's can realise how Mr. C. T. Studd used to bowl, only slower. His batting was never perhaps so sound as that of Mr. C. B. Fry, but that is the nearest contemporary type; only the style of Mr. Studd was one absolutely satisfactory to witness. The game sustained a national loss when he left it to undertake missionary labour in Asia. Mr. J. E. K. Studd, who came into the Cambridge eleven a year later, thus establishing a record of three brothers all simultaneously playing for their University, was never so good as either of the others, but he was a hard-working cricketer, and a difficult bat to dislodge, while his punishing powers were of no mean order.

In 1881 both teams were powerful, the public opinion that Cambridge were far the stronger being quite properly reversed. Three innings of the match were moderate, principally because the Cantabs all drew away from the fast bowling of Mr. A. H. Evans, who claimed thirteen wickets for 10 runs apiece. But the grandest feature was the innings of 107 by Mr. W. H. Patterson, who carried his bat clean through the second Oxford innings, although suffering from a badly-injured hand. It was one of the greatest innings ever played at Lord's, and foreshadowed the fine service he subsequently rendered to Kent. That brilliant disappointment, Mr. C. F. H. Leslie, whose phenomenal batting at Rugby evoked anticipations never realised, played a splendid innings of 70, his partnership with the old Harrovian arresting the succession of Cantab victories, which were destined to be resumed for the next two years. A conspicuous Oxonian recruit was Mr. M. C. Kemp, a capital wicket-keeper, and a most lively, not to say venturesome, bat, and a wonderful judge of a run. But it was his exciting personality and wonderful enthusiasm which made him of such moral value to any side. That attractive Wykehamist bat, Mr. A. H. Trevor, unfortunately elected to watch rather than to play cricket after he went down from college.

1882 saw a striking contrast between the treatment meted out to the two Universities by the greatest of all Australian teams. Mr. Murdoch's combination opened their campaign on the Christ Church ground, and the Colonial who took first ball scored 202. This was that magnificent batsman, Mr. H. H. Massie. Mr. E. D. Shaw alone of the home side could offer much resistance, as was also the case in the first innings against Cambridge. Although this match was on 15th May, ten Oxford blues were on the home side, the eleventh man being that energetic, if erratic, bowler, Mr. C. J. M. Godfrey. Cambridge gave a vastly different exhibition. Mr. C. T. Studd signalised his first appearance against an Australian eleven by scoring 118 and taking eight wickets.

From a Water-Colour, attributed to G. Cruickshank.
THE CORINTHIANS AT LORDS IN 1822.

The triumvirate of brothers were responsible for 297 out of 393 from the bat, and thus had a large share in the triumphant victory by six wickets, the only defeat of the Colonials till 11th August. The slow bowling of Mr. R. C. Ramsey, an old Harrovian, himself a Queenslander, had also much to do with the success, for he claimed twelve wickets for 179 runs. On 17th August, for the first time, Cambridge Past and Present met the Australians, and, after one of the most spirited contests, effected a victory by 20 runs. The bowling of Mr. A. G. Steel and Mr. C. H. Alcock—who never obtained his blue—and fine batting by Mr. Alfred Lyttelton against Messrs. Spofforth and Boyle at their deadliest, were the main agencies. That phenomenal 66 of Mr. G. J. Bonnor, compiled in half an hour with four sixes and six fours, was one of the most astounding things ever perpetrated in cricket. The University match was a good one, including a really artistic 120 from Mr. G. B. Studd, fine form in both departments from his more illustrious brother, and an innings of great force from one of the hardest hitters who ever played at Lord's, Mr. Henery, a man of iron strength though diminutive physique. Lord Hawke, then merely an energetic and interesting bat, was not in his University days so valuable a cricketer as afterwards. Indeed, his powers steadily ripen with years, and in 1902, at the age of forty-two, he batted at the Oval in grander style than ever before, although down at Taunton they say his 126 against Somersetshire was the best innings of all. Long may he continue to advance. The day of his retirement will prove a sad blow to cricket throughout the country. On the Oxford side, Mr. J. G. Walker was nothing like the fine bat to which he afterwards trained on, but at point he has rarely been matched, save by Dr. E. M. Grace.

Though Cambridge won in 1883, the side was by no means phenomenal. Mr. C. W. Wright, who was remarkably effective during his residence at Trinity, was the "centurion," and Messrs. C. T. Studd and C. A. Smith were responsible for the attack. The latter was a vigorous, bustling cricketer, whose curious method of approaching the wicket has rarely been emulated. Of the Oxonians the most notable newcomer was Mr. H. V. Page, a bat with fine nerve, and an equally fine "pull" stroke, keen field, and by no means bad bowler, perfectly indifferent to punishment. Considering that the phenomenally stubborn Mr. C. W. Rock obtained his blue in 1884, most imperturbable of bats, and destined a year or two later to be about the best contemporary amateur bowler (of moderately medium pace, be it mentioned), and further, that two notable county captains, Messrs. H. W. Bainbridge and F. Marchant, both old Etonians, came into the eleven, it is hard to say why Cambridge was so poor. But the fact remains, they were somewhat of a slack side, and neither of the Etonians was then the masterly exponent of batting which in diverging ways they subsequently became. Oxford had a big repute, including the sensational presence of Mr. (now Sir) T. C. O'Brien, who, having gone into residence solely to get his blue, had the memorable misfortune to bag a brace. Mr. B. E. Nicholls, a senior from Winchester, was perfectly extraordinary in the slips; against the Australians, for example, he nipped no less than seven catches. But the comparative falling off of the two Universities can be gathered from the fact that no one from either team represented the Gentlemen against the Colonials in either match, though three Oxonians were on the victorious side against the Players at Lord's.

The Cambridge victory of 1885 was due to some Oxonian half-heartedness in shaping at Mr. C. Toppin at the outset, and to a partnership of 142 by Messrs. C. W. Wright and H. W. Bainbridge, who just ran into the coveted three figures. Cricket was played to a different tune next year, when two great Oxonians effected a stand of 243. The heroes of this were Mr. K. J. Key and Mr. W. Rashleigh. The burly successor to Mr. J. Shuter as Surrey skipper was in his third year, and at that time was a singularly fine bat. It may be confidently asserted that no other amateur of the present generation has so triumphantly exploited the "pull," and he played the game with cheery energy. Mr. Rashleigh, who at Tonbridge had been as sensational as Mr. Leslie a few years before at Rugby, did great things for Kent, but nothing better than this fine display. Those who note with bewilderment that no one else ran into double figures in the Oxonian total of 304 ought to be told that the side purposely played themselves out. Finely as Mr. Bainbridge again played (his scores were 44 and 79), his side was hopelessly unsuccessful, but the absurdity of playing Mr. C. M. Knatchbull Hugessen remains to all time the biggest blunder in University selection, for there was already a deft stumper in Mr. L. Orford. Both that match and a year later that genial sportsman and capable cricketer, Mr. E. H. Buckland, bowled best for victorious Oxford.

The match of 1887 is known as "the last choice game." The eleventh place in each team was only filled at the latest possible moment. The Light Blue final selection, Mr. Eustace Crawley, scored 33 and 103 not out, and the Dark Blue one, Lord George Scott, contributed 100 and 66. Oxford fielded superbly, and their new wicket-keeper, Mr. H. Phillipson, was absolutely one of the finest who has ever donned the gloves, and it is a great pity that his impetuosity and tremendous punishing powers overpowered his otherwise remarkable capacity as a bat, which at Eton caused him to be regarded as exceptionally excellent. Deplorably weak bowling on both sides left the Light Blues in the minority only because of their liberality in the matter of dropped catches.

In 1888 Cambridge obtained the assistance of two amateurs whose combined services will be remembered as long as the game is played. These were of course Messrs. Gregor MacGregor and S. M. J. Woods. Undoubtedly in his prime the Scotchman has never had a rival among amateur wicket-keepers, except Mr. Blackham. The way he used to take Mr. S. M. J. Woods, the way too in which he handled the deliveries of Mr. C. J. Kortright for the Gentlemen, will never be forgotten by those who witnessed them. He was also a stubborn bat, who came off when things were at their worst, and he remains one of the distinguished cricketers of his lengthy period. Even more emphatically can this be remarked of Mr. S. M. J. Woods. The value of his bowling may be gathered from his analysis in his seven University innings, when his victims were 36, at a cost of under 9 runs apiece; moreover, for Cambridge he annexed 190 opponents at a cost of 14 runs each. To say that he was a terror is but to be truthful. His great break back, in combination with great pace, with a magnificent slow ball, made him for many years unrivalled as a fast bowler. A magnificent field, gathering the ball as he rushed in to meet it, and a great hitter, in those days somewhat less judicious than when so serviceable to Somersetshire, he combined all the aptitudes of a redoubtable cricketer. As a combination of bowler and wicket-keeper, in University cricket, Messrs. Woods and MacGregor have no parallel. But as often happens, the two stars gathered some notable men into their constellation.

Senior among these must be named Mr. F. G. J. Ford, youngest and best cricketer in a family of sportsmen. Like all big hitters, more especially perhaps left-handers, he was uncertain. During his four years at Cambridge he was not, except at Brighton, the terrifically punishing bat he subsequently became. But he was in those days a very useful bowler, as well as a formidable run-getter. Mr. R. C. Gosling, an excellent bat of the Eton type, actually was not dismissed by Oxford until his third University match, a curious feat for a man going in seventh. Another Etonian bat, but essentially fast wicket player, was Mr. C. P. Foley, who fairly won the match of 1891 by his steadiness. An even better bat was Mr. R. N. Douglas, whose play was freer than subsequently for Middlesex, and who was always attractive. Mr. E. C. Streatfield would have taken prominent rank, had he really cared more for the game. Batting with a trace of the style which made him a capital racquet-player, he could lay about him with perilous rapidity, whilst his fine bowling claimed five for 14 when Oxford was dismissed for 42, and his ball removed the bails each time. It would be idle to suggest that at Cambridge Mr. D. L. A. Jephson showed much of the great ability he subsequently developed. Indeed, he only once scored 50, and his over-arm bowling was far below the standard of his later lobs. But his fielding was invariably excellent. Mr. A. J. L. Hill was an excellent all-round cricketer. His placing was always excellent, and his dash in meeting the ball, and when bowling his capacity for suddenly sending in a ball which whipped back unexpectedly quick, proved that he was of value in all departments. Finally comes Mr. F. S. Jackson. Possessing a huge school reputation at Harrow, he did not at first effect any sensational cricket. A steady fast bowler and sound bat, was perhaps all that could be reported until his third year, when he became captain, and signalised his skipperdom by heading both tables of averages. In 1893 he improved materially on his batting figures, and was by this time recognised as the great cricketer whose finest triumph was his batting at the pinch in the test matches of 1902. A phenomenal self-reliance has always characterised his play, but it is certain that since Mr. S. M. J. Woods no such fine all-round amateur has come into prolonged participation in good matches.

It may be noted, with reference to a contemporary cry of the difficulty of freshmen in getting their blues, that in 1890 there were five vacancies in the Cambridge eleven, and the five freshmen who appeared in the first match, *v.* C. I. Thornton's eleven, all obtained their colours. These were Messrs. R. N. Douglas, E. C. Streatfield, D. L. A. Jephson, F. S. Jackson, and A. J. L. Hill. In the second innings of the game just mentioned, Mr. S. M. J. Woods took all ten wickets for under 7 runs apiece, after capturing five for only 19 runs in the first. Going to Brighton that year, Cambridge scored 703 for nine wickets, the chief scores being: Mr. F. G. J. Ford 191, Mr. G. MacGregor 131, Mr. C. P. Foley 117, Mr. R. N. Douglas 84 and 62, and Mr. F. S. Jackson 60. Next year the Light Blues against Sussex totalled 359 and 366, without an individual century. In all probability no University ever had such strenuous games with a county as Cambridge about this period played with Surrey, then in the zenith of their fame.

Now occurs the opportunity to refer to two incidents which created an enormous sensation, and eventually led to an alteration in the law of following on. The facts can be briefly put. Oxford in 1893 needed 8 runs to save the follow-on, when the last men were at the wicket. The Cambridge captain, Mr. F. S. Jackson, instructed Mr. C. M. Wells to bowl a no-ball to the boundary, and after the batsman, Mr. W. H. Brain, had covered a very wide ball, to send down one even more off the wicket. In 1896 Oxford needed 12 runs to save the follow-on, when Mr. R. P. Lewis, a notoriously bad bat, came in eleventh. Mr. F. Mitchell then told Mr. E. B. Shine to bowl two no-balls, each of which went to the boundary for four, and then a ball which scored four for byes. The hostile demonstration from the pavilion was one of the most demoralising ever heard on a cricket ground. In sober truth it must be confessed that the captains were within their legal rights in ordering unprecedented action to obviate the possibility of their opponents purposely getting out. Yet all that is not forbidden by law cannot be perpetrated without censure. Having written so much, we prefer to pass on, glad to have briefly finished our allusion to the only unpleasantness in the long series of University matches.

CRICKET

A MATCH IN 1805.

Oxford now demands some attention, for Cambridge has latterly held the chief place in these pages. Mr. M. R. Jardine was not successful until his fourth season, when he amassed a valuable 140, thus redeeming long-deferred expectations. Yet at all times it was felt that the runs he saved by his wonderful fielding were of more value than those he made from the bat. Two cricketers who have been before the public ever since, and who in different ways have proved notable exponents of batting, are Messrs. E. Smith and L. C. H. Palairet. The latter must to the present generation be the pre-eminent example of distinction and graceful perfection. Mr. Ernest Smith has always been a redoubtable and rapid run-getter, making his scores without apparent exertion, yet contriving to entirely baffle the opposing captain by the pertinacious skill with which he places his rapid hits. As a fast bowler he enjoyed days of great success, and was always efficient in the field. A senior from Winchester, only participating in one University match, was Mr. V. T. Hill. Left-handed, and possessing much of the dash and vigour of Mr. H. T. Hewett, he hit 114 in 1892 in a fashion which frankly earned the epithet sensational. Possibly owing to the exceptional interest it always arouses, the encounters of the Blues have produced a remarkable number of notable innings, but none surpasses that of Mr. Hill in vigour and "fireworks." It was altogether a great game, that of 1892. Oxford, having lost Mr. Palairet and Mr. R. T. Jones without a run on the board, amassed 365. Cambridge, in a minority of 205, followed on, and put their opponents in for 186, which were knocked off with five wickets to spare.

New men coming into the teams about this time were not less excellent than their predecessors. Cambridge in 1893, in his third year, tried K. S. Ranjitsinhji, who was third in the averages, his chief scores being 40, 55, 38, 58, and 40. Mr. J. Douglas, a capital bat, with a delightful way of scoring neatly off all bowling alike, used in those days to bowl slows which obtained a fair number of wickets. Mr. A. O. Jones, carefully coached by Arthur Shrewsbury, of course showed barely a glimpse of the great powers he subsequently displayed for Notts. Mr. L. H. Gay was a wicket-keeper altogether above the average, who had singular ill-luck in finding so many of his terms at Cambridge tally with those of Mr. MacGregor. He was a lively hitter, whose wicket was uncommonly hard to obtain. One graceful bat remains to be mentioned, Mr. P. H. Latham, who, good as he was, ought to have been still better, and would have been if he could have resisted the temptation to lash out at an insidious slow. Treading on the heels of these came another remarkable group of bats. The brilliancy of Mr. N. F. Druce has hardly been excelled. His batting was once described as "the champagne of cricket," and certainly the epithet is deserved. Practically his connection with the game ceased after his residence at Trinity Hall, except for one tour in Australia; so it is the more necessary to emphasise how very fine, as well as captivating, was his method of run-getting. It may be added that he has the highest average of any Cantab, namely, 52.47 for an aggregate of 2414, and *v.* Mr. C. I. Thornton's eleven amassed 227 not out, the highest score ever made at Cambridge, the opposing bowlers including Mr. F. S. Jackson, Hirst, Woodcock, and Hearne. Mr. W. G. Druce never attained the same standard as his more famous brother, but he was a valuable run-getter and also a most useful wicket-keeper. Mr. F. Mitchell, despite a remarkable start, did not in his University cricket display the form which culminated in his great batting of 1901. Mr. T. N. Perkins was a notably punishing bat, but the great Cambridge weakness lay in the miserable quality of the attack. Oxford in this respect was not much stronger, though Mr. G. F. H. Berkeley in his day was above the average. At this period, which coincides with that when one of the present writers heartily enjoyed his own University career, there were some distinguished bats to be added to those noticed above. Prominent, of course, was Mr. C. B. Fry, in those days a much slower run-getter than when he amassed those six consecutive centuries for Sussex. Mr. R. C. N. Palairet was often a formidable scorer, and when he and his brother went in first for Oxford v.Cambridge in 1893, it was for the first time since 1878 that two brothers had done so for the senior University; it had then been the two Webbes. Cambridge furnishes only one such incident, the case of Messrs. G. B. and J. E. K. Studd in 1882. Mr. G. J. Mordaunt was a capital bat and an absolutely beautiful field in the country, the amount of ground he covered and his rapidity in returning the ball being quite extraordinary. To these must be added that attractive bat, Mr. H. K. Foster, with his graceful strokes, some of them learnt in the racquet-court. At least one prominent judge maintains that his forlorn effort of 121 on fourth hands in 1895 was the superb gem of the whole series of big University scores since 1878. His efforts for Worcestershire have shown how little of a lucky accident was this brilliant achievement. Few sounder bats ever appeared than Mr. P. F. Warner, and if more prolonged praise be not added, it is only because the warm friendship and admiration of the two writers regard it as superfluous. His scores have been made in many climes, but the best of them all have been compiled at headquarters.

In 1901, one of the present scribes contributed to an article written for the *Badminton Magazine* by the other the following account of the close finish of the University match of 1896, and it is felt that no more sincere record could now be penned; hence its partial quotation is perhaps pardonable:—

"The last choice, not made until the morning of the match, lay between G. B. Raikes and G. O. Smith. Now as the attack was rather tender (P. S. Waddy was the only real 'change' to F. H. E. Cunliffe and J. C. Hartley), it was universally thought that the former as a bowler should have the preference (he had played in the two previous years); but he was bowling none too well at the time, and eventually the decision was in favour of strengthening the batting. As events proved, this selection settled the match. Cambridge batted first, Burnup and Wilson making a long stand; Bray hit confidently at the finish. I think, however, it speaks well for Oxonian fielding, that on a fast true wicket, against only four bowlers (C. C. Pilkington also went on), it took six hours to amass 319, Mordaunt's work in the country being especially fine. We did none too well in the first innings, and owing to the no-ball incident we saved following on. This incident, to my mind, was an error of judgment. The Cambridge eleven had not had a long outing, the discrepancy of 120 is a lot in a 'Varsity match, and to follow on between five and seven is not to enjoy the best of the day's light at Lord's. At the same time, the reception Cambridge had at the hands of the members of M.C.C. was unpardonable, and certainly prejudiced their play in the second attempt. Whilst saying so, I am not detracting from Cunliffe's performance, who, for the first hour, bowled better than he ever had before. Norman Druce, the best bat on either side, stemmed disaster. So with two wickets in hand Cambridge on the second evening led by 217, and directly play ceased rain fell heavily. However, that rain proved our godsend, for a light roller on it, binding the wicket together, made it better than at any previous time in the match, which was saying a good deal. Eventually Oxford was left with 330 to win, and up to that time the highest total ever recorded on fourth hands in the University contest was 176. A bad start was made, for at luncheon three good wickets were down for 81, Mordaunt, Foster, and Warner being disposed of, the latter having the unique experience of being twice run out in a University match. With Pilkington and

G. O. Smith together, it dawned on the Oxonian supporters that, after all, victory was not out of the question. From this time, helped by a few errors in the field, we never looked back. I had an enjoyable partnership with the hero of the game, and before I was caught at the wicket, a possible victory was in sight, for the sting had gone out, to a great extent, of the Cambridge attack (G. L. Jessop, C. E. M. Wilson, E. B. Shine, and P. W. Cobbold). Bardswell followed me, full of confidence, and hit with bland imperturbability, scoring the winning stroke, being missed off it, by the way, by Burnup. Of G. O. Smith's innings of 132 it is impossible to speak too highly, and he thoroughly deserved his memorable ovation, the whole pavilion rising and cheering him. All said and done, looking back, apart from unbounded admiration for his prowess, the great factor of Oxford's success was undoubtedly the fielding. We had precious little bowling, and conventional fielding would have given us no chance. The game was won by the work of the eleven in combination, and if only the fielding in first-class matches were what it should be, drawn games would be very rare. Reform the fielding, and then the laws of the game will need but little reformation."

By this time it will have been noticed that the Light Blues had been reinforced by that prince of hard hitters, Mr. G. L. Jessop, who was a tearaway bowler to boot, and that admirable batsman, Mr. C. J. Burnup, the new Kent captain. The succession of clever Cambridge wicket-keepers was kept up by Mr. E. H. Bray, than whom no one ever kept his hands closer to the sticks. After this, for the next few years University cricket undoubtedly fell a little flat. It was overshadowed to an unfortunate extent by the more absorbing interest evinced in county cricket. There were excellent cricketers on each side, but the teams were not so cohesive as that of 1896, had not the same proportion of really prominent amateurs as heretofore, and—here is the chief point—the idea had become prevalent that the keenness of the game was relaxed in the trial matches. So thoroughly was this re-established in 1902, so keen was the big match that year, and so bright the prospects of the game in the immediate future at both Universities, that it is permissible to frankly state so much, and to regard the years between 1896 and 1902 as ebb years, in comparison to the onward flow from 1889 to 1896.

But there was one gorgeous piece of cricket performed by the greatest of recent undergraduates. Mr. R. E. Foster, the one batsman since Mr. Norman Druce equally perfect to watch, played in 1900 a score of 171, a new record in the match, the previous best contribution having been Mr. Key's 143 in 1886. An eye-witness wrote in that cricketer's Bible, *Wisden*: "The innings was not only a great one in a numerical sense, but was in every way a magnificent display of batting. He only took three hours and ten minutes to get his runs, and, so far as anyone noticed, he did not give a single chance. Apart from the fact that he once failed to bring off a more than usually daring pull, and that just before he was out he made a dangerous stroke beyond mid-off, we did not see any fault in his play. As a matter of record, it may be added that he hit twenty-four fours, three threes, and thirteen twos. Hitting more superb than his can scarcely have been seen since Yardley played his great innings of 130 in 1872. He was equally strong all round the wicket, driving magnificently on the off side, pulling with the utmost certainty, and making any number of late cuts that were as safe as they were effective." It will be remembered that ten days later he followed this up by scoring two separate hundreds for Gentlemen *v.* Players at Lord's, a feat never performed in this match by any other cricketer appearing for either denomination. His average for Oxford was 77 for an aggregate of 930, and he led his team through a victorious season, as five matches were won, none lost, and four drawn.

Of other undergraduates, Mr. B. J. T. Bosanquet worked hard, getting a good many wickets and scoring with reliable consistency. A superb wicket-keeper was produced in Mr. H. Martyn, for with a style that was a model of neatness, he was particularly strong on the leg side, as well as a forcing bat. Not nearly enough credit was given to Mr. C. H. B. Marsham for his exceptionally meritorious century on fourth hands, and in disadvantageous circumstances, in the University match of 1901. It was not until a year later that he came to be generally recognised as a batsman of judicious temperament, possessing a very pretty knack of placing the ball hard on the off side. On contemporary Oxford it would be unfair to pass judgment, but it is at least permissible to express the belief that Mr. W. H. B. Evans (nephew of the once-renowned bowler) will fulfil our high expectation, and that Mr. W. Findlay is one of the best custodians of the sticks to be found in current cricket.

Turning to Cambridge, the brothers Wilson have emulated the feat of the brothers Foster at Oxford, and each scored a century in the University match. The elder, Mr. C. E. M. Wilson, in his four University matches scored 351, with an average of nearly 44, and took twelve wickets at a cost of 21 runs apiece. The younger, Mr. E. R. Wilson, in a similar series of fixtures, averaged 42, with an aggregate of 296, and captured nineteen wickets for less than 22 runs each. These meritorious figures were achieved by steady cricket, which never pandered to a gallery, never took a risk, nor for one moment became really brilliant. For comparison, it may be added that Mr. R. E. Foster averaged 48 for a total of 342. Of the other Cantabs, Mr. T. L. Taylor, of course, has been the soundest and greatest bat. Indeed, on a wet wicket he has rarely had a superior. Mr. S. H. Day has proved himself to be amongst the best of young cricketers, and Mr. E. M. Dowson with bat and ball has done yeoman service. As a singularity, it may be mentioned that in 1902 Mr. E. F. Penn reappeared in the eleven, after being two years absent at the war.

To mention the legion who have passed from their University eleven into that of the Gentlemen would take up too much space, but it may be of interest to give a list of those who have represented England in the test matches at home:—

Oxford	Cambridge
Sir T. C. O'Brien.	A. P. Lucas (Uppingham).
Lord Harris (Eton).	A. G. Steel (Marlborough).
E. F. S. Tylecote (Clifton).	A. Lyttelton (Eton).
C. B. Fry (Repton).	C. T. Studd (Eton).
L. C. H. Palairet (Repton).	G. E. MacGregor (Uppingham).
	GF. S. Jackson (Harrow).
	K. S. Ranjitsinhji.
	G. L. Jessop.
	A. O. Jones (Bedford).
Batting—25 inn., 404 runs, 16.4 average.	69 inn., 2316 runs, 33.39 average.
Bowling—18 runs, 0 wicket.	1265 runs, 36 wickets, 35.5 average.

And further, one of the writers, who is in the habit of perpetrating statistics, has made out that against Australians in this country, in eleven-a-side matches, Oxonians (past and present) have scored 10,439 runs in 527 completed innings, averaging 19.426 per innings; and Cantabs (past and present) have scored 17,834 runs in 924 completed innings, averaging 19.276 per innings. The Oxford bowlers have claimed 270 Colonial wickets at a cost of 6202 runs, thus costing 22.282 runs apiece; but the Cambridge bowlers, though they captured 392 wickets, did so at an expense of 43.36 runs apiece, the aggregate being 16,892.

Passing from figures to matches, it may be as well to sketch the programme of each University season. Directly term commences, usually in April, when the weather is miserably cold and wet, and no one has had any practice, comes the Seniors' match. As the object of the executive is to find new bowlers, it is obvious that the bowlers in this game are none of the best, even judged by the low standard of amateur attack. There is, as a rule, a large amount of heavy scoring, but the fielding is slack, and the fixture is invested with little real keenness. Far more enthusiasm is aroused by the Freshmen's match. Here is the pick of the public schools of the year before, with a stray candidate from a colony or a private tutor's. The cricket is not co-operative, for each is trying to make a good impression "on his own." In the heat of modern competition, it is particularly difficult for a batsman to obtain his blue as a freshman. With bowling it is different, but the captain is prone to wait till the promising undergraduate has acquired some experience in county cricket. Other trial games are XII. *v.* Next XVI., the XI. *v.*XVI. Freshmen, "Perambulators" *v.* "Etceteras." The "Perambulators" are composed of those who come from Eton, Winchester, Harrow, and Rugby, whilst "Etceteras" are selected from those from other schools. Then come the University fixtures. The opening is against a Gentlemen of England team, of which one of the present writers has latterly had charge—a very pleasant game for all concerned, and one provocative of no little curiosity to see how the new men shape. As a rule a couple of counties, M.C.C., and latterly Dr. Grace's club, with the Australians, if on tour, form the rest of the home fixtures. Thus far the University captain has probably been varying his side a good deal, and has had one or two extra places available for trials, because blues may be in the schools. But by the time the out matches begin, if the eleven be not pretty well together, matters cannot be altogether favourable. Good cricket at the Oval and heavy scoring at Brighton are the preludes to the final trial *v.* M.C.C. at Lord's. Half the Oxford eleven now never play in this latter engagement, and it must be said that there is some reason for this, for whereas Cambridge get a clear three days' rest before the 'Varsity match at the Oval, Oxford sometimes only get one day. The final place is often a matter of the most dubious difficulty. There are often two men whose merits are almost equal, and the decision, if wrong, may ultimately ruin the big match.

What a game it is, Oxford *v.* Cambridge, unrivalled for its sporting keenness, and if it has proved a triumph to many, it has also been a game of cruel disappointment in those who have been expected to do best. The importance of the match to the funds of M.C.C. can be gathered from the annual balance-sheet of the club, and considering the difficulty of affording sufficient money for professionals and other expenses at the Universities, it may be open to the consideration of the committee if it would not be judicious were the premier club to increase the amount of the annual donation to the rival centres of education, whose delegates provide such an immense share of the club revenue. If the University match were to be removed from Lord's—*absit omen*—it is obvious that the club in St. John's Wood would suffer far more than either Oxford or Cambridge. Such an exodus is not probable, but the old order changes, and it would be wise as well as generous if the committee could give more lavishly where it receives so bountifully.

A survey of all the University matches seems to authorise two deductions: Firstly, that, all else being equal, it is better to choose for places in University teams men who have already played before a crowd, because nervousness is so apt to overtake the novice when participating in this fixture. Secondly, that the presence of a formidable fast bowler is the best agency for victory. Matches, as a rule, have gone to the team which backed up a destructive attack with competent fielding, and there seems no reason why in this respect history should not repeat itself. We may be permitted to conclude with an expression of the sincere hope that University cricket may maintain its high position, and that the big match will remain something in which all the Empire shall continue to take legitimate pride and interest, because it is the contest between the best of England's youth fought in true sporting fashion.

CHAPTER XI

COUNTRY-HOUSE CRICKET
BY H. D. G. LEVESON-GOWER

I have not the least idea where my genial editor is going to put the present chapter in this book, but I am willing to wager that it will prove the lightest and most frivolous in his team. In the literary menu I sincerely hope some one will find it the savoury of the meal, because personally I like savouries best, and naturally I prefer my own chapter to any other—parenthetically, I have not seen any of the rest, except the one which I had a share in writing. No one has perhaps played more country-house cricket than I have, and certainly no one has derived more enjoyment from the matches. So I can write with agreeable memories. But as the games are the least formal in the whole range of cricket, therefore I feel this chapter needs no apology for being a trifle desultory. We are now taking our ease after dinner, and chatting in quite a happy-go-lucky way.

"What good times I have had in country-house cricket, to be sure," ought to be the observation of any one who has had much to do with such games. If not, there has been something wrong with the individual. So he is not you, gentle reader, and, if that is the test, most certainly he is not me.

All the same, I have not enjoyed the prime of country-house cricket. That must be a tradition among my seniors. Don't you know the type of jolly old buffer, aged anything between fifty-five and seventy, with a big voice, bigger presence, and cheery disposition, when the gout does not give him a twinge, who lights a cigar, pulls down his shirt-cuffs, and has a twinkle in his eye at the very mention of country-house cricket?

Men of this type made country-house cricket a thing of gorgeous merriment. Possibly at college they had paid more attention to May Week than to Plato, and to Eights Week than to Smalls. But they played for their runs in life as keenly as they tried to make them at cricket, and if they are not on the roll of fame, their names are in letters of gold on the list of English gentlemen. And mark you, it's no light thing to be a real English gentleman. A goodly number of those who call themselves such don't behave as such, perhaps have no conception of the true decencies of that most honourable walk in life. But that's another story, and my theme is cricket.

Moreover, I am not an old buffer, and I am going to have my say in this chapter. So having patted the elder generation admiringly on the back, I shall confine myself to my own.

Therefore I am compelled to repeat that, as far as I can judge, the palmy days of country-house cricket were before my time. I have had a rattling good experience myself, but each year I see some perceptible shortening in of the amount of this class of cricket. Not that there is not enough for anybody, in all conscience, so long as he is in the swim. But it is more difficult to get just the right men to play, and just the right places to play at. No one who ever met me would bring up any charge of pessimism. I am merely stating a fact for the benefit, say, of school-boys of to-day, who may not be able to get quite such a golden time in just the same way as I and scores of my contemporaries.

CRICKET

From a Picture by John Collet.
MISS WICKET AND MISS TRIGGER.

"Miss Trigger you see is an excellent shot. And Forty-five Notches Miss Wicket's just got."

The multiplication of clubs has not only spoilt to some extent the fixtures of the elder clubs, but also prevents the younger ones from getting exactly the matches they want. The next detrimental is the multiplicity of first-class fixtures. In 1881 there were about eighty such matches. Last year 154 matches were played in the county competition, and there were quite seventy others which had claims upon the compilers of statistics. The ratio of time available for a genuine amateur good enough to play in matches of this standard to snatch for the relaxation of an off-day country match therefore differs perceptibly. Moreover, there is an even worse obstacle, and it is that, nowadays, gentlemen take up professions much earlier. Men who are going to practice at the Bar can no longer afford to be idle during several summers after they have come down from the University. If they are going into business, into the City or on the Stock Exchange, it is, to-day, at the earliest possible date, not at the latest. Truly the old order changes, for formerly where a young man might laugh and disport himself in the days of his youth, now he must work to earn a living wage in the struggle for life. Fourthly, there is the insidious beguiling of golf, which attracts many a man from Saturday cricket. All these changes are marked on the sheet which records the difficulties of country-house cricket.

Going one step further, look at the Herculean task of collecting a team. You must offer good enough matches to get the aid of really good cricketers; and even then the bulk are off on tours. A mere village match, be it ever so cheery and enjoyable, will not induce a man to travel a long distance, to come to a strange place, where he knows no one but his skipper. It is not human nature in the twentieth century, and nowhere does human nature come out more plainly than at cricket. Show me the spirit in which a man plays a cricket week, and I will tell you his character; it is often easier to gauge than his true form, which may be affected by ill-health or adverse weather, or even genuine bad luck. A great deal too much is heard about luck in cricket. I do not say it does not exist. For example, I would say Haigh had shocking luck in not being chosen in a test match in 1902, and that Mr. J. H. Brain had a real spell of bad luck when he scored 0, 1, 0, 0,

0, 2 in Oxford *v.* Cambridge and the two Gentlemen *v.* Players matches of 1885, when at the very top of his form. But for the most part "luck" is made the excuse for other things at cricket.

Let me sketch an ideal week of country-house cricket, such as I have myself experienced several times. People are asked to stay in the house who are all previously acquainted with one another, thereby removing any stiffness and undue formality. There have been cases where, from almost undue kindness, host and hostess have had a house full of cricketers, many of whom they do not personally know, and the guests themselves, however much they enjoy themselves, must be conscious of the feeling that they are practically staying in a hotel, so little do they really come in touch with their hospitable entertainers. I do like a hostess to act as mother to the team, and for the old sportsman who entertains us to stand umpire. A bevy of nice girls are needed to keep us all civilised, and the merriment is then tremendous. Perhaps if a match is over early there is a ladies' cricket match. Anyhow, there is a dance one night. On the others, songs, games, practical jokes, any amount of happy, innocent nonsense, as well as perchance a flirtation as hot as it is hopeless. Boy and girl alike know they may never meet again, but they won't waste time meanwhile. Another of the charms of country-house weeks, if you are invited to the same one regularly, is that year by year you meet a group of very nice people you never perhaps see at any other time, but who inspire you with sincere regard. "Don't you remember?" and "How's so-and-so?" enable you in five minutes to pick up the old threads.

These form the background. The cricket itself ought to be of sufficient importance to interest everybody, but not be allowed to degenerate into an infatuation, and therefore a nuisance to the fair sex. The ground ought not to be too good, for a perfect pitch takes the heart out of the bowling, and long scoring can be over-indulged in. All the four totals over 100 and under 200 was A. G. Steel's ideal game, and it is about the best. The games should have local interest, and should if possible bring over one or two cricketers known to the house party. As for the cricket lunches, most delightful of all Benedick meals, on no account let hospitality spoil them. Champagne lunches are being horribly overdone. Men do not play good cricket on Perrier Jouet, followed by *creme de menthe*, with two big cigars topping a rich and succulent menu. No, give us some big pies, cold chickens, a fine sirloin of English beef, and a round of brawn, washed down by good ale and luscious shandygaff. That is all that cricketers want, and kings only fare worse. If the county folk drive over in the afternoon the host is afforded an opportunity of providing an enjoyable diversion for his neighbours. It is quite true that lots of men, unless they know that they will be extremely well done, infinitely prefer to be put up at a hotel in the nearest town. But that is partially because of their bachelor shyness, and partially because they fear they will be too hampered both in the matter of taking their ease and also about tobacco. Formerly it was the exception to smoke, now the exception is not to. I remember when Smokers *v.* Non-Smokers was played at Lord's. The former eleven all took the field with cigarettes in their mouths, and freely declared that some of their opponents had not been lifelong total abstainers in the matter of tobacco. It was a rattling good game, all the same. Those big amateur matches at Lord's had something of the charm of country-house cricket on a large scale, thanks to a slight relaxation of formality and a good deal of cheery hitting. The best of these functions was the I Zingari jubilee match, when the famous wanderers opposed the Gentlemen of England in 1895.

In connection with the immortal gipsy club, it is interesting to quote its motto, "Keep your promise—keep your temper—keep your wicket up." Founded in 1835 under the title of the Beverley Club, it was renamed by Sir Spencer Ponsonby Fane, who with the late Mr. Lorraine Baldwin and my own uncle, Mr. Chandos Leigh, will be for ever associated with its welfare. The rules are unique, and a trifle whimsical; for example: "Entrance be nothing, and the annual subscription do not exceed the entrance." At the election of a new member, it was enjoined that the candidate should take his stand at the wicket with or without a bat, as the committee may decide. Being a vagrant body, the I Zingari have never boasted a ground of their own, and it is a pity that more serious cricket should have lessened the importance of their chief matches.

Now, having announced that I am going to be desultory, I propose to reel off a batch of anecdotes. The bulk will be anonymous, which is a pity, because individuality always gives point to a tale, but I have no wish to hurt any one's feelings.

Some years ago, at the period known as "when we were boys together," the late Lord Leconfield one summer holidays had a boys' cricket week at Petworth, having teams of Sussex, Surrey, and Hampshire youngsters to play. He daily entertained all the teams at dinner, which, by the way, was served on silver plates. Suddenly, in one of those silences which sometimes fall on assembled eaters, a big lad shouted, loud enough to be heard even by the late Lord Leconfield himself, "I do hate eating off these beastly tin plates; in a decent house like this they might give us china ones." This lad never proved good enough for first-class cricket, so please do not father the tale on to any prominent run-getter.

A certain amateur of a team staying in a country house, who was a bit of a wag, by the way, much annoyed the rather pompous host by addressing the family butler as "waiter." The skipper of the team remonstrated, but with no result. At breakfast the cricketer in question never seemed able to get the right dish; if he meant eggs, he received kidneys, and so forth. This was because, the menu being in French, he used to point at random to some item, not wishing to betray his ignorance of the language. On the last morning of the week, when the usual bill of fare was brought to him, he retorted in stentorian accents, "Rats to you, waiter; I'll fetch it for myself."

I have had so many happy years of comradeship with "Plum" Warner that he must forgive me if I spin a yarn or two about him. I was in the habit of taking an eleven each year against Mr. Charles Goschen's team, an ideal country-house cricket match. To my dismay, for I was always anxious to win, we were once decidedly weak in bowling, and we knew Warner was playing for Mr. Charles Goschen's eleven. So after grave consultation we decided that, as we were never likely to bowl him out by fair means, we would do it by foul. We pressed on him to accept an invitation to stay overnight before the match. Now, my old friend is most abstemious, but on this occasion the far-famed claret of our host, dexterously administered by the opposing team, had considerable effect. He was earnestly solicited to give his opinion on every vintage we could find, and the spoon might have stood up in the whiskey dashed with soda which was mixed for his nightcap. On the morrow, when he was out before he ran into double figures, we decided that Bacchus was the best bowler on our side.

The next story is not a country-house cricket story at all, but as it is new in print, it may be allowed to slip in. It happened when I was captain of Oxford, and I think the match was against the Australians. Those who merely study cricket scores may not be aware that Warner has a high opinion of his own persuasiveness as a change bowler. His actual figures for life up to 1902, in first-class cricket, drawn from Mr. Home Gordon's *Cricket Form at a Glance*, are only three wickets for 196 runs, which only shows how bad is the judgment of modern captains. If he had been permitted the persistency of K. S. Ranjitsinhji, he would probably have captured more wickets. Last season, when he was captain, he failed to disturb the bails to the tune of 51 runs, which proves his modesty. I have known captains go on to bowl first and stay on through the whole innings, but of such certainly is not my old friend. However, in the match in question, when our opponents wanted about six runs to win, and I don't know how many wickets to fall, I chucked the ball to "Plum." "Ridley and Cobden won't be in it," observed one of the fieldsmen, and in memorial was written this rhyme:—

Little Plum Warner stood in a corner,
Thinking he'd like to bowl.
The captain said, "Hum,
I *will* put on Plum,
He may get me out of this hole."

But sad to relate, he did not.

Captain Trevor, the popular "Dux," used to tell a cheery story about the demoralising effect of first-class cricket. Mr. A. S. Archer had been a big scorer for the Incogs; then he went with Lord Hawke's team to the Cape, and on his return had changed his style, and could score no more. Captain Trevor plucked up courage enough to suggest he should forget that he had ever "figured in averages," and should play in the old way.

"You want the golf shot?"

"If you please."

"And the tennis scoop towards third man?"

"Certainly."

"And a pull?"

"Three in each over."

"Right."

He went to the wicket and made ninety without a chance that was accepted.

Any one who has much to do with getting up matches can tell eloquent tales about being chucked. Perhaps nobody quite appreciates the force of the parable in which they all with one accord began to make excuse, until he is running a cricket week. This telegram was positively sent by the man on whom everything depended, "Can't come; am summoned on a jury." The wretched captain retorted, "Rot, you are not a householder," but he had to fill the vacancy. Not long ago Mr. A. D. Whatman, wrote begging forgiveness, but the fact was, he was off fishing. As for the accident which keeps a man who is passing through town "laid up and unable to come on," it is nearly as ancient and as annoying to the manager as that hoary chestnut, "prevented by an illness in my family." However, these things will occur in the best-arranged teams.

A COUNTRY HOUSE CRICKET MATCH.

There is a comfort and ease about country-house and minor cricket, which you do not get in the charmed circle of first-class matches. The good-humoured chaff is most healthy, and certainly tends to prevent mannerisms, into which many engaged in prominent cricket find they are apt to drop. Also the search-light of publicity is conspicuous by its absence.

Next, I would like to quote a story which my old friend Mr. C. W. Alcock relates, and which, I fancy, he personally overheard on a tram: "No, Bill didn't get much out of his day's cricket. He had to pay eight bob for his railway fare, and lost 'is day's screw, and was fined a shilling for being late next morning, and 'e didn't get no wickets, and 'e missed four ketches, and 'e got a couple of beautiful blobs. He did feel sold, he did." If anybody observes that is what can be euphemistically described as a chestnut, my retort is, that it will be new to a great many people. Certainly we all thought the story of Mr. "Buns" Thornton making a mighty slog, and Mr. Bonnor subsequently observing that he had a sister who could hit as hard, was a hoary veteran. You will remember Mr. Thornton's reply: "Why not bring her over and marry her to Louis Hall? You could then combine the two styles." That was said at Scarborough, but this very story in the cricket week of 1901 in that very town was hailed as a diverting and fresh anecdote. Wherefore I take courage to proceed in my own garrulous fashion.

Among the pleasantest of all country matches are the military weeks. The play is brisk, hard hitting, keen fielding, usually a Tommy who sends down expresses which it is a treat to cut to the boundary, and, of course, the most unbounded hospitality and good-fellowship. Then there is always the regimental band in the afternoon, and one can do a little dance step to beguile the tedium of fielding, or should you be dismissed for one of those conspicuous oval blobs, it is at least consoling to retire to a tune from the last musical comedy. And of course, at soldier fixtures, all the ladies of the garrison muster in their brightest frocks, and I can truthfully say that a match where none of the fair sex are spectators loses one ray of sunshine for me. The follies of girls who do not understand the game may sound funny set down in printer's ink, but spoken by merry lips, they only provoke laughter, while, as a matter of fact, lots of ladies understand cricket quite as well as most of men do; moreover, they are singularly quick at noticing idiosyncrasies in the players.

School tours are splendid things at the beginning of the holidays. Eton Ramblers, Harrow Wanderers, Marlborough Blues, Old Malvernians, Uppingham Rovers, Old Cliftonians, and last, but chief in my eyes, Old Wykehamists—the very names cause a glow at our hearts. There you get boys leaving school playing side by side with a schoolmaster or two as comrades, and no longer *in statu pupillari*. The former gain confidence, the latter rub off the corners which may have become rather sharp during the half, and both are leavened by a further batch of old boys who have names still respected at the school. The cricket is keen, and the talk over the pipes after dinner is clean, healthy, and tends to put them all on good terms with one another.

I purposed to have written quite a valuable treatise on clubs, but when I dipped into the books, I either found that the serious matters would be dry-as-dust at this stage of my article, or else that it was difficult to collect information. So I shall merely emphasise the cordiality of the sides which do battle each summer. I Zingari come first to my thoughts, for not only have I the honour to wear the red, yellow, and black, but my uncle, Mr. Chandos Leigh, is one of the presiding potentates—more power to him. No longer do these wanderers figure on the card of the Canterbury Week, but it is still their festival. Theirs is the big tent, theirs the admirable theatrical performances, and theirs the true traditions of the historic Week. It is the most delightful function in county cricket to-day, just as it was formerly the greatest boon in old-time cricket. I feel that some of the graceful irresponsible matches which were contested at Prince's in the 'seventies still cast a pleasant reflection on the Week at the old minster town. Also, I heartily wish I Zingari could revive that one-time match v. Gentlemen of England at Scarborough, but the difficulty of collecting competent sides seems insurmountable. But let no one think I Zingari do not keep up their pristine value. Have they ever had a finer record than in 1902? It reads: matches played, 29; matches lost, 1, Silwood Park winning a one-day game by 46 runs. So I think the spirit of I Zingari can look very beaming when she is pleasantly embodied for the epilogue of the Kent festival.

It is impossible to run over the list of clubs. Free Foresters, of course, recurs to memory—cheery, bright, with a military leaven, under the admirable guardianship of Mr. E. Rutter. Their annual volume yields an admirable statement of bustling, hard-fought cricket on many welcome swards where reporters do not scribble nor the public give heed. Amateur cricket owes a great debt to them, and also to the Incogniti, in which the present governor of Jamaica has taken such keen interest. With varying sides, but unvarying good-fellowship, these pilgrims of cricket show how many withstand the attractions of golf, and prefer to drive the leather rather than the Haskell.

Each University has one club noteworthy to the community at large. Cambridge boasts the Quidnuncs, the cap of which is so familiar in county matches, because hardly any old blue seems to wear his 'Varsity colours. Against Yorkshire at Lord's in August 1902, four of the Middlesex side wore those colours of dark blue with the narrow blue stripe, these being Messrs. Cyril Foley, C. M. Wells, R. N. and J. Douglas. Though it is limited to fifteen members in residence at Cambridge, practically everybody who is tried for the eleven appears to outsiders to be entitled to wear the caps, though no undergraduate in his first year is eligible.

Of the Harlequins I must write more briefly than I should like. They are very dear to me, and I had the honour in 1902 of being elected Vice-President in succession to Mr. A. J. Webbe, who became President in consequence of the death of Mr. C. J. B. Marsham, who had occupied the position since the foundation of the club in 1845. One annual meeting is held each year on the first day of the match with the Gentlemen of England, when the elections take place. Only seventeen members may be in residence, and no one can be put up as a candidate until his fourth term. There is always one pleasant function, the dinner given by that keenest supporter, Mr. T. B. Case. If the Harlequins do not play so many matches as of yore, it must not be ascribed to lack of enthusiasm, but to the more lengthy programme of the Authentics, who possess a wider range of selection. The Harlequin cap, in its bold contrast, has been seen on every ground, and at Lord's, to the end of their keen careers in the field, it was invariably worn by two very fine Oxonian cricketers who never obtained their colours, Messrs. T. S. Pearson and J. Robertson-Walker. Of yore, half the Oxford eleven used to be seen arrayed in the coloured shirt of the Harlequins, which was gaudy when new and looked shabby when it had been for a short period the sport of the elements. I am not speaking by book, but my impression is that Mr. "Punch" Phillipson and Mr. J. H. Brain would be the two last who have donned the garment in first-class cricket. Long life and unabating good fellowship to Harlequins, present and future! There is every sign that the wish is destined to be fulfilled.

The Authentics Cricket Club was founded by Everard Britten-Holmes, in November 1883, who, from its birth in Brazenose College, Oxford, has acted as its Hon. Secretary to the present day (1903), G. R. Askwith of B.N.C. being its first Hon. Treasurer, then followed by H. Acland-Hood of Balliol (1884-89). During the summer of 1884, arrangements were made to tour during the summer vacation, and what was at first but a week's cricket, has become one of several months, and a membership then of 19 has become one of nearly 800.

During the winter of 1885, it was decided to place the club upon a more solid and active basis, and a large gathering of prominent 'Varsity players and others was held at Oxford, a question at that time coming up, as a suggestion, to include Cambridge 'Varsity players and others, when it was unanimously resolved and carried, that the club be called "The Oxford University Authentics," and confined to members of Oxford University only. Special rules were drawn up for membership, etc., and many matters of detail arranged. More important matches were played during the summer vacation, with a view of unearthing latent cricket talent, and giving members an opportunity of being brought more prominently before the cricket authorities at Oxford, and their respective counties—an opportunity they could not otherwise then have had. Above all, it had in view the keeping of old 'Varsity cricketers of the past in touch with the present, and the present in touch with the future. Professor Case of Corpus Christi College—the well-known old Oxford cricket blue of 1864, 1865, and 1867—readily consented to become the President, and took much interest in the club, and to him we owe its motto: "By Jove's authentic fire." It may be mentioned that the name "Authentics" was given to the club by the founder, who, being a musical enthusiast, coined the word "Authentics," as from an authentic cadence in music, and as derived from the Greek [Greek: authenteô], "to rule"; and from Professor Case's happy thought the colours of the club were suggested—"Blue" for the sky, "Blood Red" for Jove's arm, and "Old Gold" for the lightning.

Reverting to country-house cricket—aye, and the observation does for all club matches—the great aim is to induce those participating in first-class cricket to don flannels in the minor game. There is one great inducement, and let all managers take note of it. Tempt the crack amateur by offering him plenty of opportunity to bowl. In county cricket the amateur, with not a dozen exceptions in 1902—all I recall are Messrs. F. S. Jackson, D. L. A. Jephson, E. M. Dowson, E. E. Steel, J. R. Mason, W. M. Bradley, G. H. Simpson Hayward, W. W. Odell, C. M. Wells, H. Hesketh Pritchard and B. J. T. Bosanquet—field out while the professionals conduct the attack. To most amateurs bowling is a joy all the sweeter for its rarity. The amateur will not resist the bait, and will come if he possibly can. There is no cricketer so easy to get on with, or who makes a house match go better, than a distinguished amateur. The bulk are absolutely without "side," and having learnt the sterner discipline of first-class cricket, absolutely revel in their sporting holiday, while the effect of their presence on the rest of the side is electrical.

With that I conclude. I could write more, if I ventured to trespass further on your attention. Should I have had the good fortune to divert and not to bore, I shall consider myself the luckiest in this band of writers, and after all, I have had the best of all topics. So, hurrah! and long life to country-house cricket!

CRICKET

From a Painting by Louis Belanger, belonging to H.M. the King.

A VILLAGE MATCH IN 1768

CHAPTER XII

VILLAGE CRICKET BY C. F. WOOD

Constant readers of the *Pall Mall Gazette* will not have missed a most amusing article on "Yokels at Cricket," which appeared over the initials "R. E. M." during the summer of this year of grace 1902. With a felicity of exaggeration which would do credit to Mark Twain, the writer describes his experiences on a pitch where the blocks were too large to begin with, and too numerous; where all that could be said of the fielding was that the men in the lost-ball region did their ferreting well; and where the fast ball shot, rose five feet, and shot again. Sometimes, he pathetically adds, the five-feet rise came last.

Something of this kind possibly still exists in the remoter parts of our sportive country, but as it is my intention in the present paper to set down nothing about village cricket that has not come within the scope of my own experience, I must forego at the outset the attractions of these humorous irrelevancies, and speak the truth as far as I know it, even at the risk of making my contribution to this historic work unnecessarily serious.

For the same reason I must deny myself the pleasure of dishing up once more the innumerable funny stories about village cricket that appear periodically in books of this kind; and I have further registered a solemn vow to leave the top-hat period severely alone, and make no reference to Fuller Pilch, Caffyn, Mynn, or any other belted heroes of prehistoric days. So what it comes to is this: I am going to put down here my own experiences and opinions of village cricket as it is played to-day by my own village eleven, of which I have the honour to be captain, and if the result turns out unsatisfactory and of little interest, kindly believe that the fault lies in my incapacity of expression, not in any lack of excitement in the cricket. *That* at least is beyond reproach.

Please don't think from the above that, unlike the heroines of most of our modern stuffy plays, our club has no past! On the contrary, I have before me now the accounts of our village club right back to 29th July 1865, when we expended the sum of £1: 7s. in the following irreproachable manner:—

Umpire	£0	10	6
Dinner for ditto and scorer	0	8	0
Six *Bell's Life* papers	0	1	0
Stamps	0	1	0
Ball	0	6	6
	£1	7	0

Four shillings apiece for the umpire's and scorer's "dinner" may seem expensive in these modern half-crown days, but judging from the next entry, we can only consider it an exceptionally moderate occasion. On 21st September of the same year, when, if we may judge by 1902, the summer was just beginning, the same entry reads:—

Dinner for ditto, scorer, and beer £0 11 0

Whether the extra 3s. represents the amount of liquid refreshment required by the umpire and scorer alone, or in conjunction with those acting in similar capacities on the other side, whose integrity they thus thought to drown, does not transpire from the account.

All these and many other like interesting matters are at the disposal of the gentleman who may still do for Kent cricket what Lord Alverstone and C. W. Alcock have done for Surrey in their *Surrey Cricket*, just published; but I must not break through my self-imposed rule and enlarge any further on these exploits of bygone days. Good old Kent! Where is the historian that shall do justice to your past glories? Or is it that the part is after all greater than the whole, and that when Philip Norman finished *West Kent Cricket*, there was nothing left unsaid?

Now of all the various sorts of cricket that are played in and out of this country, I am prepared to maintain against all the writers in this or any other book that village cricket is at once the most amusing to watch, the most exciting to play, and of the greatest educational value to the English race. Notice, I do not call it the most scientific form of the game, though there is a special sort of science required to finish a match between 3 and 7 P.M. every Saturday afternoon! Let us first compare it, from a spectator's point of view, with county cricket; and it will help to emphasise my point if I quote one or two reports of county matches culled at random from the daily press in August this year:—

Notts *v.* Kent, at Nottingham. "Kent, holding a lead of 91 runs on their first innings, did not hurry themselves unduly in their second venture. Dillon took forty minutes to register a couple of singles"!

Leicester *v.* Sussex, at Brighton. "On Saturday, Dr. Macdonald was in three hours and three-quarters for 48 runs, having in the previous innings made 33 in about two hours. In other words, he was batting five hours and forty-five minutes for 81 runs"! And the poor reporter adds drowsily, "It was a terribly monotonous performance."

Is not this a veritable caricature of cricket? Why, rather than watch such a game drag its dreary trail over three summer days, I would vow never to go near a ground again, and take to German skittles. Compare this "terribly monotonous performance" with the compressed interest of a whole match completed in four hours on a village green, with the supporters of each eleven shouting each other down, as the sun sinks all too rapidly in the western sky, and both runs and wickets are freely given away as the excitement rises to fever pitch. Which would you rather do, candid reader, if you had the choice? Stand on your hind legs in the field all one day, sit and smoke your tongue sore in the pavilion all the next, with a chance of getting a knock on the third, or join our village eleven on Saturday afternoon, and have four certain hours of unadulterated joy? Well, most of us would choose the county eleven, I suppose, though we should find it weary work.

But here it strikes me I am poaching on other people's preserves, and before I commit the indiscretion of mentioning country-house cricket, which is a subject my friend Mr. H. D. G. Leveson-Gower is treating in his usual masterly way, let me hasten back to my own little corner, from which I was an ass to stray.

And yet, having gone so far, I ought perhaps to explain why I consider village cricket to be of so great an educational value to our race. And by education I do not mean the mechanical stuffing of an unwilling agent with knowledge for which he can never have any possible use, but rather the formation of all those characteristics which help to build up what we call a man—pluck, temper, self-restraint, respect for others, abnegation of self, *et hoc genus omne*. Now the people who play first-class cricket are divided into two categories—those with means and leisure who play for love of it and because they are good at it, and those who play because they are good at it and can make a living out of it; and though most of the above virtues can be cultivated to a certain extent in a team made up of these two classes, yet it is certain that the same spirit does not animate an eleven of amateurs and professionals as will work wonders in a village team made up of every rank in life, the parson, the cobbler, the squire's son, and the blacksmith, all playing on an absolute equality, all playing for their side and not for themselves, all playing for glory and none for averages or talent-money.

And now I really must tell you a little about our own village club. In the old days we always used to play on the Common, where the turf was excellent and the boundaries out of sight; but as London got nearer and nearer, and every train belched forth a volume of trippers right across the ground, we had to shift our quarters, and for £10 a year we now have a large but not exclusive interest in a ten-acre field. A large square, capable of providing about a dozen good wickets during the summer, is enclosed with posts and chains, and the patient labour of our groundman and umpire (who in his leisure hours is also a shoemaker and a lamplighter) is year by year producing better results. For although it is unwise to have a perfect pitch for half-day cricket, yet, on the other hand, it must not be dangerous, and with the limited means at the disposal of a village club, the happy medium is not easy to attain. As the seasons roll on, patches are repaired with turf "sneaked" from the Common, weeds are removed (some of them), manure and fine soil is bush-harrowed in, seed is sown, and every summer we congratulate ourselves that, if not yet quite like the Oval (which we do not want it to be!), at all events our ground is the envy of our neighbours. I should add that this year (1902) we had a whip-up and laid the water on, but only used it twice!

Perhaps, in connection with our wicket, I may be allowed to recount a little reminiscence, still fresh in my memory, of the days when the pitch was not what it is now. A short-tempered and fiery member of an opposing team was batting, as he always did, in spectacles, when a rising ball from our local Lockwood hit him right in the face. Seeing what I supposed was his eye drop out on the pitch, I dashed forward to field and return it, only to discover one glass of the spectacles unbroken on the turf. Beyond a cut on the bridge of his nose, the man had suffered no hurt, but it was long before he paid us another visit, or the scorched grass recovered from his language.

It is not necessary, but it is useful, to have some sort of a pavilion, even for Saturday afternoon matches, and we were lucky to get, some five or six years ago, for the cost of removal, an old Norwegian house, built of wood, with a corrugated iron roof, which suited our purpose admirably. It originally consisted of three rooms, two bed-rooms and a sitting-room between, and, by putting all the windows in the side facing the ground, altering the doors, and fitting up the interior with lockers, washing-places, store-room for the groundman, bat-racks, etc., we have quite sufficient accommodation for our purpose. We are also the proud possessors of a tea-tent, where every Saturday throughout the season, when there is a home match, our kind lady friends provide our opponents and ourselves with an excellent tea. This smacks perhaps of luxury, and wastes a little time, but you must remember that our matches are nearly always over before the time for drawing stumps arrives, and it is a great attraction for those of us who do not always get such a good tea for nothing! But more than this, it makes our weekly matches a cheery social gathering, it provides an enthusiastic gallery of lady friends and admirers, and thus adds a charm to the natural beauty of our ground which we should be extremely sorry to lose. In fact, I attribute much of the prosperity of our club to the kind interest of the ladies in the village, who do so much for us, and I should like to see their excellent example more generally followed elsewhere.

Well, now we have got our ground, our pavilion, and our tea-tent, what about our officials and our members, and the all-important question of "subscription"? We have a president, captain, vice-captain, secretary, treasurer, and a committee of six members, all being elected fresh every season at the annual meeting. However, so far as my five years' experience goes, no change has been made except to fill up vacancies caused by death or removal, and the meeting is a merely formal affair where we re-elect each other *en bloc!* The president in our case has always been the *persona*, or parson, of the parish, and where there is a curate, he is the best man, in my opinion, for the secretaryship. The advantages of this arrangement are obvious, for he is probably the only gentleman in the place who is there all day; he knows where all the villagers live, and it is easier for him than any one else to go round and get up the teams. For however much you print on your match-cards that "members wishing to play in any match should send in their names to the captain before

Thursday evening," or words to that effect, the fact remains that no villager has ever yet been known to *offer* to play; and though a man may be thirsting for a place in a certain match, and would be seriously hurt if he were not asked, yet the only reply he will make to your pressing invitation is a half-hearted, "Well, I don't mind if I do"! *But*, if the curate is not a good player, he should content himself with his secretarial duties, and not appear in the field. However excellent he may be in other ways, if he cannot hold a catch or keep his bat decently straight, he ought not to give the enemy occasion to blaspheme. As Dean Hole says in answer to his own question, "Is it right for a clergyman to hunt?" "On one immutable condition—*that you ride straight to hounds.*" We limit our committee to six members, chosen from every walk in life—a merchant, a farmer, a solicitor, a gardener, and so on—and in the diversity of opinions there is sometimes much wisdom. As a matter of fact, I have never found gardeners, as a class, of very much use in connection with cricket. They may know a little about turf, but, barring a few exceptions, they do not make good players. The reasons are not far to seek. From the very nature of their work, they have fewer opportunities than others of taking part either in practice or matches: in summer, there is always a lot of mowing, watering, and so on to do, and when a man has been working with his back, arms, and legs all day, he feels little inclined for more violent exertion. This too is probably why they are slower in their movements and clumsier with their hands and feet than most other people. But at least they take their waistcoats off, which a stableman never does. Now, why is that? It is almost a rule without an exception that a man who works in the stable in trousers, belt, and shirt, adds a waistcoat to his outfit before he goes in to bat. Still, waistcoat or no waistcoat, he is generally bright and quick, and with practice makes a smart field. Perhaps the best village cricketers, taking them all round, are recruited from the ranks of carpenters, footmen, blacksmiths, and schoolmasters, rather than from the stables and the gardens, but in any case it's more than half the battle to get them young. There must be disappointments, of course. Some of the most promising boys lose their interest in the game when they think they are men, and become loafers; some go out to work in other places, and the team knows them no more; but you are amply repaid if two or three of one generation at last find their strength, and after a year or more of painstaking duck-eggs suddenly blossom out into consistent scorers, to the no small astonishment of their friends and their own huge delight. Don't think from this that we set too much store by good batting. On the contrary, all our matches (and other people's too!) are won or lost by fielding, and I can never tell my men too often that it does not do to give your opponent two, or even three, lives, when he has made up his mind to take yours at the very first opportunity. Only, as at golf the good drive gives one the greatest pleasure, though the high approach may be the prettiest shot, and the deadly put wins the hole, so at cricket the greatest pleasure of the greatest number is to make lots of runs, though they may not be wanted, when a good catch in the deep field or a smart return may win the match.

CRICKET

From a Sketch by Robert Seymour.
"OUT, SO DON'T FATIGUE YOURSELF, I BEG, SIR!"

From a Water-Colour by J. Hayllar.
A CRICKETER.

I mentioned just now the ominous word "subscription." The question of finance is one which must enter to a large extent into the prosperity of a village, or any other, club, and happy those who have enough cloth to cut to ensure their coats fitting! In our own case we generally seem to have succeeded in making both ends meet, though, as will be seen from the following typical years' figures, times were not always prosperous:—

1867.	Receipts	£34	4	0	Expenses	£34	0	6
1877.	"	18	1	0	"	17	0	2
1887.	"	14	1	11	"	12	7	6
1897.	"	31	5	2	"	34	19	6
1902.	"	47	8	6	"	38	11	5

I ought to add that these amounts represent only annual subscriptions and current expenses, and do not include special collections made for special purposes, such as enclosing the pitch in posts and chains, laying on the water, and so on. If a "round robin" is not sufficient to cover these extras, I generally find a good village concert in the winter is sufficient to wipe off any deficit. We have a minimum subscription for the villagers of 2s. 6d. a year, which is readily paid when they find it is a *sine qua non*; but the rule must be rigidly enforced, even to the exclusion of your best bowler, if he prove refractory! The amount collected in this way is of course trifling, yet without it I believe the club would very soon stop for want of members; for it is the experience of all who have many dealings with their village neighbours, that they do not value or take any interest in the thing which costs them nothing. Free education has been a sufficient curse to our villages without giving them free cricket too! The rest of our income is collected by the lamplighting, shoemaking, groundman and umpire, who goes round with a book to all the houses in the parish at what he considers the psychological moment, generally after dinner in the evening; for which extra labour he is accorded a commission of 1s. in the pound collected. The details of expenditure require no elucidation; they are the same in all cricket clubs; only the healthy countryman, with plenty of muscle, but no skill to apply it, will require at least twice as many bats every season as an ordinary cricketer. And mind you, they don't go at the edges; they come right in half. Is it the stiff wrist? But when all is said and done, what fun it is! I have played most sorts of cricket—country-house cricket, club cricket, touring with my old school eleven, and so on, and once I even appeared for the county second eleven, when I was run out by a local tradesman before I had a ball; but none of them ever touched village cricket for pure, unadulterated amusement. My earliest recollection takes me back to a pretty little ground not far from Croydon, where a local schoolmaster enjoyed a great reputation as a demon underhand bowler. It was not so much the pace or the pitch that proved so disastrous to the batsmen, as the man himself. He *looked* destructive from the moment he began his run, and as soon as the ball was delivered he used to ejaculate fiercely, "That's got yer!" Whether such a remark at such a critical moment was entirely in accordance with the customs of the game, it never entered our heads to inquire; we only knew it generally had the desired effect.

It was on this same ground, I remember, that Edward Norman, one of a distinguished family of Kent sportsmen, coming in last when his side wanted six runs to win, hit the first ball he received, a straight one well up, clean out of the ground to square leg, over the boundary road and a high wall into the kitchen garden of the local squire.

Here too the head gardener of the same squire annually disports himself in spotless white, to his own huge gratification and the vast amusement of his numerous underlings. Not that they would dare to smile while the august eye is on them, for he is an autocrat in his way, and can both look and say unutterable things. Once, I remember, when he was taking part in a Married *v.* Single match, one of the under-gardeners had the misfortune to clean bowl him for a duck. He looked first at his shattered wicket, then at the spot where the ball had pitched, and proceeded to march solemnly towards the trembling and penitent bowler. We held our breath, fully expecting that some fearful tragedy was to be enacted, and that, having first brained the poor man with his bat, he would follow it up by giving him the sack on the spot. But when he had reached the middle of the pitch, he pulled himself together in the most dignified way, merely remarked, "Well bowled!" and stalked off to the pavilion. So even in his moment of defeat he was superior to most of us, for I have noticed it is generally considered etiquette in this class of cricket to *run* to shelter as fast as you can, if you have taken no exercise between the wickets.

VILLAGE CRICKET IN 1832.

CRICKET

From the Painting by R. Wilson, R.A.
CRICKET AT HAMPTON WICK.

It would be in the highest degree imprudent for any one in my position to say a word against country umpires. And, to give them their due, I have almost always found them, in what some would call these degenerate modern days, to be as accurate and as honest as their brethren in more exalted spheres; but there are brilliant exceptions! "To play eleven men and an umpire" is, I am told, a chestnut in Gloucestershire, and one story I can vouch for certainly bears out the theory. It was a match between two old-standing village rivals, and contrary to custom, the visiting team turned up with twelve men, owing to the unexpected arrival of a fairly good player. Another member of the team, conscious of his own weakness, but with perhaps more cunning than good-nature, promptly offered to stand down, "for," said he, with a sly wink to his captain, "I can be of more use to the side if I umpire!" That comes from Gloucestershire, but it is easily beaten by the remark of the real umpire in a village match in Oxfordshire last August. "How's that?" shouted the wicket-keeper proudly, as he captured the ball straight off the edge of the bat. "Not out," said the umpire, "*but it was a damned fine catch if he hit it.*" I do not wish for a moment to insinuate that our friends in the north are not always the good sportsmen we believe them to be, so we will put the following tale under the head of "exceptions." The match, a two-day one, was being played at Whitehaven, in Cumberland; things had gone badly with the home team, and all the morning of the second day the local umpire had been engineering his opponents out in the most courageous way. But to everybody's astonishment, when a confident appeal was made against the last man on the side, he gave him "Not out." Struck by this sudden conversion, a friend asked him what the meaning of it was. "Well," he said, "if I'd a given 'im out, they wouldn't 'a stayed to loonch, and my father does the caterin'"!

In one of the keenest matches I ever took part in (it was on the 16th of August 1902, and we won by four runs), two men of the opposite side were batting, one a very fair bat, and dangerous when set, the other a dubious quantity at all times. The bowler sent down a fast one to leg which the wicket-keeper failed to stop, and both men started for a bye. Meanwhile, short slip, backing up, had stopped the ball, and threw the near wicket down, while both men were apparently in the middle of the pitch. The good batsman refused to go, and the indifferent one apparently held no views on the subject, but stayed where he was, while the two umpires (I blush to record it) gave, almost unasked, an opinion favourable to their respective sides. Party feeling was running high, but I never allow any discussion in the field, and it was properly left to the umpire at the end where the wicket had been broken to give a decision. Unfortunately, it was their umpire, and the weak batsman had to go! And it was a fair decision. There was obviously a doubt, and he gave his own side the benefit of it. Who could do more? But we had our revenge on the gentleman who refused to go. He hit a lovely half-volley to square leg, which did not quite reach the boundary. My man was after it like a hare, and while they were trying to get the fourth run, he threw the wicket down full pitch from where he picked up the ball, at least 90 yards off, and with only one stump visible. A fluke, of course, but when I complimented him afterwards on his brilliant performance, which practically won us the match, he simply said, "Oh! that's nothing, sir; I was always a bit of a slinger"!

Our great annual event is, of course, the Married *v.* Single match, which takes place on the last Saturday of the season. In the old days, when we played on the Common, this was the occasion of what one might almost describe as a village orgie. Men turned up from everywhere, who never honoured the club with their patronage at other times, some even dressed, most appropriately, as clowns, and the cricket was distinctly of the "Dan Leno at the Oval" variety. Well, well, *Tempora mutantur et nos mutamur in illis.* It was doubtless very amusing, but there were objections, latterly even objectors (whether of the conscientious variety or not doesn't matter), and the present tea-tent is in every way preferable to its rival "down the road." So we play on our own field now, and get a very fair amount of amusement out of it, even without the clowns. I have tried for years to get up some sort of a representative married team before the day of the match, but it's no use. They are all too old, or too stiff, or too busy. Yet when the eventful afternoon arrives, there are generally some fourteen or fifteen Benedicts ready to do battle for the honour of their wives and families, against a meagre dozen or so of the less fortunate Bachelors. Public enthusiasm, at all times keen in village cricket, reaches its high-water mark on this great day, and the ladies especially assemble in large numbers to do honour to the brave. Sympathy is invariably and entirely with the married men—I suppose because part of the audience are the wives of the team now stripping for the fray, and the other part hope that by next summer at latest they will be in the same proud position. On paper there can be no question that the Bachelors have the strongest side, but against their youth, their practice, and their skill we place our experience and our considerable numerical advantage, so there is not much in it. Then again, they look rather contemptuously at our weather-beaten ranks; say we have no bowling, can't run (two of us are over seventy, certainly!), and are altogether as sorry a collection of prehistoric peeps as ever took the field. *Nous verrons!* The Bachelors win the toss and start batting. An old man of sixty-seven, who has recently contracted a second matrimonial alliance to make sure of his place in the team, asks to keep wicket, and after buckling on a pair of lovely old faded yellow pads, he goes to say "Good-bye" to his new "missus," and get her to pull his waistcoat down and stuff it inside the back of his trousers (this I saw myself). Then I arrange the rest of my veterans in a sort of inner and outer circle round the wickets, in places where they are least likely to be hurt, and the game begins. It is true we have no bowling, in the modern sense of the term, but it's quite good enough for the Bachelors. At one end I put on our village umpire, who bowls fast straight underhand, literally "daisy-cutters," and at the other a newly-married groom, just come into the parish, whose methods are precisely the same. Scoring is out of the question. You may stop the ball as long as your patience lasts, but you can't get it away, and wicket after wicket falls, as the pick of my village eleven try in vain to turn fast sneaks into slow half-volleys. I feel quite sorry for them when the end comes, and twelve promising young cricketers, with "Mr. Extras," have all been dismissed for 76. Then our turn comes, and the umpire and I make a good start by putting on 30 for the first wicket. But it's not all over yet! Six wickets fall for an additional 9 runs, and the audience begins to hold its breath. We have still eight or nine batsmen, but can they possibly make 5 runs apiece? We are soon put out of suspense. The groom goes in for hitting, knocks up 15 in a few minutes, which demoralises the field, the best bowler is taken off at the critical moment, and the rest is easy. We have had a most thrilling afternoon's cricket, and no one is any the worse except the old wicket-keeper, who is so stiff he cannot come downstairs for two days.

I feel I ought to apologise for appearing in such august company as this book affords, but it is our cheery editor's doing, not mine. My enthusiasm for the subject is the only excuse I can offer, and that he has kindly accepted, so I need say no more. Only I shall always regret that no more capable pen than mine was found to do justice to such an inspiring theme as "Village Cricket."

AN EIGHTEENTH CENTURY CARICATURE

CHAPTER XIII

FOREIGN CRICKET BY P. F. WARNER

In this and the following chapters I shall endeavour to give some account of the many cricket tours in which I have been fortunate enough to take part, in the West Indies, the United States, Canada, Portugal, South Africa, New Zealand, and Australia.

The days have long gone by since England was the only country in which the game flourished; for cricket is played, and played well, too, in the most remote corners of the British Empire.

It has been my good luck to play cricket from Trinidad to Auckland, and from Buluwayo to Vancouver, so I hope there may be some interest in a record of the game under conditions widely different from those of Lord's or Old Trafford—upon grounds that are within easy distances of volcanoes, and in towns that have since undergone siege and bombardment. In the course of my wanderings with bat and ball, I have covered nearly 80,000 miles by land and sea, and I have enjoyed every mile of my long journeyings, for the memories that one carries away from such tours as these are innumerable. May not one hope, too, that these touring teams are not altogether without value from the political side, for they must assuredly lead to a closer understanding and better appreciation of our kinsmen in Greater Britain.

One hears nowadays so many remarks—as a rule far from complimentary—as to the status of amateur cricketers, that I take this opportunity of enlightening those whom it may concern as to the arrangements made with regard to the financial part of the six tours which are dealt with in this chapter.

On the first tour to the West Indies we paid our own steamship tickets, and our wine and washing bills, cabs, etc., throughout the tour; all other expenses were paid by the clubs in the various islands. The trip to Oporto was a purely private affair, into which no question of expenses entered one way or the other. On my two visits to America, and the South African and New Zealand tours, all our expenses, excepting again our wine, washing, cabs, etc., were paid for us. Not one penny passes through the hands of either the captain or any other member of the team, and we have no interest whatever in the gate—that is the affair of the club which has invited the team out. The expenses of the tour are paid out of these gates, and the profits—and there is nearly always a profit—go to the body which has undertaken the risk of the tour. We are, in fact, the guests of the various places we visit.

As captain of two teams in America, no money whatsoever passed through my hands. Our tickets were invariably taken for us, and we just stepped on to boat or railway, as the case might be. The hotel bills, with the exception of our bill for wine, washing, and smaller items, were sent in to the Associated Clubs of Philadelphia.

Lord Hawke's South African and New Zealand teams contained professionals, who, over and above their ordinary expenses of travelling and hotel bills, were guaranteed a lump sum of money, which was paid them by instalments. The amateur receives his expenses only; the professional his expenses *plus a lump sum*. There has been so much misunderstanding on this subject, that I shall, I hope, be excused for having dwelt upon it at some length.

The West Indies

Before the visit of R. S. Lucas's team in the early part of 1895, the West Indies were quite unknown to the majority of English cricketers. That tour, however, showed that there was plenty of cricket scattered over the islands, which only needed encouragement to develop into a good class; and such delightful accounts did Lucas and his team bring back of the West Indies, that Lord Hawke had little difficulty in getting together an amateur side to go out a couple of years later.

We sailed from Southampton in January 1897, and after a pleasant fortnight's voyage arrived at Port of Spain, Trinidad. Here we opened with a big score against the Queen's Park Cricket Club, but came to grief when opposing the island team, chiefly owing to some excellent bowling by two black men, Woods and Cumberbatch, on not a very easy wicket of the kind where one ball bumped and the next shot. But admitting that they received considerable assistance from the wicket, Woods and Cumberbatch bowled excellently, and took thirty-nine out of the forty wickets that fell in the two matches. As it happened, these two defeats were the only ones we experienced in the fourteen matches which we played, and though I do not by any means wish to make excuses, Trinidad certainly caught us at a disadvantage, as we had not become acclimatised to the great heat, and, moreover, had not had sufficient opportunities to get into form. But the Trinidad side were a good one, their strength lying in their bowling. The batting was, with one or two exceptions, rather rough, but the fielding was excellent, and this, coupled with the bowling of Woods and Cumberbatch, proved too much for us.

Cricket is, or was at the time I was there, established on a firmer basis in Trinidad than in any other of the West Indian islands, and the game was well supported by all classes.

From Trinidad we went to Grenada and St. Vincent, where our opponents were no match for us, though the St. Vincent eleven ran us close for a couple of days. The match was played on a matting wicket, which played fast and true, though every now and again the ball turned very quickly.

At Barbados we had two splendid games, one of which we won after a most exciting finish, and the other ending in an even draw. Barbados and Trinidad were certainly the strongest teams in the West Indies five years ago, and there was little to choose between the two sides, Trinidad having perhaps the stronger bowling, and Barbados the better batting.

Antigua, St. Kitts, and St. Lucia were weak, but Demerara were a very fair side, though they did not show their true form against us. In the smaller islands, such as Grenada, St. Vincent, Antigua, St. Kitts, and St. Lucia, we invariably met black men in the opposing teams, but in estimating the respective merits of Trinidad, Barbados, and Demerara, it must not be forgotten that Trinidad played their black professional bowlers against us, while Demerara and Barbados did not. In the Intercolonial Cup, which is played for every other year between the above-mentioned colonies, the custom was to exclude the black professionals, but I am glad to say that this has been altered since I was in the West Indies, and they are now allowed to take part in the Cup competition. The admittance of black professionals into the best games cannot but do good, as they add considerably to the strength of a side, and their inclusion must instil a universal enthusiasm for the game amongst all colours and classes of the population.

Jamaica we did not visit, but I was told by more than one of the team which went out to the West Indies in the early months of 1901 that the cricket there does not attain to any high excellence.

The wickets are not as a rule good, but there are exceptions, and the grounds at Barbados, Demerara, and Antigua provide excellent wickets in fine weather. It is hard enough to make runs on a sticky wicket in England, but it is easy in comparison with a West Indian wicket after rain, for under the influence of a powerful tropical sun, the ball not only takes any amount of break, but gets up perfectly straight as well. The Trinidad ground is the largest, and has the best pavilion and seating accommodation, while of the many grounds I have seen in various parts of the world, none surpasses it from a picturesque point of view; but the wicket is a very bad one, and I really think the authorities would be wise to lay down matting.

The West Indian team which came to England in the summer of 1900 played seventeen games, won five, drew four, and lost eight, and when one considers that the team had never played together before, that they were quite unaccustomed to our climate, and to the strain of three days' cricket, and that they lost the toss twelve times out of the seventeen matches the tour comprised, I do not think their record was at all bad. At the start the side were quite at sea, but they improved immensely as time went on, and towards the end of the tour showed some uncommonly good cricket. The result, too, of the visit of the last English team—by far the strongest of the three sides that have visited the West Indies—gave evidence that the cricket had improved in the islands, for out of the three test matches played, the West Indians won two, while Demerara twice defeated the Englishmen, and Barbados once.

A PARLIAMENTARY MATCH.
The Duke of Wellington, Sir Robert Peel,
Lord John Russell, and others.

At the same time, it was generally felt that West Indian cricket had not altogether made the progress expected. There are several good bowlers, notably Burton, the best bowler in the West Indies, and Woods of Demerara, Lane of Barbados, and Smith of Trinidad; but though the fielding is excellent, the batting is weak, and of real knowledge of the game, especially in the art of placing the field, there is little, while the idea is far too prevalent that they have nothing more to learn about cricket. This comes, I fancy, from their having on three or four occasions beaten the English elevens which have played in the West Indies, quite forgetting that these sides are never more than fairly strong amateur combinations, with no pretensions to being called first-class.

From every point of view, there can be nothing more enjoyable than a cricket tour in the West Indies. The climate is, at the time of year we were in the West Indies, quite delightful, and although the sun is undoubtedly very hot, it is by no means harmful, if ordinary precautions are taken. Abler pens than mine have painted the exquisite charm and beauty of the islands, and the hospitality of the people is beyond measure, the visit of an English team being an event which is eagerly looked forward to. The black portion of the population is especially enthusiastic. They climb the trees round the ground, and keep up a running comment on the game, and it is somewhat disconcerting to hear a huge shout of "Bowl him out, Clif," go up as the bowler runs up; but this was what happened in Barbados when I was batting, "Clif" being Clifford Goodman, the great Barbados bowler. Lord Hawke was a source of joy to the native mind. On going out to bat he was generally greeted with shouts of "Welcome, my lord," followed by an exhortation to the bowler to "give the lord a duck." Once, indeed, at St. Vincent the bowler did not disappoint the crowd, for Lord Hawke retired first ball, whereupon the scene which followed was, I venture to think, unique. First of all the bowler turned a somersault on the pitch, a way of evincing delight at the dismissal of an opponent one does not usually see at Lord's or the Oval; but after he had gone through his acrobatic performances, it was even more interesting to watch the crowd, who threw their hats in the air, danced about in front of the ring, shook hands with one another, chattering and shouting the while. It was the most extraordinary scene I have ever witnessed on a cricket ground; but the West Indian negro goes quite mad about cricket, and when A. E. Stoddart was in Barbados, hundreds of them used to gather round his hotel on a chance of getting a glimpse of the great man. With more coaching from English professionals, and with a readier desire to assimilate the lessons taught, there is no reason whatever why cricket in the West Indies should not attain a high standard, for the West Indian seems to take quite naturally to the game, and the climate is admirably suited to the bringing of cricket to perfection.

One or two of the grounds, notably that of Georgetown, Demerara, are well cared for, but, speaking generally, there is much ignorance displayed in the preparation of wickets, and it would be almost worth while to have some man out from England to put the various grounds in order, and impart instruction to the native groundsmen. The Trinidad ground is infested with mole crickets, and the wicket is so impossible that, unless matting is put down, cricket will languish, for no young cricketer can be taught to bat really well on such a wicket, and a bowler may be in danger of thinking himself a good one, when in fact he is only just beginning to bowl.

My second tour was to America in the autumn of 1897, when I captained a fairly strong team, which included, amongst others, G. L. Jessop and F. G. Bull, the latter about that time the best slow bowler in England.

In discussing the strength of American cricket, it is as well to bear in mind that American cricket means Philadelphian cricket, for nowhere else in the United States does the game really flourish, though a few enthusiastic supporters do their utmost to keep it going in New York and Baltimore.

In Philadelphia, base-ball is quite a secondary consideration, and there is a genuine enthusiasm for our great national game. The grounds themselves are superb, but the wickets are not good, though English cricketers are scarcely, perhaps, in a position to pass judgment on them, seeing that teams from this country never play in Philadelphia before the middle or end of September, when, owing to the abundance of what is termed "fall grass," it is no easy matter to obtain a good wicket.

The Philadelphian eleven, as I saw them on the occasion of my first visit, were a distinctly good side. They had quite a lot of batting, a brilliant wicket-keeper in Scattergood, and, in J. B. King and P. H. Clark, two bowlers distinctly above the average of amateur cricketers. King, indeed, on his day is a remarkably good bowler, while Clark has been almost invariably successful against English elevens. My eleven played two matches against the Gentlemen of Philadelphia. The first we lost by four wickets, and the second we won by seven wickets, though it is only right to say that in this game the Philadelphians were without J. A. Lester, the best batsman in the States.

On the second tour to America, in September and October 1898, I had not, perhaps, quite such a strong team as in the previous year, but as the side included F. Mitchell, C. O. H. Sewell, C. J. Burnup, V. T. Hill, B. J. T. Bosanquet, and J. L. Answorth, it was not weak. On this, my last visit to America, the cricket in Philadelphia seemed to have fallen off. J. B. King and P. H. Clark were as good as ever, Scattergood was the same brilliant wicket-keeper, and the fielding was absolutely A1, but the batting had gone off deplorably. Our first match was fought out on a sticky, difficult pitch, when we won very easily by eight wickets, hardly any of our opponents having any idea of playing on such a wicket. The return match was played on a good wicket, certainly by far the best I have seen in America, and again we won, but this time only after a desperate battle. When the sixth wicket went down, we wanted 30 runs to win, and as the side possessed a most distinct tail, the result was decidedly open to doubt. However, some fine hitting by Hill enabled us to pull through by four wickets.

K. S. Ranjitsinhji and B. J. T. Bosanquet have both taken teams to Philadelphia since I was last there, but Ranjitsinhji's eleven was absurdly strong, and won anyhow, though the Philadelphians had the worst of the luck in having to bat on slow wickets, on which they do not shine. B. J. T. Bosanquet's eleven won one and lost one match with the Philadelphians, the Americans being seen to great advantage in the game they won, and quite outplaying the Englishmen, who lost by no less than 229 runs. Bosanquet had, too, a very fair team, including E. M. Dowson, E. R. Wilson, R. E. More, F. Mitchell, and V. F. S. Crawford, but the Englishmen admittedly played very much below their true form.

There seems to be more good cricket played in and around Philadelphia to-day than was the case some two or three years ago, and, generally speaking, the game seems on the up-grade, so that I shall be surprised if the team which is to visit England this summer does not prove to be the best that the Philadelphians have ever sent us.

I have already mentioned that Philadelphia is the only place in America where the game has taken a firm hold, but New York has in M. R. Cobb a distinctly good cricketer. He is a very fair bat, and an excellent slow to medium right-hand bowler, of the type that one would wish to see more of in America, American bowlers being as a rule of the tearaway, erratic type. Cobb's record against English teams is a very good one, and he was, next to J. B. King, the best cricketer I saw in the States in 1897 and 1898.

On my first American tour, except for a visit to Niagara, we did not go to Canada at all, but matches were arranged at Montreal and Toronto for the second trip.

At Montreal we played against XIV. of Eastern Canada, and won by 88 runs; but the ground, which is used as a skating-rink for six months in the year, is appalling. There was a certain amount of keenness for the game, but to enable cricket to flourish, a cricket ground must be obtained.

The ground at Toronto is a very fair one, and the Canadian eleven was certainly the best side we met, next to the Philadelphians, but little enthusiasm was shown, and cricket is not, I fear, in a very satisfactory condition.

A MATCH AT IGLOOLIE, BETWEEN H.M. SHIPS "FURY" AND "HECLA".

Outside Philadelphia there is, as I have pointed out, little or no cricket in America, but in Philadelphia itself the game flourishes, and our matches were followed with the greatest enthusiasm. The ordinary writer on cricket in America knows little about the game, but his headlines and comments are exceedingly amusing. We were invariably referred to as "British Lions," and we were assured that the American girl had "just a little liking for sure-enough Englishmen." Again, when the Philadelphians defeated us, one of the Philadelphia papers came out with a long leading article entitled, "Waterloo for Englishmen," in which the fact that we had been beaten at our own game was duly rubbed into us.

Cricket has many difficulties to contend with throughout the United States. In the first place, the Americans are a busy nation, and have no leisure to devote themselves as energetically as we do to cricket, while, except in Philadelphia, base-ball always has been, and always will be, the national game. But in Philadelphia the future of cricket is assured, for I have met there some of the keenest and most ardent followers of the noble game.

A great many people would, I imagine, scarcely believe that cricket is played in Portugal; but wherever two or three Englishmen are gathered together, there will wickets be pitched and creases marked out, and as the English colony in Oporto numbers a few thousands, it is not surprising to find the game in full swing in the beautiful town on the banks of the Douro.

It was as a member of T. Westray's eleven that I had the pleasure of playing cricket in Oporto in the spring of 1898. Our captain, a former leader of the Uppingham team, had got together a very fair side, which, with L. C. U. Bathurst and H. R. Bromley Davenport to bowl, and R. N. Douglas and S. A. P. Kitcat as the principal batsmen, proved far too good for our opponents. We won the first match against an Oporto eleven by an innings and 103 runs, Douglas making 106, and our two crack bowlers, with the assistance of A. C. Taylor, dismissing Oporto for 33 and 118. Our total was 254, but had the Oporto eleven possessed even a moderately good fast or medium-paced bowler, we should not have got 100, for the wicket was almost dangerous. I have a vivid recollection of being hit on the forehead by a slow half-volley which jumped straight up. The Oporto fielding was good, but the bowling very poor indeed, half-volleys on the leg stump and long hops being frequent.

Our next opponents were Portugal, three Englishmen coming over from Lisbon to take part in the match; but here again we won almost as easily by an innings and 75 runs, though the cricket of our rivals showed some improvement, the bowling being of a better length, and the fielding decidedly surer. But cricket in Oporto is confined to twenty or thirty enthusiasts, so that the game cannot be taken at all seriously. Something will have to be done to the wicket, which at present is deplorable, for the soil itself is very sandy, and plantains seem to take root again as fast as they are cut out. The best plan would be to lay down cocoanut matting, but the cricketers in the *leal e invicta citade* (the loyal and unconquered city) are rather proud of the fact that theirs is the only ground in Spain or Portugal in which a grass wicket is obtainable.

None of the Portuguese took even the slightest interest in our visit, beyond a paragraph in the local paper stating that the "afamados loquedores de cricket" had arrived, and that the enthusiasm for cricket in England was even greater than that shown for bull-fighting in Spain, and that the names of Grace, Abel, Ranjitsinhji, and Maclaren were in England as well known as the names of Guerita, Marrantini, Perate, and Carajello, the famous bull-fighters, were in Spain.

CHAPTER XIV

CRICKET IN SOUTH AFRICA BY P. F. WARNER

On 3rd December 1898 I left England on my fifth tour abroad as a member of Lord Hawke's South African team. The side was a powerful one, including such men as F. Mitchell, C. E. M. Wilson, the late F. W. Milligan, Trott, Tyldesley, Cuttell, Haigh, and Board.

CRICKET

After a delightful voyage in the *Scot*, we arrived at Cape Town, and during the next four months played cricket from Table Mountain almost to the Zambesi and back again, visiting Johannesburg, Pretoria, Kimberley, Port Elizabeth, Grahamstown, King William's Town, Graaf Reinet, and Buluwayo.

Lord Hawke's was the fourth English team to go to South Africa, Major Wharton, W. W. Read, and Lord Hawke himself having in previous years taken out sides.

In any review of South African cricket, the first thing to be remembered is that, from one end of the great continent to the other, you never by any possible chance see a grass wicket, matting being used everywhere. On the Newlands ground, Cape Town, and at Port Elizabeth, the matting is stretched over grass, and this makes a wicket which enables the bowler to get considerable work on, though the ball does not come off the pitch very quickly. It is not an easy wicket, for a half-volley does not seem the same thing as on grass, and forcing strokes generally are at a discount. This kind of wicket affords most excellent practice, for it teaches one above everything else to watch the ball.

Tyldesley did make a very fine 112 at Cape Town, and Sinclair, the South African cricketer, an equally fine 106, but the ball nearly always beat the bat, and Haigh in particular brought off some great bowling triumphs. The work he used to get on the ball was prodigious; he thought nothing of pitching six inches outside the off stump, and then hitting the leg stump. Trott, too, did one or two fine performances, while Rowe, Middleton, and Sinclair were at times almost equally successful.

At Port Elizabeth the out-field is of grass, but the wicket seemed to me even more difficult than at Cape Town, for the ball, besides taking a lot of break, turned very quickly. Perhaps, however, I am unduly influenced by the fact that I made "spectacles" at Port Elizabeth—a favourite ground, by the way, for Englishmen to fail on, for more than one well-known cricketer has "bagged a brace" there.

Cape Town and Port Elizabeth are the only two cricket grounds in South Africa which can boast of a grass out-field; all the other grounds are absolutely innocent of a blade of grass, being nothing, indeed, but a brown-reddish sand—somewhat like the colour of the sand on the seashore—rolled into a flat and hard surface. The matting is stretched on this sand, and makes a hard, true, and very fast wicket, while the ball, once past a fielder, simply flies to the boundary.

The Wanderers' ground, Johannesburg, is by far the best ground in South Africa, for the wicket is exceptionally fast, and the out-field level and true. At Kimberley there is a good wicket, but the out-field is rather rough, which may be said with truth of nearly all South African grounds, except the Wanderers'. Natal we did not visit, but I am told that the Maritzburg Oval is in almost every respect the equal of the Wanderers' ground.

It will be seen from what I have said that matting wickets differ according as to whether they are laid on grass or otherwise. Matting stretched on grass gives the bowler more than a two-to-one chance, but matting on the bare grassless ground favours the batsman, though I am inclined to think that a really good bowler ought always to be able to make the ball "nip" a bit. Haigh certainly made the ball turn every now and again on the Wanderers' ground, and both he and Albert Trott have told me that they would infinitely prefer to bowl on the best matting wicket in the world rather than on a really hard, true turf pitch.

A STATE MATCH.
The Duke of Wellington bowling out Lord Brougham.

But the matting at Johannesburg is good enough for the most fastidious batsman, for it plays very fast, and though the pace of the wicket is apt to put a batsman off on first going in, once a man has got his eye in, he can make any amount of forcing strokes on both sides of the wicket, for the ball does not often hang on the pitch. Drives between cover and extra cover, and push strokes between the bowler and mid-on and past mid-on, can be made with great frequency, while the ball travels to the boundary at a great pace.

Bowlers of the type of Haigh, Tate, or Howell (the Australian) are the most successful on matting wickets, but slow bowlers are not, as a rule, effective, and fast bowlers, unless really great ones, are usually heavily punished.

The ordinary spikes one uses in England are quite useless on the matting, and have to be replaced by a sort of flat nail.

The length of the matting varies in different places, and this,

I venture to think, causes great inconvenience. At present the matting may be any length up to 22 yards, and often I found myself standing at one wicket with both feet off the matting, at another time with both feet on, and at another with one foot off and the other on the matting, while at Cape Town the pins which keep the matting down were placed just where the ordinary batsman puts his right leg. The South African Cricket Association might very easily pass a law making the matting uniform throughout the country, and in my opinion the matting should stop about a foot in front of the popping-crease. This is the length at Johannesburg. A captain may if he desires have the matting stretched tight at the commencement of each innings. In that case the pins are removed from the end and side of the matting, which is then well stretched by scores of Kaffirs, and afterwards firmly pinned into the ground. As a rule, however, merely the end pins are removed for a minute or two, the matting is given a pull, the pins replaced, and the matting swept, for pieces of grit and sand are very apt to collect on the mat, and a batsman has to look out for this while he is at the wickets.

    The great difficulty which frequently besets a captain on turf wickets, as to which roller he will put on at the commencement of his side's innings, or at the beginning of the day's play, is removed, for no rolling of the matting is necessary. Towards the end of an innings the matting is apt to get a trifle loose, and batting is no fun then, for should the ball pitch on one of the creases in the matting, it will probably break very quickly; and in this case the last few batsmen have the worst of the wicket. Winning or losing the toss, of course, makes no difference whatever, and rain, too, has little or no effect on the state of the pitch. One great advantage of these sandy grounds is that play is nearly always possible within a few minutes after the heaviest shower. I have seen the Johannesburg ground absolutely under water and resembling a lake, and yet play in progress within three-quarters of an hour after the rain had ceased.

    Cricket on matting is not half such a good game as cricket

on turf, but as there is no turf worthy the name in South Africa, South Africans have no other alternative but to play on matting. There is at first, to one accustomed to grass wickets, an air of unreality about the whole thing, and the game does not seem to be quite the same cricket we learnt in England. For the first few weeks I hated the "mat," but after a while one becomes more at home on it, and at the end of the tour I was quite fond of a matting wicket—though I never could agree with those who said that they preferred it to grass. One thing is certain, and that is, that playing for three or four months on matting wickets does improve one's batting, and makes one a more resourceful player. At Johannesburg, Kimberley, and the grassless grounds, forward play and hard forcing strokes score tremendously, but at Cape Town and Port Elizabeth forcing forward strokes are at a discount; the man who can play back well will make the most runs.

Lord Hawke's team played seventeen matches, won fifteen, and drew two. Five eleven-a-side matches were played, viz. two games *v.* All South Africa, two against Cape Colony, and one against the Transvaal.

At Cape Town we played a couple of games with XIII. of the Western Province, the remaining fixtures being chiefly against XV's.

At Cape Town we just won our first match by 25 runs against a Western Province XIII., chiefly owing to some grand bowling by Trott, Cuttell, and Haigh, the Yorkshireman taking five wickets for 14 runs at the crisis of the game. The highest total in the match was 149, and the highest individual score 45 by H. H. Francis. Murray Bisset, who captained the South African XI. in England, batted well in both innings, and Rowe and Middleton took seventeen of our wickets between them.

The return game saw us victorious by 106 runs, for we were all in better form by this time, and more accustomed to the eccentricities of the mat. Rowe and Middleton did even better than before, taking nineteen wickets between them, while Trott and Haigh bowled splendidly for us.

From Cape Town we went in turn to Graaf Reinet, Port Elizabeth, Grahamstown, and King William's Town, victory awaiting us at each place. At King William's Town we drew lots for the order of going in, and F. Mitchell and Tyldesley put on over 100 runs for the last wicket; but the most interesting thing about this match was a splendidly-hit innings of 66 by Giddy, who scored his runs in three-quarters of an hour. He twice hit Milligan out of the ground, and scored 16 off one over of Haigh's (there were five balls to the over at that time).

Engraved by R. Dunkarton. After W. Redmore Bigg, R.A.
THE SOLDIER'S WIDOW OR SCHOOL
BOY'S COLLECTION.

We had a long railway journey from King William's Town to Johannesburg, but after forty-five hours in the train arrived at the "Golden City," where a warm welcome awaited us, the station platform being crammed with cricket enthusiasts.

CRICKET

We stayed about three weeks in Johannesburg, and in that time played three matches—the first against a Johannesburg XV., which ended in a somewhat uninteresting draw; the second against a Transvaal XI., whom we defeated by an innings and 201 runs; and the third against All South Africa, which we also won, though only after a desperate struggle.

Sinclair batted and bowled well for the Johannesburg XV., and Halliwell kept wicket superbly, while Frank Milligan did a very good bit of bowling, for in the Johannesburgers' first innings he sent back ten men for but 64 runs, keeping up a good pace all the time, and making the ball do a bit every now and again.

In the match against the Transvaal, Tyldesley played splendidly for 114, Mitchell made an equally fine 162, and Trott knocked up 101 in a short time, our total of 539 for six wickets being, I believe, the highest total ever made in South Africa.

We won the game against South Africa by 33 runs, Lord Hawke's XI. making 145 and 237, and South Africa 251 and 99. It was a splendid fight, and at one time we looked hopelessly "in the cart"; but Trott, Haigh, and Cuttell bowled magnificently when our opponents went in to get the runs, while the fielding was extremely smart, and in our second innings I was lucky enough to get 132 not out. But fortune was on my side, as I was missed at point when I had made 94, and I rather fancy I was stumped when I had got about 70.

For South Africa, Sinclair played a fine free innings of 86, and was unlucky in being run out, and Llewellyn got 38 in the first innings, and Bisset 35 and 21 not out. Llewellyn, Middleton, and Rowe, all left-handers, took the great majority of our wickets, and we ought really to have lost the match, but one or two of the South Africans played rather recklessly in their second innings, and the dismissal of Sinclair in the second over—caught at mid-off from a tremendous skyer, by Cuttell off Haigh—seemed to destroy the confidence of the side, though Bisset played some bowling of the highest class with great skill.

The loss of this match was a tremendous blow to supporters of cricket in South Africa, and the disappointment in Johannesburg was keen. The game was followed with the closest attention, and on the second day about 8000 people were present, the takings at the gate, irrespective of stand money, amounting to £470. At Lord's or the Oval one can see the best cricket in the world for the modest sixpence, but half-a-crown was the lowest sum one could get into the Wanderers' ground for during Lord Hawke's visit to Johannesburg. As a proof of the interest taken in the match, the scores were posted up at various centres in the town and along the reef at intervals of an hour.

Just before meeting the combined South African team we had played a two-day match against a local XV. at Pretoria, whom we defeated by nine wickets. Braund, the Somerset professional, was at that time acting as coach to the Pretoria Club, and his all-round cricket was splendid, for he made 41 runs, took six wickets, and brought off three fine catches.

From Johannesburg we went to Kimberley, and there defeated a Griqualand West XV. by an innings and 25 runs. Most of us made runs, for the bowling was weak, and lent itself to free hitting. Shalders of Kimberley made 76 by very good cricket, late cutting and hooking particularly well, playing our professional bowlers with great confidence. The heat all through this game was almost unbearable, and we were glad to get away to the cooler climate of Buluwayo, where we played and won two matches, defeating a Buluwayo XVIII. and XV. of Rhodesia. Our bowling was altogether too good for our opponents, three or four of whom, however, showed good form. At this period of the tour Haigh was bowling superbly, and it took a really good batsman to make any runs against him.

An expedition to the Matoppos was not the least interesting part of a delightful ten days in Rhodesia, and the visit of the first English team to Rhodesia was, I think I may safely say, a great success. Certainly Lord Hawke's team enjoyed every moment of it.

On the way down from Buluwayo we played another match

at Kimberley, which was spoilt by heavy rain, and then, after spending two or three days at Matjesfontein with Mr. J. D. Logan, we returned to Cape Town for the last two matches. We beat Cape Colony by an innings and 29 runs, Haigh performing the hat trick, and Cuttell and Wilson making 98 and 69 respectively, and on Easter Tuesday wound up the tour with a victory over South Africa; but, as at Johannesburg, our opponents headed us in the first innings, Sinclair, six wickets for 26 runs, being chiefly responsible for a miserable total of 92, a score which the South Africans headed by 85 runs. Sinclair played a really great innings. He made 106 out of 147 while he was at the wicket by splendid cricket, driving with great power, and repeatedly bringing off a powerful back stroke.

Tyldesley (112) played in his best form in our second innings, and as nine men made double figures, we ran up a total of 330, which left South Africa 246 runs to win. The general feeling was that we should win by 50 or 60 runs, but after Shalders and Powell had scored 11 for the first wicket, Haigh and Trott got on the war-path, and in an hour South Africa were all out for 35! Haigh took six wickets for 11 runs, and Trott four wickets for 19 runs. Sinclair only made 4 this time, magnificently caught in the long field by Milligan.

A few days later we left Cape Town on the *Norman*, leaving Milligan behind, of whom, alas! it had been written in the Book of Destiny that he should never return to England, for fifteen months later he gave his life for his country while fighting gallantly outside Mafeking, and his bright and fascinating personality was taken from the cricket field. He is buried at Ramathlabama, but, though he lies so far away, to those who knew him well, as I am glad to think I did, his memory is ever dear.

The first English team to visit South Africa was Major Wharton's, in the winter of 1888-89. In those days the railway had not, I fancy, reached even Bloemfontein—certainly there was no railway to Johannesburg, and much of the travelling was done by ox waggon. Major Wharton's eleven played only two eleven-a-side matches—both against South Africa—and won both, the second by an innings and 202 runs.

W. W. Read's eleven beat South Africa in the only match played by an innings and 189 runs, and Lord Hawke's first team won their three test matches quite easily, but his second team, of which I was a member, only just beat South Africa at Johannesburg, and in the return at Cape Town our opponents more than held us for two days. We did not lose a match on the tour, but three or four times we had to fight hard to win.

The South African eleven which toured in England in 1901 did very fairly, showing plenty of sound cricket, and giving evidence that in a few years South Africa might hope to play the very best counties with every chance of success, while the good form shown against the Australians last autumn has gone far to strengthen the opinion which I had already formed that cricket has a great future before it in South Africa

CHAPTER XV

CRICKET IN NEW ZEALAND BY P. F. WARNER

It was on 12th November 1902 that I started from Liverpool as captain of a team for New Zealand. This was my sixth cricket tour abroad, and Lord Hawke was originally to have captained the side; but the sudden illness of his mother prevented his starting, and he did me the honour of inviting me to lead the side in his absence. Those, like myself, who have had the good luck to go on tour with Lord Hawke know full well what his absence meant, for his unrivalled powers of management, his tact, influence, and close attention to detail are important factors in the successful conduct of a cricket tour. Though the Yorkshire captain, to the regret of every one on the side, and of no one more than myself, was unable to accompany us, the team was everywhere known as "Lord Hawke's team," and we wore his colours—dark blue, light blue, and yellow—so well known on cricket grounds all over the world. The side Lord Hawke had got together was a good average English county team—that is to say, if it entered for the county championship it would at the end of a season probably be found halfway up the list, and possibly higher—and consisted of P. F. Warner, C. J. Burnup, F. L. Fane, T. L. Taylor, E. M. Dowson, B. J. T. Bosanquet, J. Stanning, P. R. Johnson, A. E. Leatham, A. D. Whatman, Hargreave, and Thompson.

The *Majestic* of the White Star Line made a quick passage to New York, whence we were whirled across the American continent to San Francisco, learning on the way that railway speed in America does not necessarily imply safety, for we had a couple of accidents, one of which ended fatally to a fireman, which delayed our arrival at San Francisco. Here we spent a couple of delightful days, on one of which we played and defeated XVIII. of California. Leaving San Francisco on 27th November, we stopped on our long voyage across the Pacific at Honolulu and Pago Pago, eventually arriving at Auckland on 16th December. A few days later we began the first match of the tour, and from then until 6th March we were kept pretty hard at work, travelling about the country and playing cricket. We played in all eighteen matches—eleven against odds—and won them all, not a single game being lost or drawn. This was in itself a wonderfully good record; but cricket in New Zealand is at the present moment up to no very high standard, and the results of three-quarters of the matches were a foregone conclusion before a ball had been bowled. We had a close game with a West Coast XXII. on a matting wicket, only winning by five wickets (on this occasion we had a long tail, for Bosanquet and Dowson were away fishing), and the Canterbury XI. and the New Zealand team in the first test match gave us a fair game; but we were almost always winning comfortably, most of our victories being gained in a single innings.

The New Zealand XI. were a very fair side, but they were in no way equal to us, for we won both matches easily, the first by seven wickets and the second by an innings and 22 runs. In both of these games we lost the toss, though in the first match it was probably an advantage to do so.

There were but seven eleven-a-side matches—against Auckland, Wellington, Canterbury, Otago, South Island, and the two New Zealand games. Auckland, South Island, Otago, and the second test match were won in an innings, Wellington were beaten by ten wickets, Canterbury by 133 runs, after declaring our innings closed, and the New Zealand XI. in the first test match by seven wickets.

The two best batsmen in New Zealand are D. Reese of Canterbury and K. Tucker of Wellington; and it is remarkable that they should stand so clearly out from the rest. Of the two,

Reese is, perhaps, the better. He scored two hundreds out of the eight innings he played against us—111 for Canterbury and 148 for New Zealand in the second test match at Wellington. He is undoubtedly a fine left-handed batsman—very similar in style and method to H. G. Garnett of Lancashire—with all those brilliant off-side strokes so characteristic of nearly all left-handed batsmen, and particularly good on the leg side. His weak point is in the slips, where he is apt to give a chance on first going in. Besides his batting, Reese is by no means a bad left-handed slow bowler, and a beautiful field at extra cover—in a word, a thorough cricketer. Tucker is a sound batsman who watches the ball well, has a good off drive and cut just behind point, and a very clever stroke between mid-on and short leg, which he uses to great advantage. He nearly always got runs against us, scoring 84, 50, 67, and 21 in four out of six knocks. On a rather difficult wicket at Christchurch, when our bowlers were turning the ball, he played very good and safe cricket—not so brilliant, perhaps, as Reese, but sounder, and a cool player. Leaving Reese and Tucker out of the question, there is no one in New Zealand who can be classed as a first-class bat. There are many very fair batsmen, who, with coaching, and with more practice and experience, would probably become first-class, but judged merely by what I saw, Reese and Tucker are the only two men whose batting attains to anything like first-class form.

The bowling is infinitely stronger than the batting, and is really quite good, Callaway—whom Mr. Stoddart will remember as bowling well against his 1894-95 Australian team—Frankish, Downes, Fisher, M'Arthy, and Upham being quite useful. Frankish and Fisher are left-handed medium pace, Upham is a fast right-hander, Downes slow right, and M'Arthy medium right.

Frankish, in my opinion, is the best bowler in New Zealand, for he keeps a good length, being especially difficult to drive or force forward, and with a nice high action makes the ball swing a good deal with his arm. On all wickets I should consider him distinctly the best bowler we played against.

Downes, even on a hard, true wicket, gets a great deal of work from the off on the ball, but his action is distinctly doubtful, and in the first test match he was twice no-balled by Charles Bannerman for throwing. He had bad luck against us in more than one innings, several catches being missed off his bowling. Downes is a splendid trier and a plucky, hard-working cricketer who can bowl all day quite cheerfully. On a sticky wicket he is bound to be very difficult, and it was on a pitch of this sort that he and Fisher dismissed the Australian XI. of 1896 for less than a hundred runs.

Callaway keeps a very accurate length, and generally makes the ball go across with his arm, though, when the wicket helps him, he can bring the ball back pretty quickly. Upham and M'Arthy can both make the ball break, but they bowl too much at the leg stump, and not enough at the off and outside the off stump. Fisher has a good action, but does not like being hit, and is, perhaps, rather past his best.

The wicket-keeping all over New Zealand is good—even in the smallest places we met a respectable "stumper"—and Boxshall and Williams are above the average, both of them being particularly smart on the leg side.

In the odds matches our opponents let an unwonted number of catches slip through their fingers; but the fielding of the New Zealand XI. was decidedly smart in both matches.

The visit of the team undoubtedly did good, and cricket may be expected to go ahead rapidly in the next few years. More professional coaches from England or Australia are wanted, and greater efforts should be made to induce the Australians to send over teams. Lack of funds has in the past militated against the spread of cricket; but the New Zealand Cricket Council, who engineered the tour, and nearly all the local centres, made money out of the gate receipts, and as a keen enthusiasm has been aroused, improvement in the future should be rapid.

There were too many matches against odds, and too much travelling and rushing about; but we saw New Zealand from end to end, and everywhere we were received with the greatest hospitality.

One word more. The loyalty and devotion of my companions made the oft-times difficult task of captaincy a joy and a pleasure, and any success which may have attended the tour—and I think I may safely say it was a success—was due entirely to the support and confidence they at all times gave me.

From a Painting attributed to J. J. Chalon, R.A.
OLD CHARLTON CHURCH AND MANOR HOUSE.

CHAPTER XVI

CRICKET GROUNDS BY MESSRS. SUTTON AND SONS, THE KING'S SEEDSMEN, READING

Without wishing to detract from the skill of the many famous batsmen of to-day, or venturing to compare them with players of a generation ago, it is probable that the former owe some of their success to the perfect wickets on which most first-class matches are now played. No apology is needed, therefore, for embodying in this work practical notes on the formation and maintenance of really good turf.

The soils on which a satisfactory cricket pitch cannot be formed are sand and an impervious clay. On the former it is difficult to establish a plant of grass, and under rain the latter becomes sticky. But loam which has been cultivated, especially when it is slightly tenacious, possesses all the qualities which favour the maintenance of fine perennial grasses, and at the same time enables the groundsman to prepare a firm and true surface.

On sandy soil the grass obtains such a feeble hold that even after rain the pitch, as it rapidly dries, crumbles and becomes unreliable. No amount of rolling will bind a soil of this quality into a firm surface, capable of withstanding the severe wear of a cricket match. Should there be no alternative site, it is imperative that sandy soil be covered with several inches of stiff loam, inclining to the character of clay. When filled with grass roots, such a soil can be rolled down into a fast, true, and enduring wicket, and the porous subsoil will ensure effectual drainage. The club purse must determine the extent of ground to be treated in the manner we recommend, but while the work is in progress, it is worth while to strain a point to make the playing square sufficiently large—say, at the very least, 40 yards in the line of the wickets, by 30 yards in width.

A different course must be adopted with adhesive land which has to be rendered porous. Possibly an effectual system of drainage, carried out by an expert, may be absolutely necessary; but this is a task which should not be undertaken with a light heart. It is a costly business, and the trenches take a long time to settle down. After a field has been levelled and sown, it is exasperating to see broad lines of soil gradually sinking below the general level, to the ruin of the ground for one or more seasons. As a rule, a good playing square can be established on clay by taking out the soil to about 1 foot in depth and replacing it with 6 or 8 inches of mixed chalk and sandy loam. On the top, return enough of the original soil, broken very fine, and carefully beaten down, to ensure a perfect level,—the surface to be finished with the rake and roller. Making up the ground should commence in October, and work ought to be completed before the end of November. In the absence of frost, February is the month in which the best results can be obtained from the heavy roller.

A slope is objectionable in many respects. It restricts the choice of a wicket, favours the hitting in one direction, and handicaps the bowlers. For these and other reasons, a level is justly regarded as one of the conditions from which stern necessity alone can warrant departure.

Whether the entire area, or only the playing square, shall be efficiently prepared and sown generally resolves itself into a question of funds. Where the limitation is unavoidable we need not waste arguments. But it must not be forgotten that, however excellent the playing square may be, unless the ball can travel evenly to the boundary, first-class cricket is impossible. This fact is now recognised by comparatively small clubs, whose grounds are laid and kept with a precision that would have excited the admiration of county teams in years gone by. And the club which is content with a well-made centre and an indifferent margin deprives itself of matches such as every ardent lover of the game desires to witness. It costs comparatively little more to prepare the whole area perfectly, and whatever saving may be effected by limiting the outlay for labour or for seed to the playing square is almost certain to be repented of.

Apart from the ground, two reserve plots should be sown and kept in the same condition as a fine lawn. From these plots turf can be cut to mend holes made by bowlers or batsmen. When one plot has been used, the surface must be made up with 3 or 4 inches of rich sifted soil, entirely free from stones; seed can then be sown and the sward be brought into condition while the other plot is cut away. Two or three years are necessary to mature the roots into a firm compact mat that may be cut, rolled, and relaid on the cricket ground.

Cricket grounds are made either by laying turf or sowing seed. In favour of the former method it may be claimed that the ground is at once clothed with verdure, and under favourable circumstances the ground is sometimes ready for use in rather less time than when seed is sown. But the difference is scarcely worth consideration.

Objections to the use of turf are so numerous and important that advocates of the practice decrease in number every year.

As a rule, purchased turf abounds in coarse grasses and pernicious weeds, which are difficult to eradicate, especially the coarse grasses.

When turf is laid in spring, the sections separate under a hot sun or drying wind, and the whole surface is disfigured by ugly seams. The gaping fissures have then to be filled with sifted soil and sown with seed.

The objection most frequently urged against turf is its almost prohibitive cost. When cut to the usual size—3 feet long by 1 foot wide—nearly fifteen thousand pieces are required to lay an acre. The expense, including cutting, carting, and laying, generally falls but little short of £100. For the same area, seed of the highest quality can be obtained for about £5, unless for some urgent reason an unusual quantity is sown; even then, an increased outlay of 50s. will suffice.

The labour involved in levelling the land and preparing a suitable surface is substantially the same for both methods.

A sward produced from a mixture of suitable seeds is incomparably superior in quality to the best turf generally obtainable. Seeds of fine and other useful grasses are now saved with all the care necessary to ensure the perfect purity of each variety. The presence of extraneous substances of any kind, and of false seeds in particular, can be instantly detected. The percentage of vitality is also determined with exactness by severe and reliable tests. The several varieties of grasses can therefore be mixed in suitable proportions for any soil or purpose with the precision of a physician's prescription.

Drainage

Should draining be necessary, this operation takes precedence of all other work in preparing the land. If rain pass freely through the soil, leaving no stagnant pools even in wet winters, the sufficiency of the natural drainage may be inferred. But it should be clearly understood that a fine turf cannot be established on a bog. Sour land soddened with moisture, or an impervious clay, must have pipes properly laid before good turf is possible, and as the trenches cannot be filled so firmly as to prevent the ground from sinking afterwards, draining must be completed at least six months before seed is sown. The size of the pipes must be determined by the rainfall of the district, the distance between the rows by the nature of the soil. The depth need not be great, as the roots of grass do not penetrate far into the earth. Fifteen feet between the rows, and the pipes three feet below the surface, are common measurements. No single drain should be very long, and the smaller should enter the larger pipes at an acute angle, to avoid arresting the flow of water. Near trees or hedges the sockets must be set in cement, or the roots may force admission and choke the drain, and the outflow ends should be examined periodically to ensure efficient working. In laying the pipes, it is necessary to employ a practical man who understands the business, and will consider the peculiar requirements of the case.

Preparatory Work

When no important alteration of the ground is necessary, deep cultivation should be avoided. Spudding to the depth of 6 to 9 inches will suffice, and this affords the opportunity of incorporating such manure as may be required. It frequently happens, however, that the surface does not present the desired conformation, and that a level plot can only be obtained by the removal or addition of a considerable mass of earth. Possibly the level may have to be raised by soil brought from a distance. In such a case it is usual to shoot the loads where needed as they arrive, tread the earth firmly down, and make the surface even as the work proceeds. This is the proper method if the whole bulk of soil come from one source, is uniform in quality, and suitable for the seed-bed. But in the event of there being much difference in the mould, it will be necessary to spread a layer of each kind over the entire plot, putting the retentive soil at the bottom, and reserving the finer and more friable portion for the top. To make up one part of the ground entirely with loamy clay, and another part with light loam, will inevitably result in a patchy appearance, because each soil fosters those grasses which possess affinities for it.

In order to ensure a perfectly level surface, pegs must be driven into the soil at the extreme points, and intermediate pegs at regular distances between. On these a long piece of wood having a straight edge can be adjusted by a spirit-level, and by shifting the wooden straight-edge from peg to peg, the level of the whole area can be efficiently tested.

Weed Seeds in Soils

A serious danger to which strange soil is liable is the presence of seeds of troublesome weeds. We have seen a lawn which had been made level with sifted soil taken from a neighbouring field. Upon every spot thus treated a strong colony of *Holcus lanatus* had grown, and as the pale green patches defied all efforts to extirpate them, the extreme course of cutting out and replacing with good turf had to be adopted.

The only certain way of ridding soil of weed seeds is to burn it. This operation is well understood by agriculturists, and we should like to insist upon it as not only essential when adding strange soil upon which a cricket ground is to be made, but highly desirable whenever the land is a stiff clay, in which case burning is often worth undertaking, for the beneficial effect it has on the growth of grass. The disintegration of the clay, which is one of the good effects of burning, may to some extent be obtained by simply digging up the ground in autumn and leaving it rough for the frost to break down and sweeten.

Should the proximity of dwellings render burning

impracticable, the only alternative as regards the weeds is to allow their seeds plenty of time to germinate, and to destroy successive crops by light hoeings in dry weather. Of course, waiting for weeds to appear is vexatious when the land is prepared and the season is passing away. Still, it will prove a real saving both of time and labour to ensure a clean seed-bed. After grasses are sown the soil must not be disturbed, and atmospheric conditions may follow which retard the germination of the grasses, and too often doom the sowing to failure. Those who are practically acquainted with gardening know that land which has been regularly cultivated for years, and is supposed to be fairly clean, always produces a plentiful crop of weeds, although no seed whatever be sown, yet many a faultless lot of grass seed has been condemned, when the weeds have had their origin entirely in the soil. Delay in sowing offers the further advantage that the soil will become thoroughly consolidated—a condition which is highly favourable to grasses, and very difficult of attainment under hurried preparation.

Enriching the Soil

In preparing the seed-bed, the condition of the soil is too often disregarded, although it is a matter of considerable importance, for grass is quite as easily starved as any other crop. After the sward is established, the enrichment of the soil has to be effected under disadvantages to which other crops are not subject. Vegetables in a well-ordered garden are changed from plot to plot, so as to tax the soil for different constituents, and the ground is frequently manured, broken up, and exposed to atmospheric influences, which increase its fertility. Grass is a fixed crop, chiefly deriving its nourishment from a few inches near the surface, and the only way of refreshing it is by raking or harrowing and top-dressing. Hence there are obvious reasons for putting the land into good heart before sowing. Well-rotted stable manure is always beneficial, but fresh manure should be avoided, because of its tendency to make the soil hollow. From twenty to thirty cartloads of manure per acre will probably suffice.

Where artificials are more convenient, 2 cwt. of superphosphate of lime, 1 cwt. of Peruvian guano, and 2 cwt. of bone dust, mixed together, make an excellent dressing. The quantities named are usually sufficient for an acre, and the mixture can be evenly spread and worked into the soil while the preparation of the seed-bed is in progress. Sutton's lawn manure also contains all the constituents essential to the luxuriant growth of fine grasses and clovers. This is a highly concentrated artificial, and as a rule not more than 3 cwt. per acre will be necessary. After the application of the manure, not less than ten days should elapse before sowing the grasses, or some of the seed-germs may be destroyed.

Surface Preparation

A fine friable surface is necessary to ensure favourable conditions for the seed, and in levelling the ground there must be a diligent use of the rake and roller. It is not sufficient to go over the ground once with each implement. Repeated raking assists in clearing the land of stones, unless they are very numerous, in which case it may be necessary to spread 2 or 3 inches of fine rich earth over the surface. After every raking the roller should follow, each time in a different direction. These operations reveal inequalities, pulverise the soil, and impart to it the firmness which favours germination. Grasses, particularly the finer varieties, are too fragile to force their way through clods, and many seeds will be lost altogether if buried to a greater depth than a quarter of an inch.

Selection of Seeds

The selection of grasses and clovers which are to form a fine dense sward should be regarded as in the highest degree important. They must be permanent in character, adapted to the soil, and free from coarse-growing varieties. On land which is liable to burn, clovers maintain their verdure under a hot sun after grasses have become brown. There is, however, this objection to clovers, that they show signs of wear earlier than grasses, and hold moisture longer after a shower. It is therefore often advisable to sow grasses only, unless the grass is peculiarly liable to scorch in summer. Then it is an open question whether an admixture of clovers may be regarded as the lesser of two evils.

The following grasses and clovers are specially suited for establishing a fine close turf, and the characteristics of the several varieties indicate the soil and purpose for which each kind is naturally adapted:—

Cynosurus cristatus (Crested Dogstail).—The foliage of this grass is dwarf, compact in growth, and possesses the great advantage of remaining green for an unusual time in the absence of rain. The roots are capable of penetrating the hardest soil, and the plant is well adapted for sowing on dry loams, especially such as rest upon a chalky subsoil, for which it manifests a marked partiality. Still, it will thrive almost anywhere, and should form a prominent constituent of most prescriptions for cricket grounds. Crested Dogstail is strictly perennial, and will increase in strength and vigour for quite two years after it is sown.

Festuca duriuscula (Hard Fescue).—This grass grows freely on sheep downs, and when mingled in due proportion with other varieties it largely contributes to the formation of a fine close turf. The plant commences growing early in spring, and seed should be sown on all soils that are not very wet.

Festuca ovina tenuifolia (Fine-leaved Sheep's Fescue).—The foliage of Fine-leaved Sheep's Fescue maintains its dark green colour for some time in hot dry weather, and is so slender as to render the term "blades of grass" almost a misnomer. Although most useful in mixture with other grasses, a homogeneous turf cannot be obtained from Fine-leaved Sheep's Fescue alone. The plants grow in dense tufts, and exhibit a decided antipathy to each other. The roots descend to a considerable depth in search of moisture. As a consequence, this grass will thrive on sandy or rocky soils that are incapable of supporting any other variety. In the early stage of growth it is easily overpowered by weeds, and for this reason autumn is preferable to spring sowing, because weeds are then less prevalent. But for cricket grounds this grass cannot be dispensed with, at whatever time of year a sowing may be made. After the plants are established they easily hold their position.

Festuca rubra (Red Fescue) possesses many desirable qualities, which give it a peculiar value. The foliage is very fine, close-growing, endures hard wear, and the plant is not exacting as to habitat. It thrives on the driest and poorest soils as well as on the best loams. The true variety is quite distinct from either of the other fine-leaved Fescues, and pure seed is difficult to obtain.

Lolium perenne Suttoni (Sutton's Dwarf Perennial Rye Grass).—Most of the perennial rye grasses are too coarse for a cricket ground, but this variety is eminently suitable for the purpose, alike for the fineness of its foliage and the dwarf branching habit of growth. It tillers out close to the ground, forms a compact sward, and retains its verdure throughout the year, unless burnt by excessive drought, from which it speedily recovers. The quick maturity of this grass is another advantage, as it occupies the ground while slower-growing varieties are developing.

Poa pratensis (Smooth-stalked Meadow Grass).—Although somewhat shallow-rooted, this grass endures drought remarkably well. Light land, rich in humus, is its favourite resort, and it will also grow, but not with the same freedom, on heavy soil. The plant does not develop its full proportions in the first season.

Poa trivialis (Rough-stalked Meadow Grass) is somewhat similar in appearance to *Poa pratensis*, but instead of being adapted to dry, light soils, it flourishes in strong, moist situations, and unless the land contains abundance of potash and phosphoric acid, the plant speedily disappears.

Poa nemoralis (Wood Meadow Grass).—From the perpetual greenness and dwarf close-growing habit of this grass, it is admirably suited for cricket grounds. The growth commences very early in spring, and it is one of the best grasses for enduring drought.

Trifolium repens perenne (Perennial White Clover) is indigenous all over the country, and may be seen growing freely by roadsides; indeed, it grows better in poor than in rich land. The seed will lie dormant at some depth in the soil, and yet germinate freely when brought to the surface. Perennial White is one of the clovers most frequently sown on lawns and cricket grounds; when constantly mown and rolled, it produces a dense mass of herbage.

Trifolium minus (Yellow Suckling Clover).—This is a quick-growing plant, showing abundantly in summer, just when the grasses are thin and the dense foliage of clover is most welcome.

Quantity of Seed

We need scarcely allude to the necessity of sowing new and pure seed, strong in germinating power. Seeds of the grasses and clovers suitable for producing a fine turf are nearly all expensive, some of them very expensive. But as fine grasses do not tiller out to the same extent as the larger pasture varieties, a liberal seeding is imperative. We recommend a sowing of four bushels per acre, and should the ground be wanted in the shortest possible time, the quantity may with advantage be increased to five or six bushels per acre. The additional outlay will be well repaid by the rapid clothing of the ground; and in favour of thick seeding it may be urged that the more closely the plants are crowded the finer will be the herbage.

Sowing

Grass seeds may be sown at any time between the middle of March and the end of September. But from the latter half of May on to about the second week in August, hot, dry weather often proves destructive to the young plants. They cannot acquire sufficient stamina to endure continued drought or fierce heat, unless constant watering is possible, and it is not conducive to sweetness of temper to see a good plant wither away. From the middle of March to the first week of May is the best period for spring sowing, the earlier the better; and from about 10th August to the middle of September for summer or autumn sowing. The clovers from an autumn sowing are liable to destruction by a severe winter, even if slugs spare them. Should there be failure from any cause, seed must be sown in the following spring.

The seeds can be more evenly distributed by two sowings than by one, however skilled and practised the sower may be; and the second sowing should cross the first at right angles. The finer grass seeds, being small and light, are readily blown to a distance by a high wind; a quiet time should therefore be chosen, and the workman must keep his hand low. On large plots the seed-barrow can be used with advantage, but even here we recommend two sowings, instead of entrusting all the seed to a single operation. Where the work of preparing the ground has been continuous, seed may be sown immediately the bed is ready. The whole plot must then be lightly raked once more, with the object of covering as many seeds as possible. Those which are deeply buried will not germinate, and those which are exposed may be scorched by the sun, or consumed by birds. As a finish put the roller over twice, first north and south, then east and west, and it must be done carefully, for on every spot missed by the roller the grasses will fail. Good work will leave the surface almost as smooth and true as a billiard table.

It frequently happens that the preparation of the seed-bed is completed in advance of the proper time for sowing, and the plot is allowed to lie fallow. In such cases, through the fall of rain, or some other cause, the surface becomes set, and it is necessary to break the top crust into a fine friable condition before the seed can be sown with a fair prospect of success.

Worm-Casts

In a very short time a thick sprinkling of worm-casts will be observed. We have no desire to call in question the general service rendered by these lowly creatures, but their movements in ground newly sown for a lawn or cricket ground are unquestionably mischievous, and the injury they cause will be greater in proportion to the looseness of the soil. A well-made, firm seed-bed is less liable to injury than one that has not been properly consolidated by the roller. Upon old turf the cast is thrown up from a well-defined orifice seldom exceeding a quarter of an inch in diameter. Worms loosen the soil of a newly-made seed-bed for a considerable distance round each burrow, and on this broken earth not a seed will germinate. It would be comparatively unimportant if the casts were few and far between, but generally hundreds of them may be seen on a pole of ground.

When and how the casts should be dealt with is sometimes a source of perplexity. A few days after sowing, a light roller will gather them up, if moist, and the implement must be scraped at the end of every run. When the casts are dry, the roller will crush them and remain clean. This light rolling may be repeated once or twice, if necessary, always taking care not to break the surface either with the foot or the roller. After the first fine spears of grass begin to show, it is generally unwise to touch the bed until the scythe or mower comes into use.

Those who care to rid the soil of worms, either before sowing or after the grass is established, may do so by means of water strongly impregnated with newly-burned lime. Fill a barrel with water, add as much lime as the water will absorb, stir briskly, and then allow the lime to settle. The clear fluid, freely used from an ordinary water-can, will bring the worms from their burrows in hundreds, and at the same time benefit the grass. The worms should be collected and destroyed in salt water.

Water and Shade

When severe and prolonged drought succeeds the sowing, there is a possibility that the seeds may be "malted." In spring the soil is generally moist enough to start seed-germs, but during continued dry weather growth is arrested, and the fragile seedlings wither away. As a rule, the watering of newly-sown land is to be avoided, but it may become a necessity if the grass is to be saved. A small plot can easily be watered by hose, or even by the water-can fitted with a fine rose. A large area presents difficulties, especially in the absence of hose, or if water has to be carried a considerable distance. In any case there must be no rude trampling on the soil. Flat boards laid at intervals, and ordinary care, will prevent injury from the traffic. The water must be delivered in a fine spray, and for a sufficient time to prevent the necessity of a second application. Still, watering is an evil at best, and one means of avoiding it altogether is to cover the entire surface, immediately after sowing, with a thin layer of cocoanut fibre, which will screen the soil from burning sunshine, check rapid evaporation, and foster the slender blades of grass as they rise. There is no occasion to remove this slight protection, for it will prove an advantage long after the grass has grown through it. To some extent the fibre is also a defence against the depredations of birds.

CRICKET'S PEACEFUL WEAPONS.

THE END OF THE INNINGS.
(WILLIAM BELDHAM, b. 1766, d. 1862)

Bird Scares

Sparrows and several of the finches are particularly partial to grass seeds, and they do mischief in other ways. The birds break up the surface, eat until surfeited, and then take a dust-bath. There are many methods of scaring them, and some plan must be adopted to preserve the seed from these marauders.

Small plots can be protected by nets, but on a large scale this mode of defence is, of course, out of the question. One cheap scare is to connect lengths of twine to tall stakes, and at intervals hang strips of glittering tin, slightly twisted, in order that they may be freely turned by the wind. Another remedy is to make an example of some of the pirates, and hang them up as a warning. When the sown area is extensive, it should be watched by a lad until the plant appears. He must be an early riser, and if it will not prove a nuisance, he may be entrusted with a gun and a few blank cartridges.

Mowing

While the plant is quite young, it should be topped with a sharp scythe. This will encourage the grasses to tiller out and their roots to fill the soil. At brief intervals the cutting should be repeated, and for this early work on the tender grass the scythe is unquestionably preferable to the mowing machine. Indeed, the risk of injury from the mower is so great that many practical men condemn its employment until the plant is fairly established. But the condition of the machine must be taken into account. We have successfully used a mower for the very first cutting, having previously ascertained by a trial on old grass that the cutters were in perfect order.

In the judicious use of the mower lies one secret of a close sward. During severe winter weather the implement may not be wanted for several weeks, but as spring advances the ragged plant should have attention, and the necessity for more frequent cutting will be evident, until in warm, moist weather, twice a week, and possibly, for a brief period, every other day, may not be too often. No rigid law can be laid down on this point. The grass should never wear a neglected appearance, nor should the work on any account be postponed to a more convenient season. Setting the mower requires the exercise of judgment. It should never be so low as to graze the surface, and in summer, during scorching sunshine, it will be advisable to raise the cutter a trifle higher than for strong spring growth.

Rolling

Next in importance to mowing comes the use of the roller, without which it is impossible to establish a fine close turf, or to maintain it in high condition. After the first cutting of the young grass, the whole plot must be gently compressed with a rather light roller, and the work needs care, because the bed is easily broken by a clumsy foot. Subsequent cuttings to be followed by the roller until the plant is capable of bearing a heavier implement, which should not always be used in the same direction.

When the soil becomes hard through dry weather, rolling can do no good, and during frost it will be injurious; but in spring and autumn the frequent use of a rather heavy roller will have a visibly beneficial effect on the grass.

The best rollers are constructed with two cylinders, having the outer edges rounded. The division of the cylinder facilitates turning, and the rounded edges prevent unsightly marks.

Destruction of Weeds

After the most careful preparation of the land, annual weeds are certain to appear, and every weed, if left alone, will choke a number of the surrounding grasses. Frequent mowing checks these weeds, but plantains, thistles, and dandelions must be taken up, each one singly, about an inch below the surface. A pinch of salt dropped upon the cut root will effectually prevent new growth. The lad who does this work should understand what he is about, for a plantain merely cut off below the collar will send out half-a-dozen shoots, in the same manner as sea kale, and prove a greater nuisance than the original crown; and the careless use of salt will kill a lot of grass plants. Daisies should be lifted separately, each plant with its root entire, and although new growth will here and there appear for a second or even a third time, the daisies will be weaker, and a little perseverance will speedily rid a large grass plot of every one of them. Another efficient mode of eradicating weeds is to dip a wood skewer into sulphuric acid, strong carbolic acid, or one of the liquid weed destroyers, and then plunge the skewer perpendicularly into the heart of the plant. The result is deadly and instantaneous; but the use of these destructive fluids needs great care to avoid personal injury or the burning of holes in clothing. The bottle containing the liquid must be kept in a place of security.

In extirpating weeds there is nothing like system. Instead of aimlessly wandering hither and thither, it is more economical in time and labour to mark off with a garden line a strip six feet wide, and clear the weeds from the enclosure. Follow with successive strips until the whole surface has been dealt with, and it is surprising how quickly a large area may be divested of weeds.

After sowing grass seeds, how soon will the ground be fit for use? is a question frequently asked. No definite answer can be given. The time depends on the period of the year, the weather which follows the sowing, and the attention bestowed on the rising plant. To these influences must be added the nature of the soil, aspect, and district. In August or early September, sowing should produce, under favourable circumstances, and with generous treatment, a good turf during the following summer. Spring sowings are specially subject to the vicissitudes of the season. When the atmosphere is genial and the plot receives due attention, the plant rapidly fills the soil, and a thick sward results towards the end of July or the beginning of August. But it is desirable not to subject it to hard use until the following year.

Except the final mowing and light rolling on the morning of the match, wickets should be prepared three days in advance. It is often fatal to good cricket to employ the heavy roller on the day the match commences. Should the grass be so dense as to make the wicket slow, a broom deftly used, followed by a hand mower, run several times between the wickets and across the ground also, will affect a marked improvement in the pace. The preparation can be finished with the small roller.

Plantains should never be tolerated on a cricket ground. When the ball happens to fall on the centre of one of these plants, it may travel in the most erratic manner.

Many cricket grounds are grazed with sheep, and if the animals are at the same time fed with cake, this is one of the simplest and most effectual means of maintaining the sward in a luxuriant condition. But we have seen sheep do immense mischief on light sandy ground, where their quick snatching mode of feeding readily uproots the plants. Of course the work of mowing is greatly reduced when sheep can with safety be allowed to graze. It must, however, be distinctly understood that without cake the sheep add nothing to the fertility of the soil.

Improving Cricket Grounds

As a rule, every cricket ground should be liberally manured in spring, with the artificials as recommended above; and before or at the close of each season—certainly not later than the middle of September—fine grass seeds should be sown over the worn parts of the turf. If the sowing can be made early in September, the grasses will have several months in which to become established, and for this reason sowing in autumn on a cricket ground is generally preferable to sowing in spring.

As a preliminary, the surface must be raked or harrowed to provide a seed-bed. Then sow renovating seeds at the rate of not less than one bushel per acre, making two operations of the work to ensure regular distribution. Rake or harrow in the seeds to cover as many as possible, and finish with a careful rolling.

Newly-made cricket grounds sometimes show depressions after the grass is up. Where these are shallow, an occasional sifting of fine loam may follow the mowing, and with patient attention a true surface can be restored; but a quantity of soil, roughly thrown down, will smother the rising plant. Should the hollows be deep, a different procedure becomes necessary. Young grass cannot be cut and rolled in the manner usual with an established sward, and if holes are filled with a thick covering of earth, it is necessary to re-sow and follow with the mower and roller, as already advised. But if the plant is fairly thick, it may perhaps be possible to cut the young turf in small square sections, and lift each one separately by means of a thin flat board or piece of zinc. After making good the level, the pieces of turf can, with care, be restored without much injury. As a finish, lightly touch the surface with the flat beater, and spray over it two or three cans of water.

Inequalities in old turf can be remedied by a simpler mode of treatment. Across the hollow spot, cut strips 10 or 12 inches wide, and roll back the sward from the centre. Make the bed perfectly level, leaving the soil with a firm but crumbled surface; then restore the turf, which will be found rather too long for the space, and tenderly compress it into the original position; beat carefully down, give a soaking of water, and in due time mow and roll. In a few days no trace of the operation will be visible, but the grass ought not to be roughly used until it is thoroughly re-established.

Fairy rings are sometimes troublesome. They are caused by several kinds of fungus. When these decay, the soil becomes charged with nitrogenous matter, and a dark green spot of grass is the result. The mycelium exhausts the soil of the constituents which are essential to the existence of the fungi, and as new supplies of food can only be found on fresh ground, the spot becomes a circle, which annually increases in circumference, until it either breaks up or the fungi are exhausted. No direct remedy is known, but it has been observed that lawns which are liberally dressed every spring with stimulating manure produce dark green herbage, closely resembling the fairy rings in colour. As a consequence the circles are less conspicuous, and they also show a tendency to disappear under the effects of the manure.

Moss is generally a sign of poorness of soil, and sometimes indicates the need of drainage. But before laying in drain-pipes remedial measures should be tried, especially as the work of draining sadly cuts the place about. There may also be a difficulty as to the disposal of the outflow. To improve the grass, either put the rake heavily over the sward, or employ a toothed harrow to drag out as much moss as possible. Then spread over the turf a compost, previously prepared, of lime mixed with rich soil free from weeds, in the proportion of one load of lime to four loads of soil; the addition of Sutton's lawn manure, at the rate of 2 cwt. per acre, will stimulate the grass. Eight cartloads of the compost should be applied per acre. About a fortnight after the dressing has been spread, a sowing of seed will quickly fill the ground with young healthy plants, and assist in preventing a reappearance of the moss. The early part of September should be chosen for this work, to give the turf time to recover before the next season.

FOOTNOTES:

[Note.—It is perhaps only the writer's personal modesty that precludes him from giving the Australian an English companion in this special class.—Ed.]
Since these words were written Bainbridge has resigned and J. F. Byrne has filled his place.
This was done by Leicestershire a few months back when Mr. Crawford was made Secretary.
The examination in bankruptcy of Mr. Gregory, the Australian cricketer, in Australia last April, proves that this is an

accurate statement.

Allusion may here be made to the match with the cumbrous title, "Gentlemen of England who had not been educated at the Universities *v.* Gentlemen of England who had been educated at the Universities (Past and Present)," which was played at the Oval, 15th and 16th June 1874. The Gentlemen "who had not" won by an innings and 76 runs, Messrs. W. G. Grace and Appleby bowling unchanged in the first University innings, which only amounted to 58. The game was never repeated.

www.ingramcontent.com/pod-product-compliance
Lightning Source LLC
Chambersburg PA
CBHW031419150426
43191CB00006B/323